BREAKING OUT OF THE BOX

'Though some have believed one system, and others another, almost all have been of opinion that a great deal was known; but all this supposed knowledge in the traditional systems must be swept away, and a new beginning must be made . . .' Bertrand Russell

D0234690

Piers Dudgeon first met Edward de Bono in 1984 when they collaborated on the bestseller, *Tactics: The Art and Science of Success*. A writer and editor since 1979, he has seeded, developed and produced a variety of books with authors as diverse as John Fowles, Ted Hughes, Daphne du Maurier, Catherine Cookson, Peter Ackroyd, Susan Hill, Shirley Conran and Josephine Cox. In 1993 he moved from London to a village on the North Yorkshire moors, where he is converting a series of 300-year-old barns into a residential arts centre. He himself has written eleven books, including the recent Number 1 bestselling biography *The Girl from Leam Lane*.

Breaking out of the box

The biography
of Edward de Bono

Piers Dudgeon

headline

First published in 2001
by HEADLINE BOOK PUBLISHING

First published in paperback in 2002
by HEADLINE BOOK PUBLISHING

Piers Dudgeon would be happy to hear from readers with their comments
on the book at the following e-mail address: kau52@dial.pipex.com

10 9 8 7 6 5 4 3 2 1

ISBN 0 7472 6452 X

Typeset by Avon Dataset Ltd, Bidford-on-Avon, Warks
Designed by Tony Cohen

Printed and bound in Great Britain by
Mackays of Chatham PLC, Chatham, Kent

HEADLINE BOOK PUBLISHING
A division of Hodder Headline
338 Euston Road
London NW1 3BH

www.headline.co.uk
www.hodderheadline.com

Acknowledgements

I wish to thank the many people who agreed to be interviewed for this book and who gave the honest and often perceptive views which provide its value. In particular I would like to thank Edward de Bono for granting me access to his writings and his time for interview. He is a busy man and very private; the book would have been less balanced without his cooperation.

I would also like to thanks members of the de Bono family, in particular Peter and Caspar de Bono and Elizabeth Vincenti, and all those who have helped me who are involved in Edward's business and education operations worldwide, including Tom Farrell and Ann Lynch, Diane and Don McQuaig, Linda and Peter Low, Susan Mackie, Kathy Myers, Russell Chalmers, Norman Demajo, Julia Pomirska, Daniela Bartoli, Linda Laird and Barry Lynch, and especially Paddy Hills, who time and again smoothed the terrain ahead.

To sources beyond family and current project, like John Edwards, Norah Maier, Paul MacCready, Ungku Abdul Aziz, Ivor Mills, Peter Serracino Inglott, Edna Copley, Jeremy Bullmore, Marjorie Wallace, David Bernstein, Simon Batchelor, Beatricz Capdeville, Dan Sharon, Bill Maxwell, Jennifer O'Sullivan, Adam Pirani, David Tanner and Eric Borg, I am particularly indebted, as indeed I am to the eminent authors of books in the areas of physics, biology, philosophy, psychology and literature, which enlightened my research. They and the works are credited in the Bibliography.

Readers who wish to contact a de Bono resource centre for training or consultation should go to www.aptt.com, thence 'Distributor Resource Center' for the appropriate distributor.

Contents

Prologue

'The train of thought that guides us into the future has already left the station, and a few brave people are aboard. Dr Edward de Bono is certainly one of them . . .' Ivar Giaever, Nobel prizewinning physicist

Since 1967, Edward de Bono has been engaged in enacting a revolution in the way we think. He began with lateral thinking, opening our minds to new ideas and giving the method the same authenticity as logic, such that 'lateral thinking' was taken up by the *Oxford English Dictionary*.

De Bono's first book, *The Use of Lateral Thinking* (1967), put into words what was going on in the magic moment of creativity and suggested ways to re-enact it. It was a huge bestseller, from Britain to Japan. He hit the spot by describing how to escape the rigid patterns of our thinking – to break out of the box, to exploit, manipulate and outwit the marvellous but rigid mechanism of the human mind – and he did so at a moment when conventions were under scrutiny and creativity was in the air.

De Bono has an academic background – he was a prodigy, went to university at fifteen, qualified as a doctor at twenty-one, matriculated as a Rhodes scholar to Oxford University a year later, and, at the time of *The Use of Lateral Thinking*, was Assistant Director of Research at Cambridge University's Department of Investigative Medicine. He has five degrees, three from Oxford and Cambridge Universities, and has held appointments at both, as well as Harvard and London University (St Thomas' Hospital). His 'vision' – the model of the mechanism of mind, out of which he designed the techniques of all his thinking programmes – was inspired by his research in physiology and an interest in the kind of thinking computers cannot do. His work represents a major contribution both to our knowledge of how the brain works and to systems science, a paradigm that is transforming our view of the universe.

Yet no one could be less interested in the academic establishment

1

than de Bono. In the late 1960s and early 1970s he devised CoRT, his thinking programme for schools, while spelling out his disenchantment with academia, calling our universities 'irrelevant centres of mental masturbation'.

CoRT (page 128) is a collection of thinking tools that scan a perception and suggest a way forward. They can be applied to information-based subjects (history, geography, science, etc), but come into their own beyond school. CoRT is *real-world* education, so that wherever you find yourself needing to consider a problem, an opportunity, or what to do in any situation, the tools can be called upon to broaden your perception of it and bring a solution into view.

He termed what CoRT teaches, 'Operacy', and would like nothing better than to see the word sitting next to Numeracy and Literacy on the national curriculum. CoRT is his play to make education relevant to life. Like lateral thinking, it was prescient. In the world beyond school, the revolution in computer technology has switched the focus from gathering information to discovering what to do with it – designing a way forward. CoRT also foreshadowed the move to vocational education, precipitated in Britain by the granting of university status to our polytechnic colleges in 1992, but still stuck in the traditional notion of knowledge-based vocational coursework (business degrees or even pop music). Whereas, uninhibited by a knowledge requirement, transferable to any situation, usable across all ages and abilities, CoRT may yet prove to be the ultimate integrated education option.

In the 1970s, de Bono conducted an unprecedented experiment involving thousands of British schoolchildren and well over a million children in Venezuela, and became the first to put thinking on a school's curriculum. In virtually every country around the world where thinking is on the curriculum today, he first introduced the idea, often in person. He saw this as his mission – alongside a more lucrative parallel undertaking: suddenly, in the late 1960s, with the adoption of lateral thinking by the Alternative Society, big business swooped and said, 'We'd like a bit of that,' with the result that the lifestyle of this Cambridge don took a lurch to the spectacular. Travelling some 250,000 miles a year, advising companies such as Nestlé, IBM, Bosch, Siemens, Prudential and Merck, he commands seminar fees upwards of $30,000, and has a licence agreement with a company that employs more than 900 trainers of his programmes worldwide.

His work has made him a very rich man, and ever more vilified by academia for that. He owns islands in the Bahamas, in the Venice lagoon, off Queensland, Australia, and in Roaring Water Bay, West Cork. He has a country house in Norfolk, a mews house in South Kensington, London, and an apartment in Albany, Piccadilly, one of the most prestigious addresses in central London. There are also apartments on the edge of Central Park in New York, Venice, and Sydney, and a 17th-century house in Malta.

What made his success more than a passing fad is that his tools are ridiculously simple – and they work. That they do is because they are grounded in a system model of how the brain works, enabling him not only to demystify the creative process but to show how, in practice, to think creatively and constructively to maximum value.

In the process, he saw that what, more than anything, inhibits ideas of value is the mind's tendency to make a judgement before the perception of a situation is complete. Feelings and emotions tend to make our decisions and our judgements for us. When they are allowed to act on a perception before the thinking has been done, we set stereotypes, clichés, prejudices, standard opinions – and, inevitably, conflict.

In the 1980s, before the world took its first step away from conflict politics under perestroika, he developed the concept of parallel thinking (page 242), which attracted the attention of thinkers in the areas of politics (including the Kremlin) and the law. Education and business again picked it up, this time through the parallel thinking structure called Six Hats, which can incorporate both lateral thinking and the CoRT tools, and is now probably his most popular methodology worldwide.

One or two people said to me that de Bono himself solves the problem of emotions and feelings interfering with good thinking by doing away with them. One aggrieved lady screamed as much from the pages of a popular magazine, saying that he has 'chips for veins'.

The question of how de Bono's life – such as his unusual and impassive upbringing, the rigid culture and conflict politics of the country of his birth and his unique lifestyle – influences his concepts, and vice versa, is fascinating to tell, and perhaps any judgements on the man should be shelved until the perception has been fully explored.

Chapter One

The Comfort of Paradox

'It is a natural thing in the brain to seek symmetry. I don't feel that compulsion. There is the notion that if you find the ultimate answer everything springs from it. But I don't think it does.'

Johnny is five years of age. He lives in Australia. One day his friends, who want to tease him, offer Johnny a choice of two coins, an Australian $1 coin and the smaller $2 coin. They say, 'Johnny, which one do you want? You can take and keep whichever coin you want.'

Johnny looks at the coins, his eyes rest on the bigger one and he takes the $1 coin. His friends laugh behind his back and say, 'Isn't Johnny stupid, he doesn't realise that the smaller coin is worth twice the amount of the larger one!' So, whenever they want to make a fool of him, they offer him the coins and he always takes the bigger one. One day, an adult sees this and calls him over and says, 'Johnny, believe me when I tell you that you are mistaken in taking the larger coin because it is worth half the value of the smaller coin.'

Johnny listens very politely, then says, 'Yes, I know that, but how many times would they have offered it to me if I had taken the smaller coin?'

Breaking Out of the Box shows you how to think like Johnny, but it is not just about making a buck. What Johnny rumbled was a concept, very basic, to which his persecutors were complacently blind. The way to rumble new concepts is the same whether you are out to make a buck or to change the world. Edward de Bono has made a buck, which is encouraging in terms of the credibility of his ideas, and if he has not yet changed the world, at the very least he has shown us how to.

In *The Use of Lateral Thinking* (originally *New Think* in America), he defines lateral thinking as a means of escaping established ideas and perceptions in order to find new ones. He uses a metaphor to show how logical ('vertical') thinking traps us in well-travelled neural ruts:

'Just as water flows down slopes, settles in hollows and is confined to riverbeds, so vertical thinking flows along the most probable paths and, by its very flow, increases the probability of these paths for the future.' He doesn't give us much practical advice about how to break out of these ruts at this stage – he more indicates the frame of mind in which to go about it. The book sets the scene for the more powerful lateral thinking tools and techniques that followed: 'Vertical thinking is digging the same hole deeper; lateral thinking is trying elsewhere.' In *The Use of Lateral Thinking* he seeks to remove our disinclination to abandon a half-dug hole.

The phrase 'lateral thinking' arose when Edward spontaneously coined the concept in an interview with *London Life*. 'As I explained this other sort of thinking, I described how you needed to move *laterally* to find other approaches and other alternatives. At once it occurred to me that this was the word I needed.'

A merchant borrows from a moneylender to finance a trading voyage, but his ship fails to come in. Come the day of repayment, the moneylender approaches the merchant in the garden of his house. When it becomes clear that the debt cannot be paid, the moneylender's eyes settle on the merchant's beautiful daughter, and he proposes an alternative to humiliation and debtor's prison. For his daughter's hand in marriage the moneylender will excuse the merchant of his debt. When his offer is rejected, the moneylender offers the merchant one chance to redeem the situation.

'I will take two stones from the garden path, one black, the other white,' the moneylender says. 'I will then put both stones into a leather bag, and your daughter will take one of the stones from the bag. If she takes the white stone, your debt will be cancelled and your daughter will remain with you. If, however, she takes the black stone, she will marry me and the debt will be cancelled. Otherwise you must pay the debt or go to debtor's prison.'

Perceiving that they could be no worse off and have an even chance of escaping the consequences on not paying the debt, the daughter suggests they agree on these terms. She then watches the moneylender carefully and sees that he actually puts two black stones into the bag. What was she to do? She could expose the moneylender as a cheat. She could take a black stone and then accept her fate or refuse to marry the fellow anyway. Either was unlikely to resolve the situation. It was at this point that she decided to use some lateral thinking.

The girl put her hand into the bag and took out one of the stones, but immediately fumbled and dropped it onto the path. Once the stone had joined the others on the path there was no way of telling whether it had been a white or a black stone.

'Oh, I am sorry,' she called.

'It was a black stone, I saw it!' exclaimed the moneylender.

'Nonsense, you couldn't possibly have seen it,' enjoined the merchant. 'There was not enough time.'

'Then we must do it again,' said the moneylender, annoyed but convinced he would yet win.

'That won't be necessary,' the girl said. 'All we have to do is look at the colour of the stone left in the bag. If it is a white stone, I must have taken a black one, but if it is a black stone, mine must have been white.'

The story illustrates well the nature of lateral thinking. The girl's idea earned her father's freedom in a surprise way, which, in hindsight, is perfectly logical and which gives her control of the situation. Few of us would have thought of it, but with practice, lateral thinkers get ideas like this all the time.

As in the case of Australian Johnny, who chose the less valuable coin and took control of the situation, lateral thinking seems like a streetwise thing to do. Indeed, streetwise people very often do well with Edward's techniques, once they get over the fear of being exposed, which invariably comes from years of failing at school. Later, we will see youngsters from borstal operating on a level playing field with those from privileged private schools when using his techniques. We will see prisoners serving life sentences in jail excelling at thinking used by top physicists. To survive on the street you've got to be sassy, ahead of the game. Lateral thinking is a very sassy thing to do.

Edward distinguishes between two modes of thinking: *perception* and *processing*. Although later he admits that this is an exaggerated polarisation – 'in practice, the two . . . tend to overlap and intermingle' – his purpose in making the distinction is to show that the brain works *differently from a computer*. The brain does both perception and processing, while computers only do processing. (Unlike traditional philosophers, Edward does not use the word 'perception' to refer to the act of seeing, hearing, smelling, tasting, touching. He uses it to denote the interaction of sense data with the neural network of the brain – seeing with the mind.)

The point of Australian Johnny's story is that if you had given the situation to a computer which had been programmed for value, it would have processed the information available and taken the more valuable coin, thereby failing to gain control of the situation. It was Johnny's human perception that allowed him to see the bigger view of the future. And it was a complex perception. How often would he see his friends? How long would he want them to go on teasing him? How many times would they be prepared to offer him the dollars? How long before they suspected what he was up to? Once you have perceived all that, you can build it into an expert system and feed it to a computer. But you have to *perceive* it first.

This distinction between perception and processing is fundamental to all Edward's thinking and arose from research he undertook in the late 1950s at Oxford University into the mathematical analysis of blood pressure waves, over the course of a DPhil in medicine. Earlier, studying psychology for his BA in psychology, philosophy and physiology (PPP), he had been dealing with how humans think. Now, in his physiological research, he found himself playing around with some of the big new IBM computers, which sparked this interest in the sort of thinking computers cannot do.

Edward had arrived at Oxford in 1955 with a friend, Peter Serracino Inglott. Both were Rhodes scholars from the University of Malta, Edward bound for Christ Church to begin his PPP degree, and Peter for Campion Hall, the Jesuit College across the road. Edward's older brother, Antony, would join him at Christ Church a year later.

Edward had started as an undergraduate of Malta University in 1948, at the age of fifteen. He had qualified as a doctor in only five years and been offered the Rhodes scholarship in 1953, but legally he had to wait to graduate until he was twenty-one, which is why it was 1955 before he took up the scholarship and arrived in Oxford. The university required him to take only two of the three PPP subjects, so he dropped philosophy. It was a three-year course, but he completed it in two. There is a note on his file saying that he had special permission to do so.

Edward was rushing his life in England as he had in Malta, and thus it would always be, although one can appreciate that having already qualified as a doctor, this 'first degree' must have seemed a bit of a bind. Later he would intimate that he had felt bogged down by the traditional, linear, cause-and-effect, stimulus-response approach of psychology, a far cry from his own self-organising mechanism of mind, with its interactions, feedback loops, triggered responses and so on. In the event, he graduated with a BA, 2nd class. 'The great men don't always get a first,' a spokesman for the university put it to me rather quaintly when I expressed surprise.

There was no upper/lower (2:1/2:2) distinction within 2nd-class degrees in those days, but whatever Edward's marks (he was told there was a first in one subject but not in the other), they were sufficient to land him a job in 1958 as research assistant in the Department of the Regius Professor of Medicine, while he studied for his DPhil in Medicine. An MA followed the BA automatically. 'I got the MA and then I stayed on and got the DPhil with Sir George Pickering at the Radcliffe Hospital,' Edward confirmed. 'Pickering was the Regius Professor of Medicine there.' Between 1960 and 1961, Edward also worked as a junior lecturer in medicine at Oxford.

Whatever discontent there may have been with the undergraduate course, Edward otherwise had a good time. In fact, Peter Inglott (now Father Peter), ensconced in his Jesuit College across the road, didn't see Edward for dust. 'He tended to move in rather different circles,' Father Peter told me. 'He played polo for the university. He had learned to play in Malta at the same club as Prince Philip. He was thus moving in the highest social circles. He went to London parties, but also at Oxford he used to organise sheet parties, where everybody went dressed just in a sheet.' At one of these, I am told, he demonstrated his playful interest in perception by experimenting with a 'placebo' (nonalcoholic) rum punch, and was thrilled to discover that half the guests actually did get drunk.

His connections were indeed good. On one occasion, when playing polo at Windsor, he stayed with Lord Mountbatten, a family friend, at his home, Broadlands. The match sticks in his mind, as he still has the scar to show for it. 'As you line up, the ball is pushed in, and on this occasion someone swung round on his horse and caught me with his stick under my chin. The grey horse I was on was all spattered with blood. I played on, but then the girth on my saddle broke, the saddle slid off and me with it. Everyone thought I had fainted. When I got back to Broadlands, Mountbatten said, "Well we'd better get you sewn up," so I went off to the local doctor and was sewn up, rather badly as it happens.' At some point, Mountbatten arranged for him to go with the Mediterranean fleet on manoeuvres, 'they, all in their battle gear, and I a student!' And when Edward had launched lateral thinking, Mountbatten was very supportive. He booked Edward to give a seminar to his admirals in Portsmouth and lecture to the Atlantic Colleges in Wales and Singapore, and later Mountbatten was the first guest at a secret series of dinner parties, paid for by a Greek millionaire, Demetrius Camino, and hosted by Edward in London, investigating how internationally successful strategists, politicians, academics and entrepreneurial businessmen actually think.

Edward had always been good at sport, particularly tennis and cricket, and played polo for Oxford University. But the most impressive sporting feat, for the unofficial record that was set, was a race against the clock canoeing from Oxford to London. 'The point was that a lot of people had been walking from Oxford to London, and I thought walking was rather tiring. There were three of us. We borrowed a canoe from a ladies' college and we just set out, we didn't do any practising. It was two people on, one person off, there are thirty-three locks on the way and we had to carry the boat round.

'When we got to the end, we discovered that the fellow who was supposed to look at the tides had got them wrong and if we didn't hurry up we were going to spend the last sixteen miles working against the tide. So we hurried up and arrived at Westminster Pier, where we had a small party. We were, I think, four hours ahead of schedule. Other people then tried it, in fact two of them drowned. You see, there are weirs, it's very dangerous in the middle of the night, you can so easily get swept over a weir.'

Given the scene in which Edward moved, and his adventurousness, it was less surprising that on the night he arrived in Oxford as an undergraduate in 1955, he went straight to London for a party. Knowing that he would not get back to the college until after 12:30 am, when the gates would be closed, he asked 'an old hand' how he could get back in. He was told that everyone just climbed in: first he would come across a set of railings, then there was a wall to climb, and finally there'd be another wall. Edward took this in and disappeared up to London for the party.

'It was late when I got back. The railings were easy. The first wall was rather more difficult. I got over it and went forward until I came to the second wall, which was about the same height as the first wall. I climbed the second wall, only to find myself outside again. My double effort had involved my climbing in and out across a corner. I started again and with more careful direction came up to the proper second wall. There was an iron gate in this second wall, and as the gate was lower than the rest of the wall and also offered better footholds, I climbed the gate. As I was sitting astride the top of the gate it swung open. It had never been closed . . .'

The point of the story would certainly have been lost on me as I staggered up to bed, but it was not lost on Edward. No matter how good you are at wall-climbing, he mused as he wound his way up to his room, you must first be sure you are climbing the right wall. You can be the greatest logician in the world, but if you start processing in the wrong place, with an incomplete perception, you will get nowhere.

Errors of logic are rare; most errors in our thinking are errors of *perception*. In *De Bono's Thinking Course* (1982), which tied in with a BBC TV series of the same name and is his best introduction to lateral thinking, Edward writes: 'In the future, we shall be able to delegate more and more processing (for which we have developed such marvellous tools as mathematics) to computers. That leaves the perceptual sort of thinking to humans. And we need to get very much better at it.'

You are about to make a salad dressing and have before you a glass of olive oil and a glass of wine vinegar. You take a spoonful of oil from the oil glass and pour it into the vinegar glass. You stir thoroughly and then take a spoonful of the mixture and put it back into the oil glass. You stop at this point. Is there now more oil in the vinegar or vinegar in the oil, or what? (It does not matter, but we can suppose the spoon to be less than one-fifth the volume of the glass.)

The answer is that there would be as much oil in the vinegar glass as vinegar in the oil glass. Edward's publishers, Jonathan Cape, refused to accept this at first, and after publication a logician wrote politely to Edward to point out his error, saying that the spoonful of oil was a spoonful of pure oil; the return spoonful was a spoonful of a mixture and hence contained less vinegar than the first spoon had contained oil. So there should be more oil in the vinegar than vinegar in the oil.

'The logic seems impeccable,' says Edward, 'but the perception is faulty.' The two spoonfuls were of equal volume. On its first trip, the spoon contained pure olive oil. On its second trip, it contained a mixture of vinegar and oil, but whatever volume of oil it contained, that volume effectively did a round trip, and since it is back where it came from (in the oil glass), its presence in either spoonful can be disregarded, leaving equal amounts of vinegar and oil spoiling the purity of each glass.

'Now I will give you another example, which most of the top mathematicians in the world get wrong,' says Edward, thoroughly enjoying himself. 'It is in the form of a TV game show. After the guest has answered some rather silly questions of the host's, he is invited to choose one of three doors. Behind one of the doors is a very nice car and if the guest chooses the right door he gets to keep the car and drive it home.

Behind the other two doors there are goats. The guest says, "I think I shall choose door A." Before door A is opened, the host opens one of the other two doors (C) to reveal a goat. The host then turns back to the guest and says, "Are you happy with your first choice, or would you now like to change your mind?"

'The question is, what should the guest do? Just imagine that you were sitting in that chair. Would you stay with A, or move to B? What would you do? This was published in the *New York Times* and the person who published it said, "You should certainly change to B, you will double your chances." All sorts of mathematicians wrote in and said, "That's nonsense." Meanwhile, people were doing computer simulations and saying, "That is perfectly correct." After six weeks everyone had to apologise and agree.

'The thinking is surprisingly simple. We need to look into the mind of the host. The host knows where the car is and is not going to open the door to reveal it. If the car is behind B he is going to open C. If the car is behind C he is going to open B. So, if the car is behind either B or C, you just open the door that the host doesn't open. How often is the car behind B or C? 2 to 1; you double your chances. It's as simple as that.'

Not to me. The probability of the car being behind B and C is initially 2:1, but once the host has selected C, the odds on A or B are surely perceived as 50:50 by the contestant, because, though the host knows where the car is, he has not revealed anything of its whereabouts other than that it must be behind A or B. Given this, there is no more reason why the contestant should opt for B than for A.

Edward looked at me sadly: 'You can't just take an instant in time. The odds are fixed, they don't change. It is like the story of two parachutists: one is falling through the air at a steady rate, one is hung up in the tree, the net sum of forces is zero, for, if it were not, he would be accelerating through the air. So why is one moving and one not moving? Because, in order to get to the steady state, he had to have been accelerating in the past. You can't just take this point in time. The odds are there beforehand, when he made the choice.'

I couldn't agree and the equivocacy bothered me enormously, but it didn't bother Edward, who is happy with ambiguity. Zeno of Elea, a pupil of Parmenides living round 450 BC, enjoyed ambiguity too. In his efforts to discredit the so-called doctrine of plurality he came up with eight paradoxes – dilemmas which logic must face, famously including the paradox of Achilles and the tortoise. If the tortoise has the start on Achilles, Achilles can never catch up; for, while Achilles covers the distance from his starting point to the starting point of the tortoise, the tortoise advances a certain distance, and while Achilles covers this distance, the tortoise makes a further advance, and so on *ad infinitum*. Consequently, Achilles may run *ad infinitum* without overtaking the tortoise.

In an essay in *Dilemmas* (1954), Gilbert Ryle refutes the implication of illogical logic by comparing the paradox to that of a cake being cut up on the principle that each child should cut a piece and leave some for the next child. At no point will the sum of the parts cut equal the whole. 'Zeno gets us and Achilles to think of each of the successive leads that are to be made up as portions which ought somehow to add up, but cannot add up, to the total course he has run.' It is the difference between 'how many portions the cake is cut into' and 'how many portions have been cut off the cake'. The latter does not necessarily give you an idea of the cake's size, but the former does.

It's a clever argument that needs to be read in its entirety, and even then acceptance can slip like grains of sand through the fingers. To philosophers, the paradox is a perfect subject for analysis and discussion, and Ryle believed that its mix of narrative, to which we can all relate, and logic, which is the provenance of mathematicians, offers the ultimate opportunity for misunderstanding. To ordinary folk, the question very soon arises as to why we should be looking for what's wrong with Zeno's paradox, when we *know* through experience that Achilles will win. Assuming that the race is of a finite length, that Achilles runs faster than the tortoise and that there are no other factors he hasn't told us about, Achilles will overtake the tortoise *in fact*. Given a certain speed difference, a certain length of track, the precise point of overtaking can be given. The onus, therefore, is not on us to show that Zeno is wrong, but on him to show, other than by argument, that we are wrong.

Edward in fact shares this pragmatic approach, but is at ease with the perception that 'in many domains people do not have all-or-none convictions about whether something is true' (*Fuzzy Logic*, McNeill & Freiberger, 1993). The first requirement when dealing with perception in neural-network systems, as opposed to processing in computational systems (where there is nothing fuzzy about the logic and everything is either right or wrong), is to shelve the notion of truth and the desire to fit everything into a cosy, unified whole, and to start looking for *what can be*. This is the bedrock of Edward's methods – constructive, creative 'design' thinking. Not getting hung up on judging what is, but moving forward with what can be.

Timothy Melchior taught Edward's thinking programmes in an award-winning school – Memorial Junior High School in Valley Stream, New York, of which he was headmaster. He wrote, 'Effective thinkers are more comfortable with ambiguity, tend not to search for definitive answers, and tend to perceive interdependencies rather than either/ors,' what Edward terms polarisation.

Edward feels no pressure to form judgements that will fit everything into a unified picture of things. He is comfortable with ambiguity, excited by paradox. 'It is a natural thing in the brain, to seek enclosure, symmetry,' he admits, 'but I don't feel that compulsion. I think there's so much to be done. You see there is the notion that if you find the ultimate answer everything springs from it. But I don't think it does. I used to know Freddie Ayer [the late A.J. Ayer, the philosopher] quite well. We were good friends. We used to have him to dinner, I used to meet him on radio programmes. In the end we had to agree that we couldn't really have a discussion because his notion of a discussion is that you define your terms and five minutes later you say something which is or is not consistent with your defined terms. My idea of a discussion is that you gradually chimney up better and better speculations and ideas and you don't know where you are going to get. But just to circle round until you get back to your original definition is indescribably boring.'

Chapter Two

Box Culture

'We still believe that winning an argument, proving you're right, proving someone else is wrong, is sufficient. It is not.'

'Humour tells us something about perception that we have traditionally neglected in favour of logic,' Edward wrote in *I Am Right, You Are Wrong* (1990). The punchline reverberates between two hitherto unconnected contexts or frames of reference. This is precisely what happens in insight, which is why the laugh is common to both the 'surprise' of the punchline and the 'eureka! effect' in creativity. Tension is exploded at the moment when the new idea becomes evident. Says Edward, 'It will be a sinister day when computers start to laugh.'

In simple pun-style humour, we set off down the main track or pattern of thought, and then suddenly the punchline switches us along a sidetrack. 'Bob Hope complained he was having a miserable birthday because as presents he was only given three golf clubs. What's worse was that only two of them had swimming pools. Simple puns indicate a pattern-switching system,' says Edward. He continues:

> Then there's the other type of humour, in which in hindsight the joke makes sense. You get taken along this channel and then in hindsight look back and see how narrow your thinking was. Like the story of the man sitting in a train compartment and the ticket collector comes along to inspect the tickets. The guy sitting down starts looking everywhere for his ticket, in his pants pockets, his coat pocket, his coat on the rack. He is looking in a flurry and much to everyone's amusement, because they can see that he's got it in his mouth this whole time. So eventually the inspector takes it out of his mouth, punches it, and gives it back. When the inspector has left the compartment his companion says, 'Didn't you feel a fool looking

everywhere for your ticket when it was right there in your mouth?'

'Stupid?' replies the man, 'I was chewing the date off it!'

Again, a married couple, very devoted to one another, agree that whoever dies first will signal back from the other world as to what it is like. So the husband dies and the wife is waiting and waiting, and two weeks later she gets a phone call and it is her husband Bill. 'Bill,' she says, 'what is it like over there?' Bill says, 'Not bad, not bad, not bad. You make love, you eat fresh salad, you make love and eat fresh salad, you make love, you eat fresh salad . . .'

'Really Bill, is that what it is like in heaven?' says his wife.

'Heaven?' says Bill. 'No, I am a rabbit in Wisconsin.'

An older one that Edward uses, which dates back almost as far as the Bob Hope joke (still enjoying currency) is about Lady Astor, who was renowned for her forthright views. At loggerheads with Winston Churchill at dinner one evening, she said to him, 'Mr Churchill, if I were married to you I should put poison in your coffee.'

'Madam,' Churchill replied, 'if I were married to you, I should drink it.'

The main track is the narrative of the joke up to the punchline, which switches our perceptions into the hitherto unassociated sidetrack. The punchline literally bounces to and fro between the two. In the same way, in normal perception, the sequence of our experience sets up a main track or pattern, which, when it is a problem we are looking to solve, can become something of a neural rut if a solution eludes us. The dominance of this main track in effect suppresses any alternative tracks or perceptual patterns. The trick of lateral thinking is to move our thinking laterally onto a more productive sidetrack. Edward's tools and techniques for doing this, which I explain in Chapter Six, force this conceptual leap (or 'break-out') from the dominant pattern or rut.

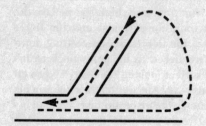

Lateral thinking is a means of escaping the dominant main track to form a new perception which is logical only in hindsight.

The purpose of logic is no longer to find the final conclusion, but to make sure it is sound once it has been found. All creative ideas of value are logical in hindsight. They have to be, however roundabout may have been the route to the new idea. Edward calls this the basic asymmetry of neural patterns. 'The path from A to B is not the same as the path from B to A. Imagine we have a tree that splits into branches, each of which splits into many twigs and then leaves. Imagine we have an ant sitting on the trunk of a tree. What are the chances of that ant reaching one specified leaf? At every branch junction the chances will diminish by 1 over the number of branches. Given an average tree the chances are about 1 in 80,000 of reaching a particular leaf. But if we have the ant sitting on the leaf, what are the chances of that ant reaching the trunk of the tree? 1 in 1! Same sort of asymmetric system as in creativity.'

It is instructive to see how new ideas are generally discovered in fact. When Edward hosted a conference for eleven Nobel prizewinners in Seoul, Korea, in 1989, one of them only had reached their breakthrough idea by systematic analysis (page 239). In *The Act of Creation* (1964), Arthur Koestler quotes Max Planck, the father of quantum mechanics, as writing: 'the pioneer scientist must have "a vivid intuitive imagination for new ideas not generated by deduction, but by artistically creative imagination." . . . I cannot recall any explicit statement to the contrary by any mathematician or physicist.' Again, the thesis of Thomas Kuhn's *Structure of Scientific Revolutions* (first published in 1962) is precisely that great advances in science are down to paradigm shifts brought about by an inspired perception or insight, which calls into question the logic of the prevailing interpretation.

Yet we love to preserve the prevailing or conventional perception, particularly of course if it embodies a lot of our own work, so that 'the one little fact which will not come inside the philosopher's edifice has to be pushed and tortured until it seems to consent', as Bertrand Russell warned in *Our Knowledge of the External World* (1914). 'Yet the one little fact is likely to be more important for the future than the system with which it is inconsistent. Pythagoras invented a system which fitted admirably with all the facts he knew, except the incommensurability of the diagonal of a square and the side; this one little fact stood out, and remained a fact even after Hippasus of Metapontion was drowned for revealing it. To us, the discovery of this fact is the chief claim of Pythagoras to immortality, while his system has become a matter of merely historical curiosity.'

In his monumental story of modern physics, *The Elegant Universe*

(1999), Brian Greene presents a picture of scientists desperately beavering away to stoke up the logic of coherence even in the face of evidence which damned their unified picture of things. It was their guilty secret that the 'two foundational pillars upon which modern physics rests,' Einstein's Theory of Relativity and the more recent quantum mechanics, were wholly incompatible, writes Greene. These large-scale and small-scale interpretations of the universe, respectively, simply didn't agree. They couldn't both be right, but for the physicists to admit as much was tantamount to admitting that their own work was way off beam.

Very often such a situation can be the prelude to a whole paradigm shift – in this case, to Superstring Theory, a version of reality which overturns the notion that matter is composed fundamentally of particles. It suggests instead that matter consists of vibrant patterns resonating at frequencies, which achieve their expression in particles of matter. 'Just as the different vibrational patterns of a violin string give rise to different musical notes,' writes Greene, 'the different vibrational patterns of a fundamental string give rise to different masses and force charges.' Suddenly there are no fundamental particles, just the 'music' of vibrating strings. The music of the heavens – the poets were right after all.

Time and again breakthrough is made as Edward describes it. The French mathematician, physicist and philosopher Jules Poincaré's view was that 'to invent you must think à coté', literally 'aside', the word precisely suggesting the obliqueness of Edward's lateral thinking. Only two or three years before *The Use of Lateral Thinking*, Koestler wrote, 'When a situation is blocked, straight thinking must be superseded by "thinking aside"; the new insight will be found in a hitherto incompatible or unassociated context and will at the moment of discovery be linked not to one associative context, but *bisociated* with two'.

When Einstein, at sixteen, began pondering on an apparent paradox in James Clark Maxwell's electromagnetic wave theory and Newton's laws of motion, he had no more facts at his disposal than the leading physicists who were also looking at the problem, but he thought *a coté*, he brought to bear a different perception, which, ten years later, when he published his Special Theory of Relativity, altered our perceptions of space and time forever. 'Einstein did no experiments, gathered no new information,' writes Edward, 'before he created the Theory of Relativity ... He contributed nothing except a *new way of looking* at information that had been available to everyone else. The experiments confirming the theory came afterwards.'

Edward's purpose is to enable a shift in perception with his tools and techniques of lateral thinking. In fact, he would have people constantly shifting perception in this way, which is how his mind works – to change perception and keep on changing perception, to shake us out of our judgemental rut of an existence. As we will see, he did an enormous amount of research with children, possibly more than anyone has done before or since, and time and again he found the child of around nine coming up with a highly original solution because he was, as yet, not boxed in to the conventional approach.

It was this 'escape from the conventional' ticket that gained him acceptance by the deliberately unconventional, anti-establishment youth culture of the 1960s. In fact, he wasn't so much anti-establishment (excepting academia) as pro-creativity, particularly in education, though he did in those days exhibit something of the idealism characteristic of the times. 'Once a new idea springs into existence,' he wrote, 'it cannot be un-thought. There is a sense of immortality in a new idea.'

The difference, then, between humour and insight is that in insight the new way of looking at things must have real value. Insight is different from intuition, but only because in intuition, after a build-up of patterns over a period of time, something happens (often by chance or mistake) to tip us into a new awareness. Edward's big project was initially to make insight and intuition happen less by chance or mistake.

Paul MacCready shows how intuition works. He is president and chairman of AeroVironment Inc. In 1977, he won the Henry Kramer Prize when his Gossamer Condor aircraft made the first sustained, controlled flight by a heavier-than-air craft powered solely by a pilot's muscles. Since then his company has produced an amazing number of pioneering and ecologically sound developments in the fields of alternative energy, power electronics, and land, sea and air vehicles. In 2000 he was named by *Esquire* magazine as first among twenty-one innovators whose work is transforming our civilisation. 'There are always a dozen interesting problems lurking around in my mind,' he says.

They may be personal, technological, to do with policy, whatever, and you are reading a magazine and another little piece fits in to the puzzle, and while you are hanging around an airline terminal and you have some time, you put in another piece. But still the problem isn't solved. Then, for some reason or other, you *stumble on something*, and it is the last piece and it *is* solved and you can now take it out and do it. So, with the Gossamer Condor you can now take it out and do it.

MacCready's Gossamer Condor succeeded because he came up with a 96-foot vehicle which weighed only 55–70 pounds. Sounds simple, but many others had failed. I asked him how he 'stumbled on' the solution.

I was solely motivated by the fact that the prize money [$95,000] was the same as a debt I had accumulated. First question, was there an easy way to win the prize that would fit into my economics and time scale and schedule? I stumbled around and tried to think of different ways of doing it, but each time it turned out that my solutions were about like those tried in England by these elegant teams and they hadn't succeeded. I couldn't hope to do as well as they had, so there wasn't any sense taking that any further.

So, I was still on the puzzle. It was one of a dozen in my mind and there were still missing pieces to it, and I went off and did some other things. You could say I forgot about it, consigned it to my subconscious. Then these other things made me take a rather broad look at some scaling laws of flying machines.

It is important to realise that he didn't just sit around waiting for a brilliant idea. Patterns of thought he had built up in connection with the Gossamer Condor were simply left alone for a while, he consigned them to his subconscious, and, most importantly, he turned to another context or framework, in which arose just the approach he needed to solve the problem in the first. He got to thinking about 'birds, this kind of bird, that kind of bird, this hang glider, that sail plane, and the scaling laws between these are very simple – you are looking at powers, power to pound . . .' MacCready believes passionately that we 'need to educate people in thinking. We are dealing with THE most powerful force on earth and de Bono is the catalyst that gets things going.'

On one occasion, the physicist Murray Gell-Mann (responsible for discovering the quark and the Eightfold Way, a method of categorising subatomic particles) made a mistake on the blackboard during a lecture, giving certain particles an isospin of 1, knowing it should have been $1/2$. The error jogged 'his brain out of a rut and down this new avenue'. As his biographer George Johnson tells so intriguingly in *Strange Beauty* (1999), Gell-Mann has an extraordinary ability to take a hazy idea that somehow feels right, then to 'tease out' its hidden patterns and give it 'a structure, an architecture, something you could turn over in your mind'. Murray would immerse himself for days in 'long streams of thought', then step back. This sort of intuition, rooted in study, sounds like that of Lloyd Morgan – 'Saturate yourself through and through with your subject ... and wait.' Another Nobel physicist, the Norwegian-born American Ivar Giaever, concurs, holding that creativity for scientists comes from constantly turning over their ideas in their minds, 'whether they drive, eat, sleep or make love. This ruminating process allows unrelated impulses to trigger associations in the brain, and eureka! – an unexpected solution suddenly appears. In lateral thinking this haphazard way of gaining insight is replaced by a deliberate method that, in a prescribed and systematic way, solves the problems.'

One difference between the biological, neural-network system of the brain and a computational system is that in the brain both the incoming information and the receiving medium work actively together. Information arrives via the senses like rain onto the landscape, organising itself and being organised into gullies, streams and river-patterns already there, the very flow increasing the probability of these pathways being followed in the future.

Threshold effects of familiarity, association, emotional bias and so on enable patterns to form, and succeeding states become inevitable. These patterns have large catchment areas that funnel in incoming data so that we tend to see the world in ways we have in the past. This is useful, making for stability and continuity. Without it life would indeed be impossible. It is how, unless otherwise provoked, the brain works. If, each morning, we put on eleven items of clothing, we would have to consider 39,916,800 ways of completing the task if it wasn't for this characteristic of the brain. The downside is that the brain tends to see only what it is prepared to see. This is the crucial, self-maximising feature of the brain. It is an environment in which *dominant* paths or patterns form, where established ideas tend to establish themselves further, where alternative pathways are naturally suppressed.

As a result, the brain is fundamentally *un*creative. 'The excellence of the human brain is that it is designed to form patterns from the world around us and then to stick to these patterns,' he tells us. 'That is how perception works, and life would be totally impossible if the brain were to work differently. The purpose of the brain is to enable us to survive and to cope. The purpose of the brain is *not* to be creative.'

In *Unweaving the Rainbow* (1998), biologist Richard Dawkins, the first Charles Simonyi Professor of the Public Understanding of Science at

Oxford University, gives a powerful description of how the brain constructs our perceptions of the external world according to what it is prepared to see. He keeps a mask of Einstein in his room, hollow side out, face against the wall. 'Visitors gasp when they glimpse it,' he writes. Why? They see the face as if it were facing them. The observer's brain actually fills in what it expects to see – the nose, the brow, the chin and so on.

Get hold of a mask of any human face, 'stand it in a good light and look at it from the far side of the room. If you look at it the normal way round, not surprisingly it appears solid. But now turn the mask so that it is facing away from you and look at the hollow side from across the room. Most people see the illusion immediately...' It is really spooky if you move from side to side, or up and down, and most striking of all when the mask is rotated. When the hollow side comes round, it becomes convex and appears to start revolving in the opposite direction.

Dawkins, whose earlier bestseller was *The Selfish Gene* (1989), shows that our senses provide us with an incomplete view of external reality and that the brain, being equipped with 'a storecupboard of basic images', literally constructs 'a kind of virtual reality', which is constantly updated. Whenever we see something, the brain is making use of a model of that thing which it carries. There is a constructed model already in the brain, a model 'constrained by' information fed in by the outside world. When one reads Dawkins, a biologist, and the cognitive psychologist Steven Pinker, one has an eerie sense of this virtual reality in which we live. Our senses give us a shorthand picture of what they feel is going on out there, what's 'news', and our brains construct a picture that keeps things on a perceptual even keel, what has satisfied us in the past. When one reads, in Pinker's *How the Mind Works* (1998), of patients who lose their sensation of colour and see the surfaces of objects as 'grimy and rat coloured', one wonders whether perhaps they are nearer reality than we are – colours are not measurable properties of objects, after all. Pinker's final conclusion that 'our conscious sensation of colour and lightness matches the world as it is rather than as it presents itself to the eye' seems completely at variance with this. Dawkins is as optimistic as Pinker – 'We are used to living in our simulated world and it is kept so beautifully in synchrony with the real that we don't realise it is a simulated world.' How does he know? Give me Edward's 'Perceptions are real even when they do not reflect reality,' any day, or the Greek Sophist Protagoras's statement, 'What seems to me is so to me: what seems to you is so to you.'

And there lies the rub. In the system universe of perception we cannot afford to judge reality, truth, and so on, only how it is, or was, *for you*. If our sense organs permit contact with reality *as it is*, then why are quantum physicists no longer in the business of classifying sub-atomic particles by mass or charge, but by isospin, strangeness, charm, truth and beauty – qualities so abstract that they do not exist within our three- and four-dimensional world. They literally cannot be perceived by our senses, but they must exist because without them nothing makes sense.

Sense perception may not be Edward's focus, but there is distinct overlap between the two fields, stemming from the sheer dominance of the brain in both as it conjures models of reality for us. Habits of natural selection that have been working on our genes for generations are, Dawkins says, among the elements forming this mental store-cupboard. And in referring to the brain's contribution as 'biases', Dawkins strays from 'seeing' with the eye to 'seeing' in the inner perceptual sense, which is de Bono territory.

Already, back in 1979, Edward was referring to an individual's set of perceptual biases, which trigger dominant patterns in the brain and determine action, as his or her *logic-bubble*. 'We can talk of selfishness, short-sightedness, limited vision, tunnel vision and self-interest and in a way we will be talking about logic-bubbles . . .' Edward wrote in *Future Positive* (1979), and demonstrated the point with two contemporary examples:

> The British government has a problem because British shipyards have no work and if they closed, the increase in unemployment would do their electoral chances no good (and in any case the shipyards are in areas where there is no alternative employment) so the government heavily subsidises the yards to build ships for Poland: ships that are going to compete against the British ships and are directly under Soviet control. So everyone is acting perfectly logically within his own logic-bubble.

At a seminar in Toronto, at a time when women's rights in the workplace were becoming a priority, Edward raised a cheer from the women in the audience by suggesting that women's wages should be 15 per cent higher than those of men. He expressed himself amazed at the response. He had assumed that the notion would be unpopular with women because it would make them more expensive to employ than men and encourage discrimination. 'All I can suppose,' he wrote, 'is that their liberation logic-bubble was too strong and too opaque.'

Our logic-bubbles embody the perceptual biases which impel us to action. Within them we act completely logically, though we may fail to act advisedly. A tendency to act in a particular direction he refers to as a logic-bubble's 'polarity of action'.

The problems of Northern Ireland would seem to exhibit intense polarities of action, and this is indeed an area into which Edward has been drawn. 'Too often people lie back and say thinking is peripheral, human nature won't change, historical enmities won't change,' he said to me recently. 'It is not true. Northern Ireland is bad thinking, bad design. I have met most of the players. Years ago I had a meeting with Sinn Fein. I have met David Trimble, who is a reasonable fellow. I met Gerry Adams recently. Mary McAleese [the President of Ireland] I know quite well.'

I asked Tom Farrell of the De Bono Foundation in Dublin how this had come about.

Five years ago he was invited to give a talk for a day by the Training and Employment Agency in Belfast. They brought him over for a conference called 'The Winning Ways', 350 people for the morning and then in the afternoon a number of people turned up to talk about Northern Ireland. There were three guys there. Definitely *not* Unionists. One of them has died since. They were late coming in and a girl called Falkener who runs the system up there, she got the chairs for these fellas, and would you believe her father was the Stormont first minister? She actually went and got the chairs for them!

After that, about two or three days later, I had a phone call: 'Would Dr de Bono meet Sinn Fein at Clonard House in Belfast?' I called Edward. He said, 'Yes.' We had a two-hour meeting with these people, and the message was they wanted him to get the business world to help the peace process. What we decided was that Paul Rowan, who was Chairman of the Foundation in Belfast at that time, would invite fifty of the top people around Northern Ireland across all divides, including trades union, Unionist, UUP, DUP, Alliance, etc, plus the commercial side, plus the head of the prison system, etc, and for one day Edward talked to them. From there came the idea that we should train a number of people in the peace process, on the ground, through the Training and Employment Agency and the Peace and Reconciliation Unit within that operation and with funding from the EU. There was a pilot of 250 people. We just completed it. We have people like Bernadette MacAliskey (neé Devlin) on this. We had the Women's Group, all sorts of fields, all able to talk to each other after a very short period.

In the meantime Edward was invited by the Northern Ireland Quality Centre, which is part of the EFQM (European Foundation for Quality Management). While he was there we had a meeting with Sean Fallon, the Minister for Higher Education Training and Employment, Bob Barber from EFQM, an organisation called LEDU. From that meeting it was decided that Edward would come to Belfast three times a year at no cost to anybody to give talks around the provinces. Subsequently, I met with Bob Barber and Michael Copeland and we are going to run Six Hats programmes around the province and a poster campaign – 'New Thinking Northern Ireland'. This is just starting now, putting things together, talking to sponsors. When we are ready Edward will come over and we will do television and have a press conference and launch the whole concept.

I said to Edward that you surely couldn't find a section of the people more firmly with lid down on the box than on opposite sides of the divide in Northern Ireland. He said,

In Northern Ireland, everyone is looking for a constructive way out without surrendering this way or that way. When I met Gerry Adams, I said, 'This business about surrendering the arms, you're never going to surrender the arms, why don't you sell them?' I said if the IRA sold them they are beyond reach, you have got the money, you could buy them back again if you need them or you could distribute the money. They talk about 'beyond reach' … I am not sure what they mean, but selling them is the classic way of getting the arms beyond reach without surrendering and yet having the benefit.

I then had a note from Ian Paisley saying he wanted to meet me. Once, I was giving a lecture in North Carolina and the people who were organising the lecture were very concerned because at the press conference in the morning there were a lot of people from Bob Jones University. Now Bob Jones University is where Paisley was trained and is fundamental Southern Baptist, really conservative. They were very concerned that when we came to the lecture it was going to be full of Bob Jones University people. I turned up. Yes, there were all these Bob Jones people. But they loved it! We need that, we need new ideas. They weren't at all threatened.

Thinking forms Edward's perception of a situation and determines his feelings about it, *not* the other way round, and this is what he encourages in his thinking programmes. Until people can allow themselves thinking time before their feelings and emotions make judgements and decisions for them, the creative process will never see the light of day. When feelings act on sense data without thinking, we get stereotypes, clichés, prejudices, standard opinions, and so on. 'Without thinking,' he once wrote, 'feeling is tyranny.'

The trouble is that for most of us, withholding judgement comes no more naturally than thinking up new ideas. Edward saw that this is so, and argued (page 244) that Socrates, Plato and Aristotle programmed us to think this way. In the 1980s, convinced that we don't have to, he introduced the concept of parallel thinking and devised Six Thinking Hats to enable the more constructive and creative approach. Its take-up by business and education round the world has been phenomenal, but what is fascinating in the present context is how natural both parallel thinking and lateral thinking were to Edward, and how his formative years provided a particularly favourable environment to develop them.

Chapter Three

Genetic Mix

'Key things about me as a boy were curiosity, a great interest in making things hapen, an unwillingness to accept that this is the only way something can be.'

Edward was born, the second of four brothers, to Joseph and Josephine de Bono on 19 May 1933, in Malta. The family lived in South Street, Valletta, an impressive city to the northeast of this Mediterranean island, commanding the Grand Harbour.

If you walk up through Valletta at dusk in the still, blasted heat of a July evening, it seems darkly redolent of the island's agonies over the last millennium, its awesome, shadowy, cliff-top architecture, iron-barred windows and plummeting depths echoing with the cries of children.

In fact, Valletta was founded in 1566, the year after the Great Siege of Malta by Suleiman the Magnificent's Muslim hordes, which so marks the island's history, but in time to savour two hundred years of rigorous control by another fundamentalist group, the Jesuits – the Roman Catholic order of the Society of Jesus, whose aim was the spiritual purification of all mankind.

Elsewhere on the island, there are reminders of a far older fanaticism. In the Blue Grotto area sacrificial temples, built around 3800 BC in honour of an androgynous god(dess) of fertility, are more impressive even than Stonehenge. Their primitive purpose brings to mind the startling image of bloody, human sacrifice by an Aztec priest, with which Edward opens *Conflicts: A Better Way to Resolve Them* (1985), the book that demonstrates the relativity of our perceptions (to cultures, to times) and discovers, in parallel thinking, a way around conflict in the process of changing them.

The strategic value of Malta's position, slap bang in the middle of the Mediterranean, made it a trading centre as early as Phoenician times (1st millennium BC), and has meant that it has suffered more than its fair share of adversarial politics and strife, not least in the last war.

Things hotted up with the advent of Christianity, which declared the island in opposition to neighbouring Arab cultures. St Paul washed up on Malta in AD 60, having been shipwrecked in the north coast bay, now a popular resort bearing his name. At that time, the Roman chief of the island was one Publius, Edward's namesake – he was christened Edward Francis Charles Publius de Bono. Publius was Malta's first bishop. The Romans had earlier made Malta a *municipium*, indicating a privileged independence, and it seems to have been a civilised and well-heeled sort of place at this time.

As in nearby Italy, Catholicism and family are key cultural focuses. Unaffected by the Greek schism in the early days of the Christian Church, Maltese Christians have always been deeply loyal to Rome. Roman Catholicism dominates every aspect of life, and the undertow of centuries of superstition could be heard in one islander's comment during the recent tussle over whether to separate a pair of Siamese twins born on the neighbouring island of Gozo – 'The [surviving] child will be cursed. This was for God and nature to decide.'

Despite all this, it was still perfectly possible in the 1930s, even for a family as influential on the island as Edward's, for religion not to dominate daily life. But you certainly couldn't avoid it, and the strong, deep-truth religious culture, political polarisations and fundamentalist history would have played a part in the developing awareness of any thinking boy – and Edward was no exception.

Following conquest by the Arabs in 870 and delivery by the Normans 200 years later, ownership of Malta seems subsequently to have passed to and fro like a shuttlecock, to no great benefit of the indigenous islanders. Then, in 1530, the Knights of St John of Jerusalem were given the island by the Holy Roman Emperor Charles V.

The Knights of St John, a military/religious order founded around the time of the first Crusade in the late 11th century, proved themselves in Malta between May and September 1565 during the Great Siege. Some estimate that 40,000 Muslims attempted to conquer the island, with its fighting contingent of less than 9,000. These were months of terrible suffering and extraordinary valour, and they put the Knights of St John on the map.

With the Knights in charge, the Jesuits, an order founded by Ignatius Loyola in 1540, formed a solid base on the island until their expulsion in 1768 – a time when they were being ousted elsewhere in Europe. The Knights' legacy is still clear in Malta; many place names refer to them, and in fact Edward's 17th-century house at Zebbug sports a Jesuit crest which suggests that the dwelling might have belonged to a senior member of the Order.

Thirty years after the Jesuits' departure, in June 1798, the Knights, made soft by years of wealth and other comforts, ceded power to Napoleon Bonaparte. The name de Bono first appeared in Malta in the 17th century, but on Edward's mother's side there is a story that he is descended from Napoleon. Besides the similarity of the names, some odd coincidences have surreptitiously helped to lend the tale credence. Edward's mother's name was, as we've noted, Josephine, as is his wife's. Then there is this thing that Edward has about islands. Besides being born on one, as Napoleon was, Edward owns four, and always says he plans to retire to a Greek isle, where he will live on love and goat's cheese. One might even point to Napoleon's dislike for the critical, judgemental way of thinking that Edward's parallel thinking system sidesteps.

But Napoleon and islands were in fact rather a poor combination (Elba can't have been much of a treat) and, well, the liaison must have been short-lived because Boney left Malta for Egypt after only six days, the island ceding to the British Crown through the efforts of Lord Nelson, who, in 1799, had put in Captain Alexander Bell as President of the Maltese Assembly. I mentioned this to Edward's younger brother Peter, who was quite unfazed: 'The dalliance was in Naples, not on Malta,' he said, sharp as a sabre. 'The girl returned to Malta, where she was then married to Baron Muscati. Her name was Judith Cohen. My grandmother is a Muscati.'

When I aired it with their half-sister Elizabeth, over a very enjoyable tea at The Randolph Hotel in Oxford, she exclaimed, 'Oh, good for Peter! That *was* quick thinking. Napoleon? Oh, please, don't. I mean it is possible, but it is not, shall we say, likely. It came from Mummy. She was a good journalist ... I can't say I grew up with that one, it emerged rather late, but she did go on about it rather a lot, even put it in the *Times of Malta*, I think.'

Elizabeth is a delight, and as it seemed that I might have unearthed a genetic tendency to mythologise (and as provocative speculation is a tool of lateral thinking), I offered her the last scone and pressed my advantage: 'Sandra Dingli told me that your stepmother had an idea about the Blue Grotto temples being connected somehow with the Egyptian pyramids in Egypt ...'

'No, keep away!' she protested, choking on the scone. 'My brother Tony [Edward's elder brother] is keen about archaeology and does know something about it. Take my advice, keep away.'

Josephine de Bono was 'a very powerful woman, a lovely person', recalls Peter. Indeed, everyone to whom I spoke, and who knew her, agreed. Edward's son, Caspar, a generation distant, gave me the warmest recommendation: 'She was a lot of fun. She used to tell stories all of the time and ended up telling you the same ones you heard last time, though always with a different twist. They got more elaborate as time went on. She was a matriarch.'

Elizabeth's mother was Josephine's cousin (their grandmothers were sisters), 'so the relationship with my brothers, Tony, Edward, Peter and David, was much closer than you might think,' she told me.

> My mother, Cora Cassar, died a month after I was born. It was on account of the birth. She was Maltese, of course, her grandfather had been a surgeon, and my uncle, Harold Cassar, a Rhodes scholar. Then another uncle, Tony Cassar, was brought up in England with Josephine, like brother and sister. Tony, the black sheep of the family, was shipped off to England after his mother, my grandmother, died, also in childbirth, and there was Josephine. This was in Belsize Park, London. I didn't even know that Josephine wasn't my mother until I was fifteen. I was told because I was sitting public examinations and I needed my birth certificate. What was worse was that it was my Aunt Mary who told me. It had a terrible impact.

With stories like this for real I began to feel guilty about doubting the other, albeit remoter, mythologies. Josephine's father had been born in County Cork in southwestern Ireland. The family, it seems, moved to County Down in the north, where the spelling of their name was anglicised from Byrnes to Burns. It was Josephine's grandfather who lived in some splendour in Belsize Park, and at some point in her childhood, around 1912, she was shipped off to London and placed in his care. His name was Agius, a name widely used among the Maltese. No. 3 Belsize Grove seems to have been an extraordinary household, teeming with children. Great-grandpapa Agius was a compelling personality and it is interesting to see what led to him being so.

'His early childhood was spent in Egypt, where his father was a wheat merchant who, for a million sovereigns, provided Lord Raglan with wheat in the mid-1850s, during the Crimean War,' Peter told me.

He persuaded the *felahin* [the people of the desert] to carry the laden barges over the rapids of the Nile to bring the wheat up over the Sudan. Then, when the boy was seven, his father was approached by the *felahin* and told, 'Now it is time for your son to spend a year with us in the desert!' Eventually the boy grew up and moved to England as a coal merchant. He spoke French fluently, and Arabic, Maltese, and English of course. He took the big house in Belsize Grove, where the top floor was the nursery, eventually to be ruled by Nanny.

This last word was spoken with some respect. By the time of her death, Nanny Porter had served the family – Edward's youngest brother, David, was the last child in her care – for no less than sixty-seven years.

'Nanny first went to Belsize Park as an under-nurse in the early years of the last century,' Elizabeth told me. 'She came from Leicester, from quite a good family, but her mother died and her father married the housekeeper, so Nanny upped sticks and left home. She then rose to become head nurse in the household, and as my great-grandmother had thirteen or fourteen children, they needed her rather. Among these children were the two sisters who became my mother's and my step-mother Josephine's grandmothers.'

Peter's more apocryphal version of the story is memorable:

Nanny came to the family a convert, had been a Baptist but converted to Catholicism. Family kicked her out and Farm Street [the Jesuits] rang up my great-grandfather and said, 'We have got this girl, what should we do?' He said, 'Send her along.' She brought up twenty-four children, all of whom were highly creative . . . and very self-disciplined.

When my great-uncles came back from the First World War, MCs and all, she would stand at the top of the stairs and say, 'Go and have a bath before you come to my nursery!' Her favourite was Richard Agius, who was killed at Passchendaele on his twenty-first birthday. The Dominican Priory in Hampstead carries a plaque to Richard because my great-grandfather was involved somewhere along the line with its establishment. Great-grandfather was a member of the Vatican order of 'Capa e Spada'.

When I was in the army I was a defending officer in a court martial and afterwards the President came up to me and said, 'Do you know George Denaro?' I said, 'Yes, first cousin.' He said, 'I thought so. Your mannerisms and everything about you said so.' He then said, 'Who is Nanny?' I told him who Nanny was. Nanny had brought up George Denaro and his identical twin, Wilfred [sons of Frank and Marie Denaro, Marie being one of great-grandfather Agius's fourteen children]. 'But,' I said, 'Why do you ask?' He said, 'Because George Denaro was a Japanese prisoner of war with me in Shanghai.' George Denaro would never, never give in to the Japanese. Although they tried to persuade him it just wasn't worth it. And all that George would say was, 'What would Nanny say?'

Stories like that (though I can't think of any other as good) make one want to down tools and pen a film.

Coal, which fuelled the Industrial Revolution, was the thing to be in, and all great-grandfather Agius's children attended expensive schools. 'My great-aunts were finished at the Sacred Heart in Paris and actually referred to their parents as "pater" and "mater",' said Elizabeth, 'which we thought was uproarious.' The tale does nevertheless source the very English colonial structure of life that fed down into the Maltese de Bonos and forms part of their character.

Continued Elizabeth:

They all grew up in England, but the tradition was for the girls to marry Maltese men and the boys, English girls. My great-grandmother came to Malta with her unmarried daughter. All a bit anachronistic because none of them spoke Maltese, only very correct English. They were all sort of caricatures really of upper class English men. Could have gone into the BBC! Terribly funny, really, looking back. After my great-grandfather died, his fortune was lost. That was in the 1920s. My great-uncles didn't have his business sense – too well educated [an observation, incidentally, which runs to the heart of Edward's disaffection for the educational establishment, as we shall see].

My stepmother was very friendly with my father's only sister, Mary de Bono, who was a nun. They were the same age. They were contemporaries. They were at school together. When my mother died, my father went away for six months. Josephine arrived and stayed with Mary. She had been a journalist in London, got septicemia and became very ill. They said that her heart had been affected and that she had come back to Malta to recuperate. She and my father met and married within about six months. Nanny arrived shortly after my brother Tony was born, and she stayed until she died except for a year when she went back to somebody else.

Josephine was very different from my mother. She was very tall and larger than life, active in politics. She got votes for women in Malta and with Edwina Mountbatten she started the Save The Children Fund.

Mrs de Bono's campaigning was intrinsic to her character. Professor John Edwards of the University of Queensland in Brisbane, who met her in the 1980s, told me, 'she was the kind of woman who doesn't sit back. If something needed to be done she would do it, not look around for someone else to do it. I remember, in particular, one afternoon Edward and I were having tea with her and she dressed the two of us down, how we weren't helping with these wars that were going on at the time, and how come "two smart men like you" aren't doing something about it instead of having tea with me.'

Joseph de Bono, Edward's father, was one of three brothers who were doctors. He was professor of medicine at the University of Malta and had a large general practice. His brother Salvina was an ear, nose and throat specialist, and Peter Paul, the eldest, was a professor of surgery.

Father Peter Inglott, Edward's Oxford contemporary whom we have already met, was for many years Rector of the University of Malta, and recalls of Joseph and his brothers, 'They were quite different in character. The surgeon [Peter Paul] was quite active in politics, became the Labour Party Minister of Health, though he only stayed as such a few months because I think he earned much more as a surgeon and the ministry was rather a bureaucratic office. He was the sort of person who, during the war, would operate on tables.'

If this sounds like another apocryphal story, I have it on good authority from one of Peter Paul's patients that table-top surgery was indeed *de rigueur* in Malta at this time. Eric Borg was a boarding-school friend of Edward's in the 1940s. Peter Paul operated on his hernia. 'We were in the hotel business,' Eric recalls, 'and he actually did it in the hotel, you know, during the holidays!'

Edward describes his father as having been 'a quiet, thoughtful sort of man,' something of an antithesis of his larger-than-life wife, 'somewhat provocative in trying things,' as Edward puts it. He sees genetic advantage in that: 'Genetically, they might have been a useful combination – the ability to be provocative and thoughtful at the same time!'

It is, indeed, a fair summing-up of Edward. When I asked him recently whether he is a natural lateral thinker, he replied, 'Provocative, yes.

Exploring and provocative.' So the design of his system was inevitable? 'Certainly the realisation that provocation was a necessary element,' he conceded.

Peter alludes to their father's studiousness: 'He studied every day, six hours a day, until the day he died. He might get up at three o'clock in the morning to study.' Elizabeth mentioned his disinterest in money or worldly goods. As I discovered when I visited Malta, Joseph de Bono's reputation as the very finest doctor lives on more than two decades after his death. I have the feeling that he was the most impressive de Bono, brilliant, modest, inscrutable, and quite unapproachable.

Peter had first-hand experience of his excellence as a doctor, for which, taken as a whole, Joseph was honoured with a CBE.

In 1970 I had my gall bladder removed in a military hospital and everything went wrong … After about three months my father got fed up, came over with all my brothers in one line [Tony, Edward and David], and the military surgeon with his lot in another line on the opposite side of the bed. They looked at me and retired and four hours later my father came back and said, 'You'll be out the day after tomorrow.' And, yes, one of the pills changed that evening and the next day the infection had gone. The surgeon said, 'I have never met a man like that.'

Diagnosis was a particular strength. As a young doctor Joseph was virtually clairvoyant, which once led him astray. Said Peter,

Father would say that he knew what was wrong with a person just by looking at them, but would take an hour examining them to prove to them that he was right. And if the person believed that he was right he could cure them. However, he hated cocktail parties because once when he was young he had a wee bit much and, as women do, one tried to get a free consultation. This woman went up to him and said, 'Doesn't my husband look well?'

My father said, 'I don't know, who is your husband?'

She said, 'Over there.'

He said, 'No. He doesn't. He's got cancer!'

Can you imagine the consternation? They took him to hospital and he had got cancer.

He is remembered, rather more often, for his steadfast principles, his discretion and deep sensitivity for his patients, however. 'When a poor person came to see him,' Peter recalled, 'he would insist on the fee being paid, but then he would put a sign on the prescription to take his fee away from the cost of the medicines. He said, "Never insult a person by telling them he is poor." Things like that stick in one's mind. He had responsibility, a hell of a lot of moral responsibility.'

Edward's brother Tony, a year older than him, attended Christ Church, Oxford, as a Rhodes scholar after Edward, and later became professor of surgery and cardiac surgery at the University of Malta. Peter was born three years after Edward, in 1936; he would go into the army via Sandhurst and later publish Edward's schools materials and design the official website. David was born eleven years on, in 1947. Recalls Elizabeth:

> David was the baby of the family. He was born into a family of teenagers. He wasn't a particularly good baby and I can remember we would all have a go at putting him back to sleep when he cried at night. The whole family would get up and offer advice. I suppose we used to treat him a bit like a toy. He was a bright little boy. At the age of three we used to show him the *Encyclopaedia Britannica* and he would recognise all the pictures and things. He was sort of adult, no contemporaries.

Edward told me that he regarded David as the genius of the family, and Peter concurs. 'Chipper first, Cambridge, Gold Medal in Surgery, British Heart Foundation Professor of Cardiac Medicine, attached to Leicester University. The British Heart Foundation scholarship is now named after him. The medical library at Leicester is named after him. He was a colossus.' Tragically, he died recently from motor neurone disease, symptoms of which appeared only a few years ago.

In 1936, after some three years' occupancy of the house in South Street, the de Bonos left Valletta. The house had been on a ninety-nine-year lease. 'It belonged to my father's family,' Elizabeth told me. 'It was where my grandfather used to live.' After a year in a reputedly haunted house called Villa Refalo, they moved to Ta'Xbiex, pronounced 'Tashbeesh', a well-to-do area on a hill leading down to picturesque Marsamxett Harbour. They took a large house, The Laurels, next door to one occupied by Peter Paul. Then, in 1940, when Italy declared itself pro-Germany, the family moved southwest, away from the coast and the centre of the action against the British naval bases, to No. 1 Dominic Square in Rabat. This was close to the ancient walled city of Mdina, the original capital city.

Nearly 400 years after Suleiman's army had besieged the island, Malta was under siege once more, and on this occasion the courage of the forces and people of Malta earned the country the George Cross. In 1940, the British occupation of this strategically important site involved the islanders in a blitz that was even worse than London's wartime ordeal.

Edward lived through more than 8,000 air raids in two years:

> We used to see the dogfights. There was an awful lot of bombing. You used to hear the whistle of the bombs coming down and if you heard the crunch, you knew you were OK because it wasn't on you. But it wasn't really traumatic. Everything was built of rock so nothing caught fire, and that limited civilian casualties. The thing I remember is that there were no toys because nothing was imported.
>
> When they were digging the air raid shelter in our house in Dominic Square they came across this tomb of some high-born Roman lady. They found gold ornaments and so on, which were transferred to the museum – so that became part of the air raid shelter. Apparently there was some slight superstition and things were changed so that no one would actually have to sleep in the tomb.

Sometimes, during the actual bombardment, Edward's mother found poetic inspiration and scribbled down stanzas which, a decade later, would form a twenty-one-page metrical story which she entitled *The Siege of Malta, 1940–1943*. It went through at least three editions. During this period, when Edward was growing up, the children rarely saw their father. 'We saw him perhaps once a month,' recalls Peter. 'He had his practice, he was looking after the hospitals and all the casualties and trying to work out how best to eke out the rations.'

In fact, Elizabeth, Tony and Edward didn't see much of their parents even before the war. Recalls Elizabeth: 'At Ta'Xbiex we had meals in the nursery. We only started coming down to meals during the war. The war was actually a great leveller. When we moved to Rabat, it was a smaller house and we seemed to have lots of relatives come and stay with us. We had Peter Paul's wife, Aunt Daisy. Aunt Mabel. There was very little food and gradually we all began to muck in a bit. And then in fact Nanny left for a year because one of the children she had brought up before she came to look after Tony and myself had married and had a baby, so Nanny left to look after her baby for a year, maybe two. So, suddenly nursery regime suffered and we all went sort of a bit wild during the war, and Mummy was always quite good at making the best of things.'

Edward's parents were distant from their children when they were growing up, and from 1940 until 1942 (when, following Rommel's defeat in Africa, the family moved back north to Sliema), Rabat offered something of an oasis in the parched desert which was usually the emotional environment of the de Bono household. Birthdays were never a big thing. If you were ill, it was bed and a starvation diet (Edward can still remember the taste of that first boiled egg when he finally got up). Emotional aridity was made a positive virtue by a lionising of the intellect: Peter remembers that when his parents didn't want the children to hear what they said, they would speak in Latin. 'They could read Greek, Latin or any language, it didn't matter ... We cannot help the blood in us and, yes, it is an important thing because we do not have that emotion as a matter of fact. Quite honestly, our upbringing has been totally emotionless. Babies mimic parents and our family was so intellectual there was none of that, and none of that with Nanny either.'

The emotional vacuum at home had one particular object or effect: it instilled self-reliance in the children. 'We were never a family that depended on other members of the family. It was simply assumed that everyone would be self-reliant,' said Edward. 'Father was pretty silent ... I never had a discussion with him ... The only time I ever asked him for anything was when I was going to Oxford [University] and needed some money. I never talked much to either of my parents. My brothers and I played soldiers together but we didn't have deep discussions. I've never relied much on discussing things with anyone else. I have always gone my own way.'

Nanny was the children's stability, but even she instilled iron self-discipline. 'She was a warm woman but if you were naughty you felt cold,' Peter said. 'You were never hit ... Nanny was always there and she held the respect of everybody.'

Elizabeth describes Nanny as 'Very disciplined, but she spoiled us in a way. When she went out she would always return with toys and things. Tony and I adored her, and once when she threatened to leave – she had a row with my stepmother – I had hysterics. You see there were four of us under six and the year I was six [1936], Peter was born in the April. She used to push one pram and pull another!'

Edward concedes that 'Nanny was a central figure as a source of affection. She was with us the whole time so she was, perhaps, a rather more direct influence on me than my parents.' But his take from her was less the affection than the self-discipline and stability and balance which she instilled: 'She was a very traditional English nanny, very strong, never lost her temper, never in despair. She was very stable, just kept going. I learned from her that you put up with things. You don't depend on people or think that people owe you something, or complain that things are unfair.'

Self-reliance and a lack of love would inevitably have an impact on Edward's life. It is natural to conclude that it did Edward harm. Edna Copley, who worked with Edward on his schools thinking programmes from the early 1970s, is not alone among Edward's friends and associates in so saying: 'Edward has a basic insecurity, which is at odds with the face that he is presenting to the world, and deep down I believe he may be an unhappy man. He must have been very lonely as a child. He knew he was different. He wanted the kind of love that the family background didn't supply.'

Another long-time friend said, 'I feel that he felt rather separated from his parents. When he was sent to boarding-school at a very early age, he *was* still on the island, close to home, so sending him was very much a discipline. Maybe his parents were of that era. They were sort of removed. I know he had a nanny who wasn't very close to him either. From what I can gather she was another of these people who sort of held him fairly far away, didn't hug . . . and that may have added to the feeling of distancing him from his mother.' Edward's wife, Josephine, said to me recently that her mother-in-law saw her first duty as being a wife to her husband rather than a mother to her children.

There is, however, an alternative way of looking at things, and that is that the de Bono family environment rather suited Edward, preoccupied as he was with thinking from a very early age. Perhaps he was even, in his quiet way, a force shaping it. In the complex triggering of family relationships, who is to say who or what creates the whole?

'Edward's lack of emotion?' queried his sister, when I iterated the trait that impels most comment and is such an issue in his thinking programmes. 'It is not Nanny because Nanny brought us all up.'

'His mother doesn't explain why there was a lack of emotion in Edward's life at all,' added another. 'Have you looked at the other children? Are they all like him? You have got to look at the others to see. Edward is a phenomenon. You have got to look at him like that and say,

"How do you do what he has done?" He may be lonely, but he *wants* to be lonely. It is more comfortable.'

I will return to this theme as we get closer to the man through his projects. For his part, Edward says, 'We were never a family that depended on other members of the family,' but claims no traumas on being sent at seven years of age as a border to St Edward's College: 'I only saw my parents during the holidays, even though they didn't live very far away [in fact, a walk away], but I didn't feel odd or depressed about it.' More than half a century on, he likes to feel he is living by the old Maltese saying, 'Quietly, quietly, with his horns in his pocket,' which means you get on with things and don't make a fuss. It's not a fashionable stance in an era contaminated with soap-opera values, but it is the way that he is: self-sufficient, self-reliant.

I asked Norah Maier, a friend of Edward's and sometime professor at the University of Toronto School for the Very Able, how far Edward's traits are characteristic of the gifted child. 'Self-reliance is very strong among the gifted, certainly, very strong. Independence is an important element.'

Control of the emotions (as opposed to suppression) is a fundamental requirement in his thinking programmes. In the 1960s and 1970s, when he first set out his stall, Edward recognised that feeling was more fashionable than thinking – although the trend had not reached industry or the military. With Vietnam fresh in people's minds, he wrote: 'Body counts in the war were just numbers on paper to be juggled with and not real people. Pollution was a necessary cost of industrialisation and not real rivers with real dead fish ... Feeling sets priorities, gives direction, and provides pressures.' But the thinking has to come first. 'You need organisation to channel the energy of feeling, and ideas to give it form. Feeling strongly about cities does not actually transform them.' In *Future Positive*, one of the four reasons why thinking is important is that it enables you *not* to follow 'the emotion of the moment'. In *Handbook For A Positive Revolution* (1990), emotions are 'the sauce of life', but 'self-improvement means gaining control of them.'

Edward's self-reliance and intelligent introspection enabled him to get on well at school. 'I was a quiet sort of boy,' he recalls, 'always thinking about things. I ended up a couple of years ahead.' Peter had to suffer the consequences of the de Bono reputation: 'The cruellest thing at school was that if we did not come first we were a disgrace to the name,' he recalls. 'Not from my parents. Never mentioned the word. But from the teachers. Expectations were high from everybody. You did not compete with the de Bonos. For five generations, de Bonos had been professors at the university, mostly of medicine.'

Edward meanwhile was attending his own 'inner academy', for his teachers had learned simply to leave him to it. 'I was lucky, very early on, at the age of eight or nine, my teachers just left me alone, they let me do my own thing,' he once said to Maier.

'St Edward's College was set up by the Strickland family. It was part of the English versus Italian culture struggle dominant in Malta at the time,' Father Peter tells me.

> The British in Malta had behaved like a garrison – they hadn't tried to influence Maltese life at all before the Fascists under Mussolini began to consider Malta as *terra redenda*, a bit of Italy not yet united to the mainland. Italian was the language for teaching at the university and law courts and so on. Lord Strickland was half English, half Maltese, and he became a pillar of the Empire, pushing this Anglicisation policy further than even the Colonial Office wanted. St Edward's College was part of this campaign.

Sir John Philip Ducane, Governor of Malta, persuaded the War Office to let the school take over a military site in Cottonera. Cottonera is across the Grand Harbour from Valletta. The building used to be a military hospital, and in the holidays, when all but deserted, it seems more military than scholarly still – regimented, flat-roofed, porticoed buildings and bastions at the back, where I saw generations of boys' names carved into the white stone and listened to a gun salute from the nearby harbour. However, it was only during his last couple of years at school that Edward attended the Cottonera site. During the war, while the de Bonos lived at Rabat, the school moved to nearby Mdina.

Father Peter continues,

> To the rest of the Maltese educational system, St Edward's stood apart, first of all because it was by far the most expensive, and only the most well-to-do could afford to send their children there. Then, because it was a boarding-school, and in Malta, with the family thing so strong, very few parents would want to send their children away from them, particularly when it is so close by. They also had a disciplinarian type of thing . . . I think they were trying to model the college on Rugby School – you know, the original English public school sort of ethos, which of course is a completely alien mode of

education to the traditional Maltese. I mean, the Maltese usually don't even put children to bed at a certain time, and if you go out at ten o'clock you'll still see small children playing around with their family, small children allowed to do what they liked practically.

The college had a Roman Catholic foundation, like everything in Malta, but the headmaster was a member of the British Conference of Public Schools, so the intention was for it to be as like a British public school as possible.

It all sounds like the worst case of colonial cringe imaginable, and provincial snobbery was rife. 'It wasn't easy for any of us, because everybody would finger you,' said Peter. '"We know who his father is, who his mother is . . ."'

Edward remained impervious to the dehumanising process of this ersatz English public school. 'I got on with things. No traumas . . . I loved science – I was the only boy with a key to the chemistry lab. Thinking was originally my hobby. Of course one could never have chosen it to be a career, but I loved making and inventing things.'

Pretty soon, his teachers realised they had something of a phenomenon on their hands. 'I jumped classes twice,' Edward recalls. 'In other words, I once went to the class above the one above me, and then a second time, so I was three or four years younger than others.' This led to its own set of problems at home.

'There was competition with elder brother Tony,' Elizabeth recalls. 'That was inevitable because there was barely a year between them, but even worse for Tony, Edward was bright. I mean, Tony was bright, but Edward was, well, he moved up to be in the same class as Tony, and that caused a lot of friction because they had to share a bedroom due to the lack of space at home . . . It was very upsetting for Tony.'

At school, it meant that Edward was rubbing shoulders with children who were bigger and often physically stronger. 'Thinking was important because I couldn't use muscle!' he says, and his inventive nature was soon put into service to curry favour with his older classmates.

Our school was in what is now the Cathedral Museum in Mdina, the old walled city, and I pioneered an escape route going down through the cellars and into the air raid shelters by making keys to open the big iron gates. We went through the middle of the girls' convent, underground, and came out in the centre of the town. So when the older boys wanted to go out for a beer they'd have to come to me and borrow the maps to use the route I'd opened up. Only the senior boys knew about that. I was never found out, never caught.

I asked his brother Peter whether Edward made many friends. 'We were all alone at school,' he replied. 'We only had, say, two or three friends. One of Edward's best friends was a chap called Borg 5 – Edward was de Bono 4 – Eric Borg was his name.'

'I was at school with Edward,' confirmed Eric Borg when I hunted him down on Gozo. 'He was in the same class as me. I haven't seen him since. I was born in 1930, so I was three years older than him. It was a very small class. There were only seven. I think about four of them are dead now. I used to go to his summer place in St Paul's Bay in the holidays.'

By this time, round 1947 or 1948, the school was back in Cottonera. Edward had caught up with pupils three years his senior and the de Bonos had moved out of Rabat to No. 83 Rudolph Street, Sliema, not far from Ta'Xbiex and close to the Blue Sisters Hospital, where Joseph was working. After David was born in 1947, Josephine began to pressure her husband to move to a larger house, away from the dust and traffic of Sliema. 'So, as a sop to Mummy, my father bought the holiday house in St Paul's Bay,' recalls Elizabeth. 'We went there in 1947, 1948, and stayed four or five years.'

Eric recalled:

Edward and I used to spend many a day there together. He was always very keen on sports and cars – cricket was the great favourite. He used to be a very good googly bowler. You never knew what he would send down to you. He was very tricky, you know? He was also very sure of himself. He never really studied, and always came first. I think he only ever studied the night before the exam and always came top. We, of course, had been swotting for ages before that.

There was a bit of snobbery. His father was a professor, you know? But it didn't bother me at all. The de Bonos, they were top of the tree. His uncle was an MP – Peter Paul – and also a famous professor, a surgeon. And his mother, she went out for the Labour Party, was very friendly with the Prime Minister, Mr Mintoff.

Rarely was his father at the house. He had a big practice and his university work. There was a nice garden there in St Paul's Bay.

I said I was surprised that Edward was interested in cars. You will never see him drive one today, and he has absolutely no interest in status symbols. But Borg insisted.

If there is one image I have of him, it is in the garden of the house at St Paul's, I have a book about cars in my hand and he is snatching it from my hands and going through it like mad. He didn't like American cars, that was for sure.

Their main house at that time was in Sliema, a very nice house. We used to meet sometimes – Easter, Christmas holidays – and we used to go up there. No one other than me used to go and see him, no one at all from our class. I was the only one.

I asked him why he thought he had been selected as a friend, if that was the case, and he seemed to indicate that he had a bit of a way with the toffs.

There was a chap who is a marquis now, Marquis de Piro. Maybe Edward mentioned him? The rest of the class, they couldn't get used to him because . . . it wasn't his fault . . . he used to talk lah-de-dah. I was always the tallest and once or twice I had representations from some of the other boys. They said, 'We can't get used to Tony [the marquis] at all. You are the biggest, so you go and sort him out,' you know? When I did, Tony said to me, 'Eric, that is just my way of talking. I can't help it.' Actually we became very good friends. Edward used to get on with him too. Fascinating!

I think he was quite a loner in his way. A lot of people didn't like the idea of his always coming first in class and never studying, though he never got into any fights on account of his intelligence. On the sporting field he was quite popular, especially in cricket, though he wasn't very keen on football, which we had to play. Easter term was mostly athletics. He was quite good at running, and of course he used his brains there too – tactics – how to stay back and then have a flurry at the end, that sort of thing.

I don't know, he was a bit . . . seemed to be in a class higher than us somehow.

When Edward transferred to the University of Malta in 1948, at fifteen years of age, there was absolutely no question as to what he would read. 'Medicine was something you did – like getting dressed in the morning,' he said.

The first two years at university were supposed to be foundation years that corresponded to sixth form, but Edward either jumped these or breezed through them rather quickly, because, as we've seen, he qualified as a doctor five years later.

At the time, there were only professional courses at the University. You could study to become a lawyer, a doctor or a priest. 'There weren't any arts or science faculties,' Father Peter recalls.

There was only teaching on the arts or science side in a propaedeutic sense. So, I was on the arts side [reading Philosophy] and Edward was on the science side.

He and his brother Tony were among the few students interested in both the literary and debating sides of the University Literary and Debating Society, of which I was secretary. At the time, the professor of English was an Irishman called Owen Fogarty, a great character who was also patron of the sports club. I think his Irish character got him the job because before the war we had a nationalist government which was basically pro-Italian and anti-British, so they thought an Irishman would be the right person. However, Fogarty's instinct was more to be against the dominant trend, the establishment, so he was in fact extremely anglophilic and became the protecting genius of the Society, which also published a magazine called *The Sundial*, there being an old sundial on the wall of the old university in St Paul's Street, Valletta, where it was founded in 1592 as a Jesuit college.

The first debate which I organised as Secretary of this debating society was, 'Should Students Take An Active Part in Politics?' And I had Edward speaking on the side which nobody wanted to defend, namely that students should *not* take an active part in politics. Edward also wrote pieces for *The Sundial*, which I think are interesting enough to look at in view of his later developments, because they were very definitely and deliberately taking the opposite point of view to the conventional. It was already his mode of thinking. He is basically a science student so he writes an article about such as the old classical techniques by the Romans of watching the flight of birds, but tries to show that this was a rational way of predicting that something was going to happen and so on.

This championing of the point of view opposite to the conventional may have been born of a cocky desire to exercise his prodigious intelligence. But the realisation that if you are highly intelligent you can use your intelligence to defend a point of view whether or not it is true would be a key influence on his thinking programmes. Paradoxically, the take was that intelligent argument can trap us into adopting poor ideas – thinking is required to ensure deliberate and thorough exploration before judgement is passed. 'So many excellent minds are trapped in poor ideas because they can defend them so well,' he would say to me more than half a century later. 'Then, if you grow up knowing that you are more intelligent than those around you, which is perfectly possible, the quickest reward or gratification is to prove someone else wrong. Using intelligence only for critical judgement, not for being constructive.'

He called this the Intelligence Trap and used it as a kind of touchstone on which to build his constructive thinking programme for schools, also used in youth custody centres, prisons, boardrooms of the world's largest multinationals and colleges for gifted children. Broadly, and with impressive results worldwide, he used it to transform self-image from, 'I am/am not intelligent, I can/can not pass exams, etc,' into 'I am a thinker,' which is not susceptible to the same competitive edge. That distinction is offered to all. Thinking is a skill which anyone can learn.

In the 1950s an incident began to build that seemed simultaneously to caricature the polarities of conflict politics, which Edward's pro-gramme of parallel thinking would later address, and to define the locked-in, parochial logic-bubble of life on the island, which, increasingly, Edward sought to escape.

In 1947, the Maltese Labour Party had come to power. This was a council, not self-government, but it signalled a whole new power base for Josephine de Bono's campaigning. Dom Mintoff (later Prime Minister) became deputy leader of the party and Minister of Public Works. Pawlu Boffa was Prime Minister. Says Father Peter:

> As you can imagine, at the end of the war the traditional pro-Italian party was out. It was the end of pro-Italianism. After that the Maltese began to speak of independence. The Labour Government was asking that we should get a direct share of Marshall Aid and Britain didn't accept that. We were given war damage compensation. Mintoff then persuaded the Cabinet to send an ultimatum – this was in 1950. Basically, they were saying unless we get a share of Marshall Aid they would ask the United States to take over Malta. But within a week of presenting this ultimatum the British government of course refused

to discuss anything until the ultimatum was withdrawn. Dr Boffa came back to Malta and, while Mintoff wasn't present, he persuaded the government to withdraw the ultimatum. So when they withdrew this, Mintoff proposed a vote of no confidence in the leader of the party. And this vote got a majority in the General Conference of the Labour Party. But the majority of MPs didn't follow Mintoff. They were for Dr Boffa. So there was a split in the party. Now, from that moment or a little bit after, Mintoff came out with a proposal which was either integration with Britain – Malta should become a constituency of the United Kingdom basically, like Northern Ireland, we should have our own MPs and so on – or independence. A proposal of union with Italy was never published, but years later it emerged that Mintoff had also written to the Italian government basically proposing that if the thing didn't work with Britain, etc, etc . . .

Into this tense, complex situation stepped 'the ineffable Josephine', as one of the protagonists would later describe her. As we've seen, she was a supporter of Mintoff, and Edward's uncle Peter Paul had for a short time been Minister of Health in the Labour Government. Mintoff's wife, who was related to the Duke of Devonshire, was a close friend. 'Mintoff's wife did a lot of philanthropic work, helping blind people and so on in a most inconspicuous manner,' said Father Peter.

Mrs de Bono was a friend of hers, but she was always more . . . conspicuous. I knew Mrs de Bono very well because I used to sit with her on various committees. One of them was the King George V Hospital, a hospital originally for the Services, which then became a private foundation. She was also a member of the National Council of Women. She was prominent in all these . . . Mintoff was also greatly supported in this integration with Britain idea by Lord Mountbatten, who at the time was Admiral in Malta, and Mrs de Bono was a great friend of Edwina Mountbatten, practically the leading figure in Maltese social life at the time.

Lord Mountbatten had in fact been a friend of Edward's mother since he was a young naval lieutenant. They were all strongly backing the Mintoff integration idea, unaware of any dealings with Italy, but in opposition to the nationalist style and even to the traditional pro-British force represented by Miss Strickland (of St Edward's College fame), who was against Mintoff due to the uncertainty and ambivalence of Mintoff's attitude: one day he was talking integration, the next in a most anti-British manner. From Mrs de Bono's own correspondence, a seven-page letter dated 20 April 1958, it emerges that she had originally become involved in the affair over tea with Mintoff's wife, when, in Dom Mintoff's presence, she was told to 'go ahead and do what I can' to convince people that he did not really want to break away from the Commonwealth, that the government still wanted integration.

Letters and memos show that Mrs de Bono had enlisted her son Peter's help in intervening between Dom Mintoff, the British and the Maltese governments. At one stage, Peter is reported to have made a mad dash to London to sort things out, and Mrs de Bono is accused of occupying the 'self-appointed role of mediator' and her son of being a 'well-intentioned meddler'.

It began to look as if the de Bonos were the fall guys in a manoeuvre by Mintoff to extract some £6 million from Her Majesty's Government, and preserve his own power base in the face of a split party and waning confidence. The whole affair centred on the mystery of a missing telegram, which never materialised, but which was supposed to have suggested a compromise between the two governments. The Commissioner General, to whom the telegram was allegedly sent, was reported never to have received it. And, rather cruelly, he lumped the whole thing on Mrs de Bono, saying that she was 'a silly busybody of a woman' who had got an idea in her head and mistakenly believed it represented the views of the Maltese Government (as no doubt Mintoff had intended).

The affair offers a window on to the irrepressible, campaigning nature of Edward's mother and on Maltese politics, which had on this occasion lurched into international significance. The affair had been brewing over a number of years, and I asked Father Peter what Edward's involvement had been. 'I think I should say that Edward always stood remarkably aloof from all these political involvements,' he replied.

I don't think he was interested in this rather parish-pump politics. Perhaps he already had something of the idea which now is very prominent in what he writes – his opposition to adversarial structures. I think his approach was always, we have one party saying, 'This is right and you are completely wrong.' So he was always of the idea that what was needed in these circumstances was not a compromise but something completely new, which both sides would see to be to their advantage.

Which is precisely the purpose of parallel thinking. I told Elizabeth this story and Edward's disinclination to be involved rang true:

When we were fifteen or sixteen we used to have these tremendous arguments, you know what teenagers are like, and Edward ... he would not say a word. At one stage our parents were quite worried about it. He used to just sit with his chair back on its heels, and we always used to wait for the crash, but it never came. He didn't join in. Mother would come out with some outrageous statement. I am sure it was deliberate. She would come out with something that was so provocative and Tony and I would jump straight in. This would be round the dinner table and Edward would be leaning back in his chair. I mean, some people don't like conflict, do they? I am sure that it wasn't because he didn't think he would win, because Edward could have won any argument.

Quiet Edward may have been, but he was emerging from his shell, had begun to go to parties and, as his sister (among many others) recalls, 'The girls would always fall flat because he was terribly goodlooking, and he played tennis,' which was a social requirement, it seems.

The Mountbattens used to give super parties. Their house was in South Street, just opposite where I was born. He had two daughters. They used to have lovely parties, and then there were the de Traffords ... We used to go and play tennis there. Edward played tennis very well, very seriously, used to play with Charles Grech-Orr, who worked on the *Times of Malta*. They were very great friends. Cecilia was a Strickland. She was Mabel's sister. So you see ... The parties, the style, it was really something, though it depended where you were coming from. The Hotel Phoenicia was the place. You used to go to dinner dances there. [The Queen, before her coronation, and Prince Philip, who had stayed with the Mountbattens in Malta at the end of the 1940s, frequented this hotel too.] We used to go and play tennis at the Club and then watch the polo and go to dinner dances there. Yes, it was very colonial, very English. It was fun if you were in with it, but if you were not it was difficult. And then you see after the war, well, the British Navy declined and the dockyards ...

Edward is not socially adept, never was. Small talk is of no interest to him ... It is very difficult but you have to cultivate that. Still, when you are twenty and gorgeous there's not much you need to do in that way. He would just say, 'Shall we dance?' and that was it. So, he didn't need to make an effort at communicating, which is maybe a pity. And then, you know, if you *are* quite bright, unless you really make an effort, you actually do find other people's conversations rather boring ...

Later, surely underlining this desperate shyness, he devised a visual alternative for chat-up – stroke the right side of your nose to indicate 'I like the look of you and want to get to know you,' pause and then do it again; in reply, squeeze the end of the nose between thumb and forefinger for, 'Not in the least interested;' stroke the right side of the nose for 'interested' the left side for 'very interested'.

When Edward left Malta in 1955 and took up his Rhodes scholarship at Christ Church, it wasn't his first visit to England. 'I had been once or twice before,' he said, 'different things, as a student, fruit picking, that sort of thing.' This, however, was going to be a long stay and had certainly been long anticipated. He had begun to look at medicine, not so much as a career thrust upon him, but as the very means of escape from the closed world in which he had been brought up: 'What one also has to think of is medicine was one of the few degrees that were international, so it was worth doing. You could learn medicine in Malta and use it in many other countries, whereas if you studied law it was not international.'

Having escaped Malta, he had entered a new land. All that he needed now was a new mystery to explore.

Chapter Four

The Mystery Explored

'Creativity has always been a black-box mystery. Showing how it is the behaviour of an asymmetric system, and how you can intervene, is intellectually very satisfying.'

Lateral thinkers are more than a bit like Edward. They tend to be autonomous and self-reliant. They never accept that there is only one way a thing can be. They feel ill at ease when things fit neatly into place. They like to disturb stability in order to create things that offer better value than before. They are of an inventive frame of mind and are good detectives – they like to hunt for clues. They also extol the eureka! moment of insight and enjoy the unexpectedness of the punchline in humour. They are at home with ambiguity and like to play with paradox. They are alive to shifting probabilities, good timing and what Edward calls the 'hump effect' – in order to get north you may first have to travel south. However, unlike Edward, they are not all born to it.

The lateral thinking frame of mind begins with a deliberate, keen focus on things and a wondering why things are like they are, what the operating concept behind them is. Lateral thinking needs a mindset attuned to challenge, to seeking alternatives, even when something is running well. 'Key things about me as a boy,' he once said, 'were curiosity, a great interest in making things happen, an unwillingness to accept that *this* is the only way something can be.' He later coined the phrase *simple focus* for looking at everything – on the dinner table, on your desk, in the street, in line for a taxi, wherever you find yourself – with an eye to new ideas, enhanced value, movement forward.

Focus and looking for clues are habits of mind that young medical students, such as Edward in the 1950s, must perfect in diagnosis. As Edward points out, Conan Doyle applied his own medical training to moulding the behaviour of Sherlock Holmes. With creativity, the difference is that there need be no problem, but a willingness to look anyway at what seems to be going well and consider alternatives. There was nothing wrong with detergent before someone came up with the concept of concentrating it. Afterwards the space it took up on the shelf plummeted, it was 45 per cent cheaper to handle, and profits soared. A subtle concept shift can revolutionise what is already a good idea.

Later Edward would give us the Concept Fan (page 98), a powerful lateral thinking tool for discovering and exploring the operating concept behind a thing, an idea or a situation and cascading alternative ideas to deliver better value. But in the very early days of his career, in *The Use of Lateral Thinking*, he recommended instead truly purposeless play to generate new ideas by chance. It's difficult, in fact, to sit down with an object and set off towards nowhere, but 'the very chance processes of play provide combinations that may never have been thought of otherwise . . .' This was pure autobiography. As a child, he had loved inventing things, loved to play with familiar configurations and well-tried patterns, trying out new and unfamiliar relationships. Now, as an adult, it was still his everyday mode, and remains so today.

Toy shops are a passion. 'Every place we went we had to find the toy shop and spend an hour in it,' said his sometime travelling PA Linda Laird. 'He would scout one side of the street and I would scout the other side. He would be looking for a toy that had something about it, not just a ball and a bat, something that had dual meaning or a couple of ways you could do it, or a way that Edward could improve on the way it might be played. I am always bringing him back toys.'

Freddie, a robot who appears in two of Edward's books, was based on part of a child's toy unearthed after a casual visit to a toyshop on Lexington Avenue in New York. 'The space age pet suitable for modern living' (a very 1960s notion now having a comeback), Freddie was smooth and black, required no food nor walking to the lamppost and back, and was kickstarted (literally). 'Once moving, he carefully avoided or retreated from objects which he encountered, generally rolling about on his own without any obvious agency, apparently claiming as much identity from his life as you or me.' On another occasion, the sight of some brightly coloured toy balloons in a chemist's shop inspired a model for studying the basic principles of some complicated system interactions, and the $2.5-million computer Edward had been using suddenly became superfluous.

He is constantly, restlessly inventive. 'Thinking is just an automatic process for him in a way that it isn't for most people,' says his ex-boss, Ivor Mills. 'He is a child of five, because he will evolve new ideas faster and more efficiently than anyone else.' The first job Edward put Linda onto, she coming from a fashion background, was the design of a travelling-suit-for-travelling-people. 'He invents lots of these sort of things,' she told me. 'Have you seen his little napkin thing that hangs round his neck?' I confessed that I hadn't. She said,

It has a bauble thing that traps the napkin in place, because he is always dropping food on his tummy. He has all sorts of little ideas. You know, in airlines, before they had the little pull-out popper to hang your coat on, he used to bring a pin thing that he had made, and he hooked it into the seat and then he could hook his jacket on it. In fact, long after they provided the pull-out hangers he refused to use them because he had invented his device first! I remember he used to carry a little case with him which had all sorts of bits and pieces in it.

Edward is a playful chap. Give him familiar, sensible, adequate symmetry, which satisfies most of us, and he will feel bound to worry it into a different shape. In the 1960s, as he was refining his ideas about lateral thinking, he was forever being photographed with, or interviewed about, some wacky invention. One Sunday afternoon somebody was smoking in his room. What to do about the problem? Remove harmful substances or get people to smoke less. 'A naive approach to the first part of the problem would involve filtering out some of the tar particles from the inhaled smoke,' he noted. 'A more sophisticated approach would involve trying to alter the chemical composition or combustion so that such substances were not formed.' Characteristically, he decided to reverse the first idea, lowering the concentration of tar by adding something rather than taking away. Pinholes in the cigarette allowed air to dilute the smoke, a revolutionary idea at the time.

Then there was the day he was casually playing around and devised a special whistle for testing lung function, replacing one that cost many hundreds of pounds – the idea eventually prompted by a whistling kettle.

While at dinner one evening, Edward's train of thought connected wine bottle and cutlery to project an amusing problem. Take four knives and three beer bottles and place the bottles upright on a table, each at the point of a triangle, the sides of which are just longer than a knife. Using no more than the four knives, construct a platform on top of the bottles sufficiently strong to support a glass of water. No knife should touch the ground.* Edward says that the form of the idea may have had something to do with the presence of an architect at the dinner table. The bottles and knives were left lying around overnight. In the morning, a little more playing around produced a further development of the idea, which would be written up into *The Five-Day Course in Thinking* (1967).

In *The Five-Day Course*, Edward also introduces the L-Game, again the result of playing around, but with a firm idea of what the final result should be. At dinner one evening in Trinity College, Cambridge, he found himself sitting next to the mathematician, Professor Littlewood. 'We were talking about getting computers to play chess. We agreed that chess was difficult because of the large number of pieces and the vast number of possible moves. It seemed an interesting challenge to design a game that was as simple as possible and yet could be played with a degree of skill.' The next morning, Edward was fishing around in his jacket pocket and found a square piece of plastic, which 'provided the focus for random playing around that led to a large number of possible ideas.' There were so many possible ideas that Edward reckoned that it would be best to look for one reason why each idea would *not* make a good game. He then took the idea that survived, and the L-Game was the result.

It is a board game for two players, each of whom has an L-shaped piece. The board is four squares by four. The Ls cover three squares on the long side, two squares on the short side. There are also two neutral pieces – disc-shaped counters, each of which fits within one square.

Each player in turn moves his L-shaped piece 'to any new vacant position (lifting up, turning over, moving across the board to a vacant position, etc.),' Edward writes in *De Bono's Thinking Course*. 'After moving his L-piece he can – if he wishes – move either one of the small neutral pieces to any new position. The object of the game is to block your opponent's L-piece so that no move is open to it.'

There are sixty alternative moves open to the first player to start, and in a certain position there are as many as 195 different moves, of which only one is successful. Overall, there are as many as 18,000 possible positions for the pieces. The strategies and tactics open to players, in what is essentially a very simple game, are widely varied. 'Break up the

---

* The solution is to use only three knives, interleave the blades so as to form a strong triangular-shaped platform and balance the ends of the knife handles on the bottle tops.

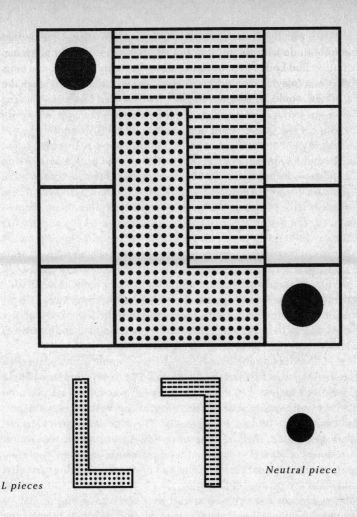

L pieces

Neutral piece

empty spaces; stay close to your opponent's L-piece; use the neutral pieces to block rows and columns; dominate the centre; keep out of the corners; force the opponent to the edge.'

Thirty-five years later he is still inventing games.

The other day I was sitting on a bus and said, let me invent a card game which has no element of chance whatever. So I did. I'll tell you how it works, we might even play it. You take out three sets of 1 to 10

– throw out the court cards. You have one set, I have one set, we shuffle the other and put it in the middle. We then cut it twice and look at the cards. So suppose we come up with 9 and 3, 12. Keep that number 12. We shuffle the pack again, then we turn over the top card. Now you have got to put in one of your cards face down. I have got to put in one of my cards. We then turn them up. Whoever's card plus the face-up card is nearest to 12 wins. Suppose I get 10 and you get 8. I am 2 points off 12 and you are 4 points off 12. You then multiply these (2Ω4) so that I get a score of 8. Now we carry on until there are no cards left. We know which cards have turned up in the pack (there are only ten). I know what you have put down (there are only ten). You know what I have put down. So there is no element of luck. You have to figure out now how close have I got to get, what is the other guy going to do ... Play it, it is fascinating. I got to it because I was saying what is not going to be luck. So we both start with equal, we both have a situation and the skill is the strategy of me figuring out what you are going to do and what is the optimum strategy. It often ends up that the winner really keeps a very strong position at the end because then you are forced to play your last card. You have to get a feel of it. But there is no luck at all. Possibly it's the only card game with no element of luck.

Did it take the whole trip to think this out? Did he miss his stop? These are questions sadly lost to the urgency of our task. In life, luck plays too big a part – originality arises during play, arises most often by chance. 'Chance has no limits,' he wrote in *The Use of Lateral Thinking*, 'imagination has . . .' Within a few years, Edward would have worked out in *Mechanism of Mind* (1969) just why, from a neurological point of view, chance plays such a part in creativity, and developed thinking tools that would make the process deliberate.

'You would not have chosen medicine if you were going to make a career in thinking,' Edward states. 'However, the advantage in choosing medicine is that it gives an insight into self-organising systems, biological systems, which you would not get by studying physics, mathematics, education or psychology. So that was, in the end, the special thing.'

Edward's DPhil thesis, *The Control of Blood Pressure in Hypertension*, was deposited in the Radcliffe Science Library at Oxford in 1961. In order to discover the dynamics of the circulatory system in chronic experimental hypertension, he had intervened first in animals' circulatory systems, then in those of humans, by altering the pressure within one or more of the baroceptors – nerve endings in vein walls that are sensitive to pressure. He then measured the responses to this in the system, and interpreted his findings. His tests of the human baroceptor system were all straightforward, simple system interventions. Some were rehearsals for his later medical research at Cambridge, which would lead him further along the path towards understanding the self-organising system, which would become his model for the mechanism of mind. In the thesis he is beginning to form concepts relevant to the dynamics of self-organising biological systems, and to see that if you want to learn anything about how such a system works, you need to intervene, perturb or provoke it and note what happens. Since 1961 he himself has spent a lifetime doing just that.

Although you could say that the circulatory system is better described as a self-regulating system than a self-organising system (because unlike the brain, where information has to get organised, there are no parts to organise once it is set up), the point is that the concept of a complex system with its own dynamics, requiring no regulation from outside, was approached here for the first time.

Following his DPhil, Edward continued his work on the circulatory system at St Thomas' Hospital in London. 'At that time I was looking at blood flow through the lung. Normal flow mechanics are well known: with pressure differential across a tube and resistance, you can work out the flow. But the flow never fitted the data.' He could look at what was before him, analyse the data every which way, but it made no sense.

> It was only when I said, 'Maybe it's not a tube, maybe it's a waterfall, and never mind how high a waterfall, it doesn't affect the flow,' that the data made sense. The new model, the new way of looking at things fitted the data perfectly. Turns out that when blood is flowing through the floppy capilliaries of the lungs, there is the equivalent of freefall. It was only when putting in that construct, bringing in that possibility, that the data made sense.

This encouraged Edward to focus on finding an underlying construct consistent with his ideas about creative thinking that would explain the character and rules that governed the neural network system. We need to understand behaviour in the context of an appropriate construct, universe or system. The capillary system has one set of rules, the waterfall system has a totally different set. There are many different systems with different sets of rules all around us. Today, in seminar, he likes to give the example of three men, each holding a piece of wood, which they then let go. The first man's piece falls to the ground. The second man's rises up in the air. The third man's piece floats in front of his eyes. Impossible? Not at all. The three men are operating in quite different systems, each with its own set of rules. The first man is standing in his garden, the second is under water, the third is in orbit around the Earth.

The very fount of Edward's own creativity – the thinking methodologies, lateral thinking, parallel thinking, and the constructive thinking of his schools programme – is his design of the conceptual construct that explains the mind's workings and yields the tools and techniques to exploit, manipulate and outwit its regulating mechanisms. Eventually, after much more work at St Thomas' and at Boston City Hospital in America, he would conclude, 'We have believed that perception and information processing are operating in the same universe. Not so. Perception operates in an active universe – the elements of information on the surface have their own dynamics. Information processing operates in a passive universe, the elements of information must be organised from outside.' He had his concept of a self-organising system, in which the incoming information and the receiving medium work actively together without intervention or control from outside, the dynamics of which we will look at in Chapter Six.

At St Thomas', Edward met Ivor Mills, who would become the first 20th-century Chair of Medicine at Cambridge University, and take Edward with him as his assistant. At St Thomas', Mills had been senior lecturer in the Department of Chemical Pathology and senior lecturer in the Department of Medicine at the same time. In 1962 he became reader in medicine full time. 'Once I was appointed to the Department of Medicine,' he recalls, 'I saw more of Edward . . . He stood out, from my point of view, in one respect. He had novel ideas.'

With his predecessor in the Department of Medicine, Hugh de Wardener, Mills had worked on experiments to determine how sodium in the body is controlled. 'In 1961 de Wardener and I published a paper saying an unknown factor in sodium control was a circulating substance with a short half-life. We didn't know whether that substance increased sodium excretion or decreased sodium excretion, but it played a part in regulation, and it could outweigh the effect of existing sodium-retaining substances and what was known on a small scale about sodium-excreting mechanisms.' Mills and de Wardener did not know, however, where the substance, a hormone, was released or how it was released. 'The most probable explanation was that there was something in the chest which either detected the need for the substance or produced it, or both . . .'

What Edward brought to the party were some dynamics of the new construct he had envisaged for the circulatory system, and he and Mills developed 'the crazy notion' that timed, intermittent pressure on the renal vein resulted in a marked increase in sodium excretion. 'Now I wanted to publish that as a paper, describing the effect of intermittent renal vein exclusion on sodium secretion,' recalls Mills. 'But that wasn't clever enough for Edward. He said, and reasoned as much in the paper, that you could in fact say what the kidney was doing was *monitoring the cardiac output of the heart*. Well, I met some of the main people in the States soon after we published that paper and the woman in particular who had worked on salt excretion for many years, she couldn't understand the paper so she threw it away. That was the feeling . . . It was so cleverly worked out, but it was very difficult for people to comprehend.'

It wasn't just Edward trying to be clever, it was Edward pointing to the system concept – the construct – that underlay and explained what they had discovered and might explain a whole lot else if they experimented with it.

The intensity and restless energy of the man was palpable at this time. One afternoon, he was working away at St Thomas' when an American appeared who had an appointment with someone else in the department. Edward fell into conversation with him. 'He had come over from Harvard. I forget who it was he came to see, but the person was busy, so I sort of looked after him, and he said, "If you ever want to come to Harvard I'll give you a job."'

Edward had talked of his ideas about the dynamics of self-organising systems with the Harvard man, who had picked up on the possibility that he might be onto something radical. The offer of a job had been serious, and Edward took it up, but then Mills was approached to take up the long-vacant Chair of Medicine at Cambridge University, and he also wanted Edward along. Agreement was reached that Edward would take up the Harvard appointment after a year as a sabbatical.

So it was, that in the Lent term of 1964, Edward was formally admitted as a member of Trinity College, Cambridge. The Cambridge equivalent of his Oxford DPhil (a PhD) was awarded 'by incorporation', which means that Cambridge University recognised the degree he had obtained at Oxford, and he took up his appointment as Assistant Director of Research in the Department of Investigative Medicine.

Although students graduated in medicine at Cambridge, there was not yet a clinical school as such; undergraduates went off to other clinical schools to do their training. Around the time Mills was offered the position, a report was drawn up saying that a clinical school was not envisaged in the future, either. Mills' department was also to be limited to a staff of one, and he was furious.

> I said what a crazy notion, who on earth did you take advice from? They said, 'We went to Oxford,' which was quite sensible, but I was sure that our set-up would be Lilliputian compared to Oxford's. I was furious and argued against the limitation of one member of staff being put in the report. 'In due course,' I said, 'you might want to change your view about the clinical school.' (There were plenty of *pre*-clinical professors on that committee.)

In due course they did change their minds and the clinical school was established under Professor Mills at Addenbrookes Hospital. As a result, the department did grow dramatically. Mills had, in any case, ensured that teaching began almost immediately.

> I was addicted to teaching, so when I came here and there were no clinical students I found myself teaching the nurses on ward rounds and Out Patients, and asked the university permission to teach some third-year students some clinical medicine. Third years knew that if they wanted to come on my ward round they were welcome, six at a time maximum, and that I would teach them how to take blood from patients, how to talk to patients. I wanted some slaves. Students came in considerable numbers to apply ... Edward would also be addicted to teaching but of course he would be teaching on his level. Now that is not always easy for everyone to grasp because he is bringing in new concepts all the time.

I said that it must have seemed pretty bad form, Edward slipping off to Harvard after a year. 'No, no, you must allow people to expand in their own way,' Mills replied. 'If you try and clamp down on them you lose their value. I knew he would learn all sorts of things from contact with different people there, so I wasn't all that bothered. I was more interested in capturing his brain when he came back.'

The Harvard appointment was sited at Boston City Hospital. 'I think it was called the Thorndyke Lab,' said Edward. 'Ed Kass was the person I was working with there. Around 1965 to 1966. I was again working on the kidneys and had to work out some concepts of self-organising systems. That really was the key to what followed. The concept of self-organising systems applied to neural networks – what happens? They wanted me to stay on at Harvard, but I said no and came back to Cambridge and was there for about fourteen years or so.'

The American trip had established contacts sufficient for *The Five-Day Course in Thinking* (1967), an idea that had arisen at a dinner party and was written up over a weekend, to be published by Basic Books of New York in the same year as *The Use of Lateral Thinking* came out in London (the year after he had returned to Cambridge). It was another example of Edward's restlessness, frowned on in this case by his new London publisher.

More importantly, his sojourn in America had helped sort out the construct, the self-organising system, which he would model in *Mechanism of Mind*, and from which would flow the lateral thinking tools and techniques, like Random Input, Provocation and the Concept Fan, which appeared in future books, the whole process proving the creative efficacy of the construct itself. As Edward put it, 'At first I developed some ideas, then I developed the system model of the mind and then the model generated further ideas – random word entry, provocation – and so on.'

Chapter Five

Sixties Tricks

'The new division has on one side all those interested in new ideas and on the other side those who feel threatened by them.'

In 1967, when *The Use of Lateral Thinking* was published there was no suggestion that Edward had come up with anything especially new. Indeed, he had expected creative people, inventors and the like to claim they knew all about it already. 'Henry Dreyfus, Milton Glaser, Misha Black, Alex Moulton, Paul MacCready were among the first to contact me,' he said, telling him that his statement had served to focus them on what they knew subconsciously but could not have expressed.

'I'll give you a quote,' said David Bernstein, creative director of the ad agency McCann Erikson in the early 1960s and with Garland-Compton when he first read Edward's book:

'What oft was thought, but ne'er so well expressed.' That's Alexander Pope. I mean, I thought, '*I* thought that! but my God he has said it perfectly!' That was the magic of lateral thinking. The Sixties was the time to be creative and to excite people. Also the thing about Edward was that he was knocking the conventions. Rebel is too strong a word, but he was knocking conventions and I was fascinated by that.

There is a tide in the affairs of men,
Which, taken at the flood, leads on to fortune.

Brutus's observation in Shakespeare's *Julius Caesar* is apposite to Edward's immediate and huge success in the late 1960s. *The Use of Lateral Thinking*, with its invitation to escape from the obvious way of looking at things, was absolutely in tune with the times. Its publication coincided with the Beatles' release of *Sergeant Pepper's Lonely Hearts Club Band*, an album inspired by Eastern mysticism and the hallucinatory drug LSD, two other means of escape to new perceptions popular at the time. The album's release heralded the Beatles' much-publicised, spaced-out sojourn in India with the Maharishi Mahesh Yogi, where they were joined by Marianne Faithfull and Mick Jagger, following the Rolling Stones' release of *Their Satanic Majesty's Request*. That year also saw the release of the Grateful Dead's eponymous first album. This hugely popular LSD-inspired band was closely allied to Ken Kesey, author of *One Flew Over the Cuckoo's Nest* and leader of the Merry Pranksters, whose trip across America in a Day-Glo-painted bus, famously documented in Tom Wolfe's book *The Electric Kool-Aid Acid Test*, had 'turned on' that country's youth to acid. These were heady days. The driver of the bus, from which the LSD-laced Kool-Aid was dispensed at challengingly crazy parties, was none other than the inspiration for Jack Kerouac's seminal Beat novel *On the Road* – Neal Cassady. With Kesey, the Beats of the 1950s somehow merged into the hippies of the 1960s, the whole thing underwritten by writers like Allen Ginsberg, William S. Burroughs and Aldous Huxley, who described his own experiments with mescalin and LSD in *Doors of Perception* (1954), a title borrowed from William Blake: 'If the doors of perception were cleansed, everything would appear to man as it is, infinite.'

So was de Bono the Bob Dylan of the thinking world? The image hardly squares with that of the polo-playing aristocrat. A picture of Edward from around 1967 shows him in a kind of hippy-style, flower-power shirt, but he is wearing a tie and the ensemble is finished with a sensible, rather itchy-looking tweed jacket. Radical youth culture was not de Bono's scene. But, hands up anyone who remembers that he was a contributor to the infamous underground magazine, *Oz*?

'Think sideways with Edward de Bono!' screamed the centre-spread issue of *Oz* 8. Even his definition of lateral thinking at that time had something of a psychedelic feel to it: 'The dynamic fluidity of lateral thinking, which is continually forming, dissolving and re-forming the parts of the situation in ever different shapes . . . to find the best way of looking at it.' Mimicking socially conscious warnings about drug abuse, he actually counsels his readers on the dangers of not being able to escape from the idiom. 'It is far more fruitful to alternate between periods of creative fluidity and periods of developmental rigidity.'

The fact is that the public's perception of Edward uniquely allowed him to straddle both camps – straight and alternative (before straight had its modern connotations). 'The reason I myself occasionally write in

Oz,' Edward explained at the time, 'is precisely because I am against the taking of drugs, but I am for some of the ideals some of the hippies express.' In the summer of 1971 he had a unique opportunity to stand up publicly, shoulder to shoulder with leading figures of the so-called Alternative Society, when the famous *Oz* trial began at the Old Bailey and Edward was called as an expert witness.

The trial, which lasted about six weeks, concerned obscenity and in particular Issue No. 28. *Oz* was *the* underground magazine in Britain, and this particular issue, known as the School Kids issue, had been given over to a gang of school kids to do their own thing, the ageing editors believing themselves to be in danger of getting out of touch with where things were really at.

Where things were really at among school children at this time appears to have been oral sex, humour, drugs and revolution. But comparing the issue's sex content today with glossy sex mags available above the counter at your friendly family store, *Oz* really does not live up to the label 'obscene'. However, Issue 28 was seized by the police, and in June 1971 editor Richard Neville and his two sidekicks Felix Denis and James Anderson were arrested and hauled up in front of judge and jury at the Old Bailey.

The *Oz* trial was a significant moment in the revolution that had taken hold in the late 1960s. It is one of a handful of events, along with the Isle of Wight festivals and the Grosvenor Square demo against American aggression in Vietnam, which English people who were kids at that time remember as hugely significant. All of it was anti-Establishment, and the Old Bailey ... well, you couldn't get more Establishment than that. John Mortimer for the defence, deliberating on a point about the merits of the inimitable Furry Freak Brothers, asked an expert witness about 'what we've all got used to calling smack and horse [cocaine and heroin] and so on.' It was a million miles away from Mortimer's later, comfy television series, *Rumpole of the Bailey*, for which millions now know him.

The Alternative Society, the underground press, the revolutionaries, the free thinkers, Mortimer and the whole world of 'smack and horse' never for one moment thought that they would not win. Shock horror, therefore, when Judge Argyll sentenced Neville to fifteen months and recommended him for deportation to Australia. Anderson got twelve months, and Denis, nine.

There would be some twenty days of evidence from expert witnesses at the *Oz* trial. Following the hugely successful publication of *The Use of*

Lateral Thinking at the very moment the alternative revolution was gathering pace, the calling of Edward to give evidence seemed faultless strategy, and it gives a fascinating glimpse of how lateral thinking was seen at this time.

When it was Edward's turn to take the witness box, Neville, who actually conducted his own defence at this stage, made the connection between lateral thinking and the underground culture as explicitly as he could. Talking about a feature by Edward in *New York* magazine, Neville said, 'One thing I noticed was that the title was upside down and in fact the picture of yourself in it was sideways.'

Edward: 'Yes.'

Neville: 'I know that this court will be confused by the techniques in *Oz* of headings not particularly related to articles and illustrations not necessarily relating to colour and so forth. What are the designers of *Oz* trying to do?'

Edward: 'I think what they are trying to do is to get away from some of the standardised ways of using a paper by different uses of visual effects, different positioning, headings, typescript ... I think sometimes this is effective and sometimes it is not effective.'

Neville: 'Would it be fair to say that *Oz* is attempting to escape from the norm?'

Edward: 'Oh, certainly ... I think it serves a very useful purpose.'

The transcribed evidence of Edward's performance in court is a wonderful picture, shorn of the bias of memory, of the energies of the man, thirty-eight years of age and about to conquer the world. Even the stenographer had difficulty keeping up with him, and at one stage, Judge Argyll brought things to a halt altogether to say, 'I am so sorry, but the witness does speak very quickly and it's very difficult to hear everything he says.'

The year before, Edward had published *The Dog Exercising Machine*, a collection of children's drawings with his comments, and the court heard that it was his insight into children's minds, and presumably how they might (or might not) be corrupted by *Oz* 28, that recommended him as an expert witness. As Edward told the court, 'I've had an interest in patterns of children's thinking, and drawings are often a very good window to look at this.'

Broadly, Edward's case was that there were five possible reactions to *Oz* 28 from children: 'not interested', 'unable to relate to it', 'regard it as remote', 'déjà vu', and finally 'able to relate to it but put off sex by it'. Late on, he hardened up this last point by saying that if you were given a brief to design something to put you off oral sex, it would be difficult to do better than this issue of *Oz*.

'In those categories,' said Mortimer, 'do you have a category of whom it would do nothing but harm?'

Edward: 'I suppose you could say that if putting them off sex would harm them then I suppose this would be harm.'

Whatever Judge Argyll made of that, the sentences he passed on the three defendants on 5 August 1971 were subsequently quashed on appeal by Lord Chief Justice Lord Widgery.

What Edward liked about the 1960s counterculture was its existential lack of pretension: 'The only thing that is really fashionable nowadays and is the essence of the culture is *doing your own thing*,' he wrote. 'In other words not accepting that culture dictates a fashion. In other words the fashionable thing nowadays is to be unfashionable.' Autonomy, independence and self-reliance, were, and still are, Edward's defining characteristics and there was huge conceptual empathy in the purpose of lateral thinking to shake us out of conventional patterns of thought, in Edward's creativity and love of paradox – all spot-on hippy things too.

However, while *The Use of Lateral Thinking* was about relaxing the rigidity of people's mindsets and looking for alternatives, in the permissive context of the 1960s there were acres of space for misunderstanding. One widespread notion was that it is only the totally uninhibited who can be creative. This caused Edward no end of problems, not least criticism that he was jumping on the brainstorming bandwagon. Alex Osborn first introduced this concept in 1938, as a way of removing inhibition and generating ideas. One can see why people confused the two. 'With lateral thinking a rapid succession of different ways of looking at something is deliberately passed through the mind,' Edward wrote, a definition that could almost pass for brainstorming. He accepts that inhibitions depress levels of creativity, but creativity *per se* has nothing to do with Werner Erhard's self-development seminars, est, or any other movement popular at the time dedicated to removing inhibitions. Edward is aware of the popular image of the uninhibited, creative rebel, and jumps on it as romantic tosh:

If you are inhibited you can't be creative, true. If you are uninhibited, you can be creative, not true. Imagine we have a man and a rope and someone comes along and ties that man up with the rope. Then a violin is produced. The person tied with the rope cannot play the violin. Everyone would agree that with your hands tied tightly to your side you cannot play the violin. We say, 'That person cannot play the violin because he is tied up.' So, if we cut the rope, is that person going to become a violinist?

A fellow injures his hands at work and is taken to hospital. The surgeon comes to see him and the patient asks whether after his operation he'll be able to play the violin. The surgeon says, 'Yes, of course.' The patient says, 'Do you guarantee that? That's very nice because I couldn't play before.'

For the last fifty years we have believed that if you are inhibited you can't be creative: if we make you uninhibited you are going to be creative. Not true. But because we have believed that, we have been satisfied with brainstorming and so on, which is a very weak approach (useful in the area of advertising, where novelty value can be important, less so in areas where novelty is not of sufficient value); we have thought it is enough to be liberated and free. It is not. You may sit there and say, 'No way is that a fair analogy because playing a violin is not a natural ability, but creativity is.' The answer is no. The brain is specifically designed to be non-creative.

Unusually for the time, Edward also distanced himself from militant revolution, which in 1968 would bring Paris to a halt. He coined a word – 'provolution' – denoting a more gradual, non-confrontational change. His whole revolution was to be non-adversarial, 'the weapons not bullets, but perceptions and values.' He would nevertheless still be questioning the *status quo* long after the revolutionary members of the Alternative Society had rejoined the Establishment.

What, at bottom, united Edward with the hippies, united him to others, too. 'There are few things which unite hippies and big-business corporations, painters and mathematicians,' he wrote in 1971. 'The need for new ideas does just this . . . The new division has on one side all those interested in creativity and new ideas and on the other side those who feel threatened by them.'

From 1967, Edward was happening in a big way. On university campuses his work was *de rigueur*, but in truth this thirty-four-year-old, however handsome, wasn't very cool. The alternative society liked Edward because he was about new ideas, about moving forward in surprising ways, questioning 'old and adequate ideas, which like old and adequate cities, come to polarise everything around them.' The drugs and mystical element was most definitely not his thing. 'Lateral thinking,' he wrote in a bid to dissociate himself from the rising tide of escapees dedicated to LSD and Eastern mysticism, 'is a matter of awareness and practice – not revelation … The New Maths makes good use of it,' he declared in rather a schoolmasterly tone. 'The psychedelic cult is an abuse of it.'

The principle of New Maths was actually big in the press at the time. It concerned the 'degrading' of numbers. If, for example, you had to add 899 and 19, you would add 900 to 20 and take away 2. Here Edward was much more at home.

Or try this: add up the numbers from 1 to 10. This is a simple task which anyone can do. Now add up the numbers from 1 to 100.

1 2 3 4 … 97 98 99 100

To do this in the same way would be laborious, so what's the alternative? Clearly one would be to change the *sequence* in which the numbers are added to one another, such as working from the outside in: 100+1, 99+2, 98+3 …

| 1 | 2 | 3 | 4 | …… |
| 100 | 99 | 98 | 97 | ….. |

As soon as you try this, you discover that each sum is the same and equals 101. Doing so for 100 pairs gives you a total of 100 × 101, which equals 10,100. However, as each pair appears twice in the sequence, the answer is 50 × 101 or half of 10,100, namely 5,050.

Another of his favourite lateral mathematical twisters is as follows: 134 tennis players enter a tournament run in the usual elimination way. What is the least number of matches to be played? Lay it all out and see how the winners are gradually whittled away and count the matches. Or shift your perception away from the winners to the losers: there are 134 players, so the least number of matches to produce 133 losers must be 133.

The Use of Lateral Thinking caught on, sold very very well and took Japan by storm. Yet Edward had barely introduced the concept in this book. 'I thought it was a good lark with some nice ideas,' said his publisher, Tom Maschler. 'Yes, it did very well, extremely well.' Suddenly Edward was hot news. The interesting thing was that the Establishment, if one can put capitalist business with that – certainly it seemed distinct from the Alternative Society at the time – cottoned on to it too.

Edward says:

When I wrote my first book, there is virtually no mention of business in it, but business came to me and said, 'What you are talking about is important to us, what we need is lateral thinking and creativity.' Interest in the business community has always been higher than in any other sector. Now, that is because they have an organisational capacity, they have the ability to pay, etc, but underlying it is that in many sectors of society, academic, legal, political, and so on, all you are required to do is to *defend your point of view*. In the business world you can defend your position until you are blue in the face, and go bankrupt next week. In business a skilled defence is of no avail if the market thinks otherwise. There is a reality test. Do people buy your stuff?

When I say this, educators and academics get very upset, you can imagine, but it is true. The business community is more interested in thinking than any other sector. So, businesses came to me and sure ... I get a lot of interest from other groups too, the law, ecology. When I was in New York recently I was seeing the head of the UN Environment Programme because I am a director of the Athena Foundation which, alongside the Olympics, is setting up a big environmental programme. The reason I say this is that when you say de Bono is involved, you get all the long-haired geeks coming out saying, 'Oh that's all capitalist exploitation.'

For a while, however, it was both long-haired geeks and businessmen who wanted him. One minute he was a defence witness at an Old Bailey obscenity trial of members of the underground press, the next he was hobnobbing with capitalist hierarchies.

Paul MacCready first met Edward at an IBM talk:

IBM back then would put on these big programmes for three or four days, put a million dollars into them and get all kinds of people together to give talks, as well as talk about their next internal programmes, something big time and exciting. In fact they were beautifully done, stimulating, fifteen projectors, five screens, some magnificent motivational speakers ... I was very impressed by his presentation that day and I sat next to him at dinner that night and found that I seemed to share all his prejudices and interests and approaches, the only difference being that these were just things I was thinking about, while he was a professional and knew what he was talking about.

* * *

'When *The Use of Lateral Thinking* was published, there was much publicity and I read it,' recalls Jeremy Bullmore, now chairman of J. Walter Thompson's holding company, WPP Group plc. It was part of Bullmore's creative philosophy already that there be 'a constant questioning of the *status quo*, a constant revaluation of the ways in which we think and work in an effort to stop perceptions from becoming pedestrian and stale . . .

> It was practice at the time to take the Creative Department away and get them to think, as you might say, laterally about things. I believe we went to the University of Sussex. We invited Edward. I was doing half and he was doing the other half. Edward was an obvious choice to invite. He opened people's minds a great deal. I have no doubt that he had a benign influence on all those present . . . That was the first time we met and we kept in contact. We didn't see a huge amount of each other, but you could say we were friends. Very engaging, fun to be with . . . he had endless enthusiasm, energy . . . Not long afterwards he did a seminar for BP in Portugal, which I also took part in, and we became involved in a television programme together, BBC2, and I did one or two of his Albany dinners [page 166]. I believe I read somewhere at the time that his next book was going to be written with me, though he hadn't mentioned it to me! But I can't write books like Edward writes books. He said to me, 'Well, come and stay the weekend and we'll have a couple of stenographers and it'll be done by Monday morning.'

David Bernstein was also a speaker at the BP seminar in Portugal. 'We got to know each other at the BP Creative Workshop,' he says. 'There was a lot of money around in companies like BP, which used to run these courses. They'd get artists, designers, architects, etc, to talk about creativity. Edward was one of the people.'

It is important to realise that Edward was still a doctor, still research-ing the physiology of the human body. He was the only person on the circuit, which Bernstein describes, whose focus on creativity was not connected to the thinking or knowledge-base of his particular pro-fession. He had actually written in *The Use of Lateral Thinking*: 'Among the most rigid vertical thinkers are lawyers, doctors and to some extent business people, all of whom prefer things to be rigid, defined, and orthodox, for it is only then that they can bring to bear their experience and technical training.' 'Also, he was the only one at the time, and still today I think he is the only one, actually to show you *how* to be creative as a skill rather than as some kind of mystery,' says Don McQuaig, a corporate consultant who first took him to Canada in the mid-1970s.

'Certainly, my impression in Portugal back in 1968 was that he went down big,' says Bernstein.

> I was very taken with what he had to say. We came back on the same plane from Lisbon and we were sitting next to each other. I was on the inside. There were just two seats and you have on your left Edward de Bono. Soon as the 'No Smoking' sign goes off, what does Edward do? He gets out a new invention of his called the L-Game and challenges me to do it. Did I beat him? Are you kidding? I don't think I ever beat Edward at anything.

Very few do, although I recently watched it happen on Australian television in an interview with Edward on one of his islands – Little Green Island off McKay in Queensland, Australia. He introduced a game of cards, which he had developed, called Concept Snap. You play your cards as in normal Snap, but they are illustrated with concepts. Players call, 'Snap!' and collect the pile of played cards when they see a link between concepts as they fall on the table before them. Edward, in his game with the TV interviewer, was the first to call, on the appearance of a ladder and a rocket: 'Both ways of going up, both ways of ascending,' he said, grabbing the pile. The cards then turned for some time and a pile was built up before the journalist shouted, 'Snap! Bucket and sticky tape. A bucket holds something and sticky tape holds something together.'

It was a very good call.

'Oh, oh, fair enough, fair enough,' Edward conceded, and it appeared that the game was in fact over. 'You mean I've won?' goaded the interviewer, knowing not only that he had won, but that he had a prime moment in the can – he had beaten Edward de Bono at his own game! 'You won that time . . .' Edward agreed, just about graciously.

It cannot be easy being the great lateral thinker in the public eye with people taking pot shots to test your skills. It will have irked Edward that the TV interviewer had in fact linked two *different* concepts, 'contain' and 'adhere', because they both denote 'hold', as it is just such vagueness of language which he holds responsible for some poor perceptual thinking. But he wouldn't have wanted to go into that during an essentially light TV interview about his island. He knew when he was beaten, albeit a tad unfairly.

Edward became a bit of a media darling in the late 1960s, always on panels on radio, and in the odd period piece on television. Says Bernstein, 'The Very Idea was one such, about 1974, a TV panel game between two teams given one problem to solve in advance and then another to solve without prior warning. If you had an idea that needed filming, it could be done prior to the programme and the video would be cut in. Edward was the question master, as it were. In the programme I was in, the four panelists were Brian Aldiss, Heinz Wolf, the psychologist Richard Gregory and me. The problem in advance was how to reduce mugging in an urban area, where they have very bad illumination. The logical answer was of course to increase the illumination, but I came up with the other thing – which attracted Edward – which was, in a sense, to increase the people rather than the lighting. I had this coat made up – it looked very good actually. When you thought you were going to get mugged you would open up this coat and out would drop a pair of legs and up would pop a head and you started talking to it. So the light being bad was quite useful! It was a dummy, you see. Edward liked that because I had turned round the question. The problem with the programme, why it didn't go beyond the first few, was this guy who did the marking. He was the wet blanket. "I don't like yours as much as so-and-so's, etc, I am only going to give it such and such." The programme wasn't about marking. It was a lot of fun with a serious concept behind it.'

Marjorie Wallace who, more recently, started SANE, the international charity helping people affected by mental illness, remembers just how sweet a catch Edward was to the media as the 1960s gave way to the 1970s. She had just graduated in psychology from the University of London and was working for David Frost on The Frost Programme.

I was one of the seven people on Frost's team, which included Tim Brooke-Taylor and Anthony Jay. I was one of the two people selected by ITV as graduate trainees. My job was to have ideas. I came across him – it was The Dog Exercising Machine that put me onto him – and I drove up to Cambridge to meet him. He was then rather handsome, you know, and I interviewed him and it was a very sunny day and everything else . . . So, anyway, we met and he fancied me and I mistook the message. He said he was going up to bed, he went up, and I sat there. So I thought, 'What am I doing sitting here in this cottage?' So I drove into Cambridge and wandered around . . . That *was* a missed opportunity, wasn't it!

Had Wallace made the mistake of stroking the left side of her nose? Alas, history does not tell:

> It has been amusing ever since. He has always laughed and said, 'Well, I told you I was going to bed.' Then I say, 'That is not the way you do it! There I was, nice innocent young girl and I took you at your face value. I thought you were really sleepy.' I was 21, 22, and what I really thought was, this man is eccentric and going to sleep, he's bored with me! That's the beginning and end of the story. I don't know whether he ever went on the programme.

The year 1971 was another busy time for Edward – paperback editions were published of both *The Use of Lateral Thinking* and *The Mechanism of Mind*. On 23 September Jonathan Cape published *Practical Thinking and Different Ways of Being Right and Wrong* in hardback, on 28 October American publishers McGraw Hill published *Lateral Thinking For Management*, and in time for Christmas, Penguin issued altogether four paperback editions of his books. He also formally established the Cognitive Research Trust in Cambridge, through which he would direct a worldwide educational programme, and in the same year married Josephine Hall-White, who was from an army family and had been a friend of Edward's brother Tony. She and Edward had met in London.

All this was going on while he was holding down a salaried position as Assistant Director of Research at the Department of Investigative Medicine at Cambridge University, as well as undertaking a busy lecture and seminar schedule that took him through Europe (including engagements at twenty-six of the forty universities in Britain), America and the Far East. He was advising corporations like Nestlé in Switzerland, international advertising companies J. Walter Thompson and Young & Rubicam, industrial giants BP and Ford, and shuttling between America and Japan to show international centres of capitalism how to think laterally. In fact, he had just recently been to New York to advise Mayor Lindsay on how to solve the problems of crime in the streets, public transport, housing shortage and drugs, and while in North America had come up with the concept of Neighbourhood Watch. 'PO: Suppose everyone became a policeman,' introduced the concept which rapidly spread through America and the UK. (PO, the lateral thinking provocation technique, is covered on page 104.)

Then, the following year, came a man who would introduce him to the country which would become Edward's number one market.

Tom Farrell was born in Malahide in Dublin and is an Irishman through and through. On the face of it, Edward and he are chalk and cheese. Early in Tom's childhood his parents moved to the west coast of Ireland, about eleven miles from Galway Bay, where he recalls one day being taken to the dockland area and seeing 'this man coming off this ship.

> He had scrambled egg all over his hat and gold braid here, and I said, 'That's for me.' Partly it was the dreamer in me, this wandering lust I always had, and the Irish are given to dreaming, but we came from a pretty poor family. There were nine of us and we really had our ass out of our trousers. Sometimes we didn't have the shoes to go to church on a Sunday. My father was earning about £2 a week, way back in the 1950s.

Tom left school just before his fourteenth birthday, and after a job on the railways and another on a boat running a line to the Aran Islands, he left home for London. 'I was going on fifteen at that stage.' He took a job with a friend of his father who lived on Hampstead Heath and had a pub called The Cruel Sea.

> I went out there to be a pot man – picked up the glasses. But what happened was my first experience of homosexuality. This asshole tried to get into the cot with me so I belted him one and I left there and went over to my aunt in Kensington and got a job in a pub there. That was my first six, seven months in the UK and I got TB. I went to a sanitarium in a place called Wokingham. Left there after about fifteen months, went to Slough, got a job in a factory until a friend said to me, 'Why are you working here? Why aren't you at sea with my son?' So I got a job as a bell boy on P&O and then as bedroom steward, as a dining room steward, as a public room steward, fell in love, made quite a lot of money for those days, then went to Australia in 1964. Once there I got a job in a pub and went to night school, and did all those things I should have done as a kid.

Self-improvement focused his politics and Tom began to join Establishment clubs, 'the Lions Club, the Rotary Club . . .

I joined all these things, but was totally self-educated, then worked with W. D. Scott, which was a management consulting group. Then a friend, a Welsh chap called Don Joynson, who was an editor on the *Canberra Times*, we had a big Friday session and we said, 'To hell with working for other people, let's do things by ourselves.' We set up a company in Sydney. Then I parted from him and set up a company of my own called Training Methods Australia – management training methods. Australia really didn't go into the management world until the 1960s, but we were importing a lot of speakers. If you sold in Australia at that time you sold anywhere in the world because we were a fairly cutthroat bunch at that time. There wasn't really a circuit in those days in Australia, though we had the Institute of Management, which was growing. You have to remember, in the 1960s there were only about 9 million people in Australia. Today there are 18 million plus, but a decent restaurant wasn't seen in Sydney until about 1975.

Then I went to London to look for new things. I went to a conference, didn't know that de Bono was going to be represented there. The conference had been announced in the *Economist*. There were about 150 booths of people selling management stuff, and I came across this guy, Derek Knight, who was managing Edward at the time, in a very tiny corner with a 16mm projector doing his thing. I was bright enough to see that he had something that nobody else had or ever did.

Edward recalls the set-up in those days: 'a film, yes, and there was a little puzzle with a triangle of coins pointing upwards. You had to make the triangle point downwards, making only a couple of moves. I think that was what impressed Tom – you had to move the outer coins round.'
Tom recalls:

I kept coming back to the booth, and eventually this chap says, 'Where are you from?' and I said, 'I come from Australia, so who is this man called de Bono?' He said, 'Well, he is a medical doctor and he is a Rhodes scholar and he developed this idea of lateral thinking.'

I hadn't heard of him, but I thought, I like this. The thing had probably been around for thousands of years but nobody had put it as simply as Edward put it. So I said, 'I have to meet this guy,' and he said, 'Well, you can't because he's working for Nestlé in Switzerland.'

I met him eventually. His office was huge when I met him and his filing was laid out on the floor. He had A, B, etc, right across the floor. So I had to walk past all this filing to this enormous desk where he was sitting. I said my name, he said, 'OK,' and I said I would like to bring him to Australia. Just like that. So he said, 'Let's go and have a beer across the road.' So we went and had a half draught of beer, and I said, 'I don't have much money, but if you are interested in coming to Australia I'll see what I can do. I'll work things out. I'll need to take the two reels of film with me to show some people in Australia.'

So back in Australia I went to Qantas and to a few friends of mine and showed them these two reels of de Bono doing his stuff, really great stuff. And my friends said, 'Well, the men in white coats will come for you. You can't teach people to think! Did you not learn to think when you were doing your mathematics, history, geography, etc?' And I said, 'We did, but we didn't learn to think as a skill.' De Bono was talking about thinking as a skill even in those days. He was also developing CoRT [his system for schools], which I am really into – constructive thinking in education. But at that stage we were only talking about lateral thinking.

So, I told de Bono I wanted him for a month. I didn't have a lot of money, but Qantas took the bait and gave me a first class air fare for him, and I arranged contra time for them. They got a day and a half of Edward all to themselves, and during that day and a half they developed the first baby care centre on an aircraft. That came from Edward . . . Then I got tickets all the way round Australia from Anset Airlines, we had a car in every state from Hertz, and we had hotels paid for by Hilton. I arranged all that, and I got the advertising free from J. Walter Thompson.

When I met Edward he was getting around $300 or $500 a day [in fact, in America, he was paid $1,000 per one-hour lecture as early as 1968]. I went to Australia and said he was worth A$2,000 a day 'in-company', but only A$25 a day if you attended his morning seminar. Anset Airline got free time at his public seminar and so did Hertz. He did a day and a half for J. Walter Thompson – they did the advertising free in papers across Australia.

But the key to all of it, the key to the success of de Bono in Australia was the following. We had to find a way to get the Australian journalists to kick down our door. So, we got stringers in the UK to write articles before he came out. Now, there's a family called Brash in Australia, into haberdashery, pianos, music, all the good stuff that the Jews get involved with. The old man apparently had a horse and cart going through Australia, selling needles, pots and pans way back in history. One of them was called Rabbi Brash, and at five to seven every morning on the Australian Broadcasting Commission [radio] he would have a five-minute inspiration slot, plus if you had an old saying or an old proverb or an old quotation and you wrote to him, he would tell you the meaning. So, would you believe it or not, he was talking about the first coming of Christ one morning, and I thought, Jeez, now wait now!

So I was driving along the highway to my office in Sydney, and I thought, what about the first coming of de Bono? And I called the guy from J. Walter Thompson, and he said, 'I don't know but you might like to talk to Jeremy Bullmore in London.' Now, Jeremy Bullmore was a great friend of Edward's. So I called him up and said, 'What if I have "The First Coming of De Bono" and just the dates and the places?' and he said, 'OK,' so that is what we did. We put it at the bottom of the advertising of every paper across Australia. And sure enough, the press called us, and we told them where he was.

Now, before Edward came to Australia several articles were written, but there was one particular article in *Woman's Weekly*. Every man and his dog read this magazine in those days in Australia. They were selling a million copies a week. They made a big story on Edward. Inside, he was in his cottage in Cambridge, dressed totally in black, with a black polo neck up here. And there he was developing something with straws.

'I was just building something,' recalls Edward of the picture. 'There is no particular invention attached to that.' However, the stories of his inventions abounded at that time. Recalls Tom:

He was developing the cigarette, with all sorts of holes at the end of it to take away a lot of the nicotine. He designed a lot of things around that time. That was 1972, and he came to Australia for a month. Whitlam was in power at the time and I was a red, red Conservative, to the backbone, and still am. My job was getting rid of Whitlam at the time. So along with getting rid of Whitlam and launching de Bono, I was having the time of my life.

The evening he arrived in Australia was a Monday and there was a very popular television programme called *Monday Conference*.

Normally they would have three people on that programme for the hour. Edward was on his own. Then there was a prime time show, the Mike Walsh show, very much a housewife's show, it came on at midday. As he was walking down the aisle he noticed that a little old lady had caught her finger in a hole in the chair and couldn't get it out, and he just did something to release it in front of the whole audience. It wasn't a set-up, but there was huge applause.

Edward remembers it well: 'I put my fist behind the old lady's hand so that she had to pull up not back. Out popped her finger.'

Tom went on:

For a whole hour he was being interviewed on that programme, and he became a household name. At that time, Australia was hungry for foreigners, to hear what foreigners had to say. So if you were a foreigner of any note at all, you got a lot of good press. It wasn't too hard to get. Not so much now. You had to be good of course, because if you weren't good they would chop your head off.

On that trip Edward did enormous interviews. He wasn't exhausted. The energy that man has is extraordinary. He still has it today. He can get off a plane from London, arriving in Australia or in Japan, get straight off and do a seminar. However, he is not good with people, unless he is sitting around a dinner table. After a conference is over he walks away and doesn't get involved with people. That's one of the downsides to him.

We went to every state – Perth, Adelaide, Melbourne, Sydney, Brisbane, and New Zealand: Auckland and Wellington. He had forty-seven hours of radio and television in that month. There was not a magazine, including a fishing magazine, that didn't interview him in one fashion or another. I judged the room bookings according to the numbers I expected to hear him. When he came to Sydney we had two morning sessions and an afternoon session, so 1,500 people heard him the first time in Sydney, and paid A$25 a head. It was at the Seble Town House, where he still stays today. We then went to Melbourne and had one day, 500 in the afternoon and 500 in the morning. Adelaide was about 120, 150. Perth was about 200. Brisbane was about 120. Wellington we had about 300 and about the same in Auckland.

During this time people would come up to him with inventions. There were all sorts of people with all sorts of ideas. I remember this old fella – he had two pieces of leather – I don't know what it was – there was a ring on one end of the leather and another ring on the other end and he told of the strength it could have if he put them together with a matchstick. 'Was that lateral thinking?' he asked.

Australia was an incredible success. He loved Australia. Why? I think he discovered that Australia is not a snobbish country. If you think of his childhood, his upbringing, Oxford and Cambridge and all the rest of it, and living with the dons and being a don himself, etc, all of a sudden here was a people among whom you are either a drongo or a dill or an asshole. Whatever you are it doesn't really matter. If you are a whingeing Pommy bastard, go home. But I briefed him fairly well at the same time, though he was very very shy. When he first came out, I had the Premier of New South Wales put on a 'do' for him at the Menzies Hotel. I had to literally carry him by hand and walk him in to talk to people. He had this great habit of standing there and working his heel into the ground, part of the shyness. He is not so shy any more.

You couldn't have found two more different people than Edward and Tom Farrell, but the combination was explosive. Hitherto, Edward had maintained a kind of academic-style management, and his degrees and Oxbridge connections had been emphasised. With the appearance of Tom Farrell on the scene all that had changed. In the global context in which Edward worked, Australia would become his playground. 'He likes the newness of Australia,' says his Australian manager, Julia Pomirska today, 'the freshness of the people, the casualness of the lifestyle here – nobody is very uptight, it is very relaxed and young.'

'I think going to Australia is very important for Edward,' agrees his long-time associate, Paddy Hills. 'There is the enthusiasm, but there is this slightly laid-back approach which he likes. He doesn't feel he is being frogmarched into one place after another. And he can have fun.'

I asked Tom Farrell what he thought of Edward's management prior to their meeting. 'None of them thought big enough,' he replied. Australia remains, to this day, Edward's most popular territory. When I told Edward of Farrell's account of his first trip to the Antipodes, he said:

One of the anecdotes which Tom probably didn't tell you is that we were in New Zealand one time and I was due to give a seminar that day and about breakfast time I said, 'Tom, I have fallen out of bed and broken my arm!' His response was, 'Which arm?' Not, 'Are you

OK,' just 'Which arm?' He was only worried that he had 300 people arriving in three hours' time for a seminar and that if it was my right arm I wouldn't be able to do the projector work! No, but he's a good fellow.

In fact, Tom did tell me the story, and the reason why Edward had broken his arm was more innocent than might appear: 'We were staying in a hotel in Wellington. We had an earthquake, about four o'clock in the morning. We were literally thrown out of the cot!'

Chapter Six

The System Matrix

'When you have the underlying system, can see how it works and what interventions will make a difference, then you can design things like lateral thinking.'

Edward mistrusts words. In 1993's *Water Logic*, he sees them as stabilising our perceptions, which is useful, but anchoring us to obsolete concepts which can inhibit creativity. Twenty-five years earlier, in *The Use of Lateral Thinking*, they inhibit creative associations by classifying concepts miles apart. A bomber plane in World War II riddled with bullets. The hydraulic system is leaking and the crew gives up until one man thinks of filling the system with his urine – the perfect solution, but few would have thought of putting the two things together because language places them conceptually so far apart. A picture, on the other hand, makes the connectedness plain. In 2000, in *The de Bono Codebook*, words are substituted not by pictures, but by a code capable of expressing high level concepts concisely and internationally.

When I challenged Edward about the emotional aridity of language code for communication, he said I would soon get used to it.

> The triumphs of language are generally description triumphs, where a poet puts together these adjectives and creates an image. The point about perception is that it is not description, it is an *intact total view*. If I say you are going to look at a Modigliani, if you know anything about Modigliani immediately you see these figures, these long faces. Or Edvard Munch – immediately you think of *The Scream*. That word has triggered a whole complex vision, and there has been no need to describe with lots of adjectives. Language is short on such words. Short on complex perception. I think that some of the primitive languages do have it, they do deal with

complexity, and it is only when we become so sophisticated at description that we no longer see the need for it.

I shake my head, only to pick up a newspaper and read that researchers from the ad agency McCann Erikson have concluded from a recent survey that a shorthand, coded language, rich in emotion and imagination, is already evolving for the purpose of text message writing on mobile phones, so that, for example, :-) not only represents a happy feeling, but if placed next to a sarcastic comment, is taken as meaning 'Only joking, no harm meant.'

In *The Use of Lateral Thinking* Edward suggests that we should avoid thinking in words and think in visual images instead. I believe that Edward does this naturally. 'The visual language of thought makes use of lines, diagrams, colours, graphs and many other devices to illustrate relationships that would be very cumbersome to describe in ordinary language.' In *Teach Your Child How To Think* (1992), he champions the imaging ability of children. Years earlier he asked a child to draw a machine that puts people to sleep. The child drew a bed on an incline with music for lulling the person and a mechanical hammer for putting him to sleep, after which he would slide down the bed and activate a switch with his feet to turn off the music. 'The concept,' Edward points out, 'is that of "feedback control". The child would never have been able to describe the concept in words.'

People who attend his seminars remember, above all, his drawings. They are a constant feature. As he talks, he draws on reams of acetate with felt tip pens, the images cast on the screen by an OHP. 'It is the way people connect with what he is saying,' observes associate Don McQuaig. 'He has a very visual way of thinking,' agreed Edward's son, Caspar. 'I can see why he wants to have shapes and pictures, illustrations.'

A child's ability to image concepts may be due to an inability to describe them in words – it is easier to draw a picture. For Edward, it is a way to escape what he sees as the conceptually boxed-up nature of language, its rootedness in a culture he wants to change.

In *The Mechanism of Mind*, he gives full rein to his talent for visual conceptualising. He uses words, but only to set up a series of overlapping, visual models which gradually reveal his *conceptual construct* of how thinking works, the mechanism of mind that he is after. Offering up different, but overlapping images not only explains the basis of his thinking system, it is itself an example of it in action. His method is appealing to our intuition, laying down and building up patterns, applying them like successive templates on our minds, the concepts overlapping so to encourage a diffuse kind of attention and an intuitive grasp free of preconceived ideas.

'Writing in ... mainstream genres is usually based on tight logical argument, with points building on each other in logical sequence to develop the argument,' writes Professor John Edwards. 'De Bono's approach is totally different. He ... commonly uses the "overlapping views" approach in order to build a fuzzier, more intuitive overall concept ... This approach can be confusing for those looking for watertight argument and logical consistency, but for de Bono it creates the type of "blurred vision" of a concept which he advocates.'

Analysis, he believes, would conceal as much as it would reveal: 'Analysis of complex systems is like dismembering a body to look for the soul.'

Edward encourages us to think of the brain as facing two environments, the outer world and the inner world. The data from the outer world are our sense impressions; those from the inner world are our emotions. We'll look first at how Edward modelled the way sense impressions organise themselves perceptually.

A limited amount of water poured over a sheet of polythene, which has been stretched over a structure of pins, shows itself prone to pooling due to minute dips and raised portions on the surface. The model demonstrates the idea of incoming sense data *organising itself into patterns*. The nature of the surface is passively to provide an opportunity for the information to be self-organising, to settle in pools and in so doing to change the contours of the surface, determine where future input will flow and direct itself elsewhere. Established ideas establish themselves further and patterns spread.

In his thousand-bulb model incoming sense data is a light source above a surface made up of a thousand separate light bulbs. The source activates a unique pattern of lit units in specific positions. Each unit or light bulb is equipped with a light-sensitive switch. This switch is sensitive to the light source (the incoming data) and to light from neighbouring light bulbs (the switch is shielded only from its own light bulb). Each switch also has an activation threshold – a concept introduced earlier as a series of leaning Lego towers of critical height, requiring just one more block before they topple over. The more you switch a switch on, the more sensitive to light it becomes (the lower the threshold) – this concept finds a match in a dislocated shoulder, something that when it happens makes it easier to happen again.

We recognise concepts in the thousand-bulb model that are similar to concepts from the polythene model, but one significant difference emerges. In the polythene model, the incoming information (the water) itself moves across the surface, while in the thousand-bulb model the input triggers a spreading pattern. Light bulbs that have been lit remain lit, and given that light bulbs activate neighbouring switches, there is no limit to spread. There is nothing to stop all the light bulbs lighting up, spasming the brain in a convulsive fit.

What is needed is a limiting factor, something that will inhibit spread. The purpose of the thousand-bulb model thus emerges: to explore the concept of *positive and negative feedback* – a circular system on which the self-organising nature of the brain depends. In negative feedback, a portion of output returns to *inhibit* input. In positive feedback it returns to *excite* or reinforce input. A lavatory is an example of a negative-feedback system. Rising water raises a ballcock that closes a valve to prevent water from rising further. Rising water inhibits rising water in this negative feedback system.

The model's excitory factor is the tendency of a switch to activate when its neighbour is alight. What is now needed is an inhibitory factor. He puts his model in a glass case and makes each light bulb temperature-sensitive. As the number of bulbs lighting up increases, so the temperature in the case rises, heightening switch thresholds and making it harder for the light pattern to spread. This creates and, with the excitory factor, regulates pattern flow. As a result of this modification, if an activated area abuts onto an area of bulbs with especially low thresholds (due to frequent activity in the past), the pattern will flow into that area at the expense of the light bulbs in the area onto which the incoming pattern actually falls. And if the incoming pattern covers less than the minimum area that can be lit prior to activation of the inhibiting factor, it will spread to the most easily activated and/or the nearest units on the surface.

Here we have the dynamics of information processing, of activation (selection), threshold effects and limitation (inhibition), the dynamics of a self-organising system in which thought flow depends on the interrelationship of these excitory and inhibitory factors. It is in this area that Edward's tools and techniques will go to work, broadening and exciting our perceptions, and foiling the brain's natural desire to make a self-satisfying fit with what has gone before.

In *The Mechanism of Mind*, these and other cognitive models of how the brain deals with sense data build up a simple, elegant and powerful construct – a self-organising, self-selecting, self-maximising, pattern-making and pattern-using system in which thought is a 'flow of activation' across a passive 'surface', rather than an active stringing together (by something called 'self') of items from memory. Once it is understood that the brain works in this way it will be seen why the attention-directing tools of his schools programme, CoRT, and his provoking lateral thinking techniques are designed as they are, to broaden, redirect and intervene in the natural flow from one stable state to the next immediate stable state – the natural point-to-point thinking for which our brains are designed.

In 1969, when many still thought of the brain as a glorified telephone exchange system, such a construct was so innovative that it would be a decade before designers of the so-called neurocomputers (computers which might think more like humans) caught up with it.

In March 1978, Edward predicted that the next generation of computer experts would 'take the pattern-making road'. John Hopfield, now at Princeton University, was then at Caltech, leading research on the mathematics and simulations of biological neural networks, and on the possible electronic and optical implementations of these. Having contacted Edward, Hopfield began writing about the connectedness which had been modelled in *The Mechanism of Mind*, and lent support to Edward's claim that 'these ideas are now the basis of the advanced neurocomputers'.

I Am Right, You Are Wrong contains yet another model for how the brain works. This, to my mind, benefits from Edward's work since *Mechanism of Mind* was published, and Viking made the book a national bestseller in 1990. While the essential points of Edward's concepts remain the same, *I Am Right* states them very much more succinctly, and only presents one model. I recommend this book as a summing-up of Edward's ideas at the time, and also as a valuable restating of the fundamentals of his system. *Water Logic*, which followed three years later, is linked to it – the chapter 'Flowscapes', shows day-to-day examples of how our thoughts/perceptions do actually flow according to patterning concepts explored in *I Am Right, You Are Wrong*.

I Am Right, You Are Wrong was written over little more than a week at the de Bonos' house at Marnisi, Malta, as many of his best books were. Palazzo Marnisi was the de Bono family's summer retreat in the island's eastern, wine-growing region of Marsaxlokk (pronounced 'Marshash-lock'), an achingly romantic seventeenth-century clifftop villa looking out across rough, stone-patterned fields to the sea. Everyone connected with Edward during his period of tenure of Palazzo Marnisi has fond memories of it. Family friend Marjorie Wallace recalls 'reading every page of *I Am Right, You Are Wrong* as he wrote it – I didn't edit it, I just commented. I didn't do anything with it really – you don't with Edward – while the boys, Charlie de Bono and my son Stephan, dived off the cliffs into the sea.'

In an appropriate maritime reference, the chapter entitled 'The Nerve Network of the Brain' images the neural network as a beach full of octopuses. Each octopus has many more than eight tentacles, representing neuro-transmitters. Each tentacle rests on the body of another octopus and is capable (when stimulated) of transmitting an electric shock. Distance is no object – some tentacles are enormously long.

The octopuses are stimulated by a light shone from a helicopter above, representing sense data. When stimulated, an octopus turns bright yellow and is prone to stimulate other octopuses. Activation – the yellowing effect – spreads via the tentacles of the directly stimulated octopuses, and would spread right across the whole length of the beach. What prevents this is that when an octopus is awake and bright yellow, it also gives off a pungent smell which, when it reaches a certain level, ensures that other octopuses resist stimulation and stay firmly asleep. The response to the stink one might call negative feedback, the inhibiting factor which ensures that the activation pattern doesn't continue to spread and send the brain into a convulsive fit.

Regular stimulation by a particular tentacle on a particular octopus causes soreness, which makes it more susceptible to a shock from that tentacle in the future. This is Edward's threshold concept of connectedness, and is of course all about association (which becomes memory when permanent) and enables pattern reconstruction, on which our day-to-day living depends. An old pattern is triggered when the brain recognises a part of it on a subsequent occasion. This is essential. We rely upon it to live normally, but, as we have seen, the tendency marks out the brain as essentially *un*creative. His lateral thinking techniques are designed to outwit this natural tendency.

So, in line with past experience, the yellowing effect in the octopuses remains limited by the stink. Eventually, however, the yellow octopuses become bored and as they get bored the stink diminishes and other, hitherto inhibited, live-wire connections are activated instead, letting the previously activated group go to sleep. This is *the tiring factor* characteristic of nerve systems and turns out to be vital. 'I once made a model of a brain on a computer, which had only five nerves,' Edward recalls. 'This brain was capable of fifty billion thoughts. Now, any mathematician would tell you that that is absurd, with only five nerves you would have just factorial five. Any electronics person would tell you it is impossible. But biologically it *is* possible, why? Because nerves get tired. Transistors don't get tired, but when this nerve gets tired the pattern's got to go another way. When that nerve gets tired it goes another way. You get huge complexity. Electronics engineers would never understand that. Mathematicians would never understand that. But coming from biology it is obvious.'

Time and again, a weakness is a strength from another point of view in the mechanism of mind, which at root explains Edward's purpose in lateral thinking, Six Hats and CoRT to get us looking for alternative perceptions whose logic lies as yet undiscovered.

Activation then shifts to other groups of octopuses, switching off here and yellowing up there, perhaps suddenly on the far side of the beach, depending on thresholds set by the relationship between the excitory and inhibitive factors – strength of firings, connectedness, soreness, tiring. But the important thing is that no one outside the system has determined the pattern flow; the system has done it. The system only behaves *as if* it had a self. A self-organising system is a system with a life of its own. What it does, it does without outside intervention.

Think of it this way. People crowd into a small room to hear an interesting lecture. The room rapidly heats up and begins to drive the less interested out, while more interested observers may yet come in. Finally the room is filled with the most interested observers. Selection and limitation. No one has made the selection; the system did it. Nothing and no one outside the cerebral system can take credit for choosing what you do. Selection is a natural function of the system, and the system decides the flow.

But what of our inner data – the emotions? Once we begin to consider the internal environment, we are no longer dealing with information for its own sake, but for its usefulness. Emotions are concerned with needs. 'In terms of survival or adaptation this may be essential,' Edward writes in *Mechanism of Mind*. 'In terms of maximising information, it may be limiting.' Emotions are the dominant influence on the patterned flow. They reflect the chemical state of the body, and, for better or worse, give this selfless system its identity. 'Experiencing the inner world eventually develops identity, and that developed identity starts developing structures or influences on the outer picture. So it is like two separate maps are developing and after the inner map has developed it says, "I have an identity, I can do things, let me look for this and that in the other map."'

To Edward, emotion is 'non-conceptualised perception'. He gives the example of remembering a holiday. You summon an image of the place – a beach or town – and attached to it (though not itself imaged) is a feeling or emotion about that place.

In addition to the ordinary expressions of anger, hatred, love, fear, joy, suspicion, jealousy, sorrow, depression, remorse, sadness, and so on, there are the ego-emotions – pride, power, insecurity, drawing attention, the need to be right all the time, playing the funny man, feeling important, not being fooled. 'In life,' Edward admits, 'emotions usually come first and then the thinking is used to support and back up the emotions. Even when the thinking does come first, the emotions give it power. All decisions and choices are emotional.'

Even if you go out of your way to make a wholly practical decision, emotion is the driving force, providing 'a system of value for reference' (telling you what you feel about a situation) and enabling 'the application of values to action' (deciding what to do about it). But it wasn't until the 1980s that Edward got to grips with the way emotion and ego dominate our thinking. Six Thinking Hats, which come out of this time, is a way of dealing with thinking processes in parallel rather than, as we tend to, higgledy piggledy, all at the same time. With the hats you can be critical, cautious, egotistical, angry, and so on – but at specific times. No one way of thinking is allowed to dominate at the expense of another. CoRT, which he developed in the 1970s, encourages completion of the perceptual stage of thinking in as thorough a manner as possible before the emotions come into play. It is, therefore, never a matter of doing without emotions completely.

Edward challenges us with the notion that all decisions are naturally based on fear, greed or laziness – 'fear of making a mistake, fear of risk, fear of losing money, fear of a lot of trouble, fear of what others say, fear of seeming silly, fear of being impractical'; greed, usually in the sense of achievement and wanting more; laziness as a kind of negative greed – lack of motivation, aversion to getting caught up in things, and so on. 'A biological system operates by moving towards what is desirable,' he writes in *Teaching Thinking* (1976), although there is also the 'hump effect, where an objective requires short-term sacrifice (a strategy first to go north in order to get south),' and similarly there is the great meta-system, religion, which 'carries man past the temptation of immediate self-gratification in order to reward him with higher things.'

He writes admiringly that, 'Over the ages religion has provided the most powerful meta-system to take people out of the self-interest of their own little systems in order to work for a higher goal. It has been extraordinarily effective, with martyrs going willingly to a cruel death . . .' In an interview in 1986, he said, 'People sometimes think that I would be unsympathetic towards religious beliefs, but actually I have the view that believing and thinking are completely separate systems and can easily coexist.'

One might read this as something of a step sideways. He once had fun shocking a party of Catholic teachers by saying, 'God cannot think and God cannot have a sense of humour. Thinking means moving from an imperfect arrangement of information to a perfect one. That implies change and imperfection, which is a logical impossibility for God. Also, God will never be surprised by the punchline of a joke because he already knows it. Fortunately, however, he does have a sense of the ridiculous, otherwise he would never have created *us*.'

His conclusion was, 'the answer to the question whether there is a God is '"Maybe!"'

In *Unweaving the Rainbow*, Richard Dawkins indirectly demonstrates the subtlety of Edward's challenge that all our decisions are based on fear, greed or laziness, with the biologist's contribution to the argument as to whether human/animal nature is essentially selfish or good-natured: 'It is now widely understood that altruism at the level of the individual organism can be a means by which the underlying genes maximise their self-interest.' So defined, it would seem that Edward's point is uncontestable.

Let's get back to the beach, away from such troubling thoughts. It appears that octopuses like music – indeed, that they have distinct preferences for different kinds. When the beach is bathed in jazz, some octopuses are clearly stimulated, while others seem more at home with country and western, and yet others are electrified by Mozart. Likewise, our emotions bathe the beach of our minds with distinct chemical mixes, and turn on some neurons but not others to a state of readiness, joining other excitory factors, such as connectedness, to influence the direction of pattern flow.

When Edward designed the self-organising system of the mind, he didn't set out to prove how the mind works, but only to hypothesise a construct, a conceptual model, which would enable him to develop his lateral thinking tools and techniques. In an article in the *Times Educational Supplement* in 1971, in which he envisaged a Concept Circus of which he was ringmaster, he wrote, 'In a child's constructor set some pieces are much more useful than others simply because they enable you to fix the other pieces together. Without these "connector" pieces one is unable to *put things together*.' That was the purpose of his conceptual model of the mechanism of mind. If the lateral thinking tools and techniques then worked, that was enough. He wanted to enable his readers.

But it confounded many. His friend, Father Peter, remembers Edward's father, 'asking me one day whether I had read *The Mechanism of Mind*. I told him, "Yes, I had read it." And he began to tell me, "Of course I don't think it's medicine!" I told him that I thought that there was a brilliant idea there, this picture of the brain, [and] that had he actually proven the hypothesis – this model that he had – in neurophysiological terms, then it really would have been a breakthrough.'

A Russian mathematician said to me at a recent de Bono seminar, 'It is not normal to use a model to prove something and not worry that the model is not true.' But is it not? Scientific genius Richard Feynman wrote in 1965, 'I think I can safely say that nobody understands quantum mechanics.' The point was, who cares? The theory works. It enables prediction!

Edward's approach is speculative, not analytical. Analysing information will allow you to use existing ideas or to combine existing ideas, but to get a really new idea you have to start it in your mind as a possibility. That was what he was doing in his physiological research with his conceptual constructs, and that is what he is doing now, in the context of thinking. People mistrust speculation, but it is, in fact, how science moves forward. As Edward says,

> That word 'possibilities' is very important. The whole of Western success in science and technology has depended on that word. They won't tell you that in universities, they'll tell you it's all data and logical deduction. That's rubbish.
>
> Two thousand years ago China was way ahead of the West. Gunpowder, rockets, bronze, paper and so on. Very smart people. The University of California has 162,000 students, 40 per cent of them are Asian, mainly Chinese and Koreans living in California. What is the percentage of Asians in the population? Four per cent, which is providing 40 per cent of the students.
>
> So what went wrong? At one time technicians were trying things out and civilisation was advancing. But then they fell into the hands

of the Mandarin class and in a sense the academics, who said, 'This is so, this is so, this is so . . .' *They never developed the hypothesis*, the possibility system . . . In technology the hypothesis is the vision. I can imagine this, now how can I realise it? Possibility is the driver of thinking.

Edward's model of the mind is, therefore, his 'vision'. When I suggested to him that from a marketing point of view it might have been as well to have done the extra work and experimentation to prove his model and put his thinking programmes on a sound scientific basis, I had his ex-boss Professor Mills's comment in mind: 'He had one defect as far as I was concerned. In order to publish things you have to be able to do the experiment repeatedly and get the same answer. He was always too impatient and wanted to get on to the next stage.'

Edward would have none of it.

So, I could have spent time giving more description. So, you have people arguing on about their descriptions, but then what do you do with that? What does it *mean* in terms of changing things? It's like taking a walking stick, and someone examines it and says, 'There's a top and a bottom.' And someone else says, 'No, no. There's a handle, and there's a metal tip at one end, and there's a middle thing.' And yet another person says, 'No, no. You've got the handle, and you've got the middle of it, and you've got the bottom, and then there are the two linking things.' So you can just go on forever describing things as you like, and it doesn't actually help.

But when you say, 'If that is so, let me design something – a process that will improve that thing I'm describing or will employ it in a different way.' Now, if that thing turns out to be effective, two things can happen: the effective practice may justify the theoretical basis, or it might turn out that the basis was erroneous. But either way, if the practice you designed is useful, it doesn't matter whether or not your theoretical basis was accurate. You've got something useful, and your erroneous basis has served as the launching point, and that's what matters.

His own approach is that of all his thinking programmes, useful, pragmatic, *design* thinking. In design thinking, *movement* forward is implicit. Movement is 'the willingness to go forward in a positive, exploring way rather than stopping to judge whether something is right or wrong'. We are not concerned with analysis and judgement.

All that being said, purists might be interested to know that in 1982, two academics *did* put the model to the test.

M. H. Lee, from the Department of Computer Science at Aberystwyth University, and A. R. Marudarajan, from the Department of Computer Science at the University of Southern California in Los Angeles (UCLA), set up a computer simulation of Edward's model in *The Mechanism of Mind*, and published their findings in the *International Journal of Man-Machine Studies* (vol 17, pp 189–210). Two main studies on the model were made, and pattern flow analysed. Lee and Marudarajan concluded that the simulation showed that Edward's system 'does in fact' organise itself and behave as he describes in *The Mechanism of Mind*. The duo then speculated as to how much of Edward's work was original and promised further evaluations.

So to the lateral thinking tools and techniques, which work on the selective processes, the dynamics of the mechanism of mind, alternately outwitting and exploiting those excitory and inhibitory factors. *Serious Creativity* (1995) is an in-depth study of them.

As we've seen, while the brain is an excellent system for adapting to a stable universe, setting up routine patterns, using them and so on, the tools of lateral thinking provide what's missing. They are creative software for the brain.

I have written about the need to focus, look for clues, challenge things (however well they may be going), seek alternatives. About almost anything you can say, 'Why does it have to be like that? Why does it have to be done that way?' But lateral thinking is a disciplined, focused skill and the first priority is targeting.

It goes against the mechanism of mind to challenge what makes for a stable or unified view of life, and it goes against the grain to challenge things which are not problems – but if you want to be creative, this is the area which you will have to consider. Says Edward,

> We take it for granted that it's just as easy for a plane to go from A to B as from B to A. Let's challenge that. Why should it be just as easy? From that we develop the idea of planes that go only one way. If planes always went east rather than backwards and forwards, could more flights be overnight? Then, could we consider a whole new design of the plane with beds and bunks instead of seats? Possibilities.
>
> When a concept has always done well then a certain sort of complacency surrounds that concept and protects it from further

evaluation. Consider plate shape. Must a plate be round? There is no manufacturing reason to stick with round plates. What other shapes could we have? What could we do with the new shapes which we couldn't do with the old? An ordinary wine glass has been the same shape for about 7,000 years. Challenge it.

In a seminar organised by Shell Oil, in London in 1971, someone challenged the usual method of drilling for oil, which of course is vertically, straight down into the ground. So familiar was the idea of drilling down that no one had considered alternatives. Once this was perceived, they began to drill vertically down and then, by using enhanced hydraulics, to cut horizontally across the stratum, producing an L-shape bore and giving wider and more productive access to one bed. Shell didn't take it up. Statoil in Norway, the state-run oil company, now has one shaft that runs 10 kilometres laterally.

Edward says:

> Many years ago I was doing work for Midland Bank and one afternoon a marketing executive challenged the idea that banks have branches. Some time later they came up with First Direct, where all the banking is done by telephone, a very successful concept; at one time they were getting 10,000 new customers a month.
>
> I was speaking to an International Lottery Conference and said, 'Why are lottery tickets all the same?' When you a buy a ticket some of the money comes back as winnings, some goes as profits to the operators, some goes to the charity committees that give out the money. Why not name tickets E, M or C? If you buy an E ticket it goes for Ecology, an M ticket for Medicine, a C ticket for children's charities. So when you buy a ticket you decide where the surplus money went, not some anonymous committee. Simple challenges. We accept *this*. Why?

The fundamental point is that creative challenge is nothing to do with problem-solving. Creative challenge is an eagerness to discover other ways of doing something.

'Challenge the stable state,' says Edward. 'Why number the pages of a book 1 to 200, when numbering them 200 to 1 has the additional value of informing you directly at any point how many more pages to go? Stable – unstable – new stable is the creative movement. The original stable state may be way below optimum value.' Challenge and alternatives are techniques concerned with *value sensitivity*. We have the technology to do virtually anything we need. What we need to do now is to apply technology in ways that will add value to our lives.

When you have a problem, what to focus the tools on may be obvious, but when challenging traditional or even successful methods, it is less easy. 'If I say to people, "Put down your problems," they will do so without difficulty,' says Edward. 'If I say, "List your creative needs," they have a hard time listing more than two or three. A creative need is not there until you make it there, and I am amazed how few people are aware of where new ideas are needed.'

So Edward came up with the Creative Hit List, which organises what to focus on. Although this is discussed in detail in *Serious Creativity*, with advice about considering focus under speciality areas, such as improvement tasks, projects, whims, opportunities, etc, I recommend also reading books such as *Opportunities* (1978), *Sur/Petition: Going Beyond Competition* (1992) and *Simplicity* (1998). Consider where you should direct your creative energies carefully. There are many seductive traps. Edward advises choosing your own race to run and being very specific about where you intend to focus the creativity tools. If you do manage successfully to challenge something that is going well, you are more likely to have found your own race to run, an area in which there is little competition.

Peter Low was trained in the use of Edward's thinking tools in 1992. Deploying them in the Pacific Rim countries and on his own business strategy has made Peter and his wife, Linda, millionaires. They live in a house in Singapore called Casa de Bono. I will look at their incredible story later. When I spoke to Peter, he was still buzzing from a three-hour seminar he had given to representatives from forty hospitals in Hong Kong.

'The response was so favourable that I was invited to draw up a programme which would incorporate Edward's Six Thinking Hats and lateral thinking,' he told me.

> This would be specifically for the medical fraternity in Hong Kong, for the CEOs running the hospitals, the chief of staff of the various hospitals, the people that head each department at the various hospitals, managers, and anybody who fell under the general term of 'doctor' – neurosurgeons, eye surgeons, physiotherapists, a very wide group.
>
> Every month I will have about seventy doctors coming to these

two-day sessions, and as many of these were heading hospitals themselves the next logical step was for them to invite me in-house to their various hospitals to conduct what we call 'in-house pro-grammes'. They wanted their top people to be exposed to the methodology as a way for them to think *in parallel*, to think more creatively but in a very structured manner.

We will come to parallel thinking later. I asked Peter how he would normally begin a lateral thinking seminar.

There are eight sessions over two days. After the introduction I go straight into something called Targeting. Targeting is a very essential part of Edward's methodology. At this point I ask the people to highlight certain issues that are of particular relevance to them. From then on, it is just a matter of application of whatever I introduce to them, to these thinking focuses. It is a hands-on approach. This question of focus is an actual strategy . . . Edward's concept of the Creative Hit List immediately allows relevant application. Suggestions become more pointed and more relevant.

After targeting, Peter moves into Sequence of Alternatives, trying to raise the threshold levels of that bank of light bulbs, reduce the inhibiting factors, widen perception, outwit the brain's natural tendency to see only what it has been prepared to see in the past.

Consider ways to make it difficult for a man to get from A to B – two points on a map. Typical suggestions might be to build a wall or set a trap. 'Because our brains have set up the main, usual routine track,' says Edward, 'it is difficult to think of anything else.' While this gives the brain an advantage over the computer in rejecting a mass of irrelevant alternatives, it also restrains its ability to accept or create new patterns. The first approach is to issue a challenge, block the routine track. 'We do something that way, yes, but why do we have to do it that way?' Instead of building a wall or setting a trap between A and B, why not make it more attractive to get to C? 'Challenge is a very powerful tool, but very difficult to use because it runs counter to our normal thinking patterns.'

Challenging things creatively means looking for alternatives. Identify the *dominant* concept behind an idea, perhaps you could change that. Remember that concepts evolve over time and are 'a summary of history rather than a blueprint for the future,' as Edward wrote in *Tactics*

(1984). Peter Low points out how Swatch watches swung the dominant concept of a watch away from a timepiece to a thing of fashion. Challenge *assumptions*; challenge anyone who, at any time, says, 'Either we have to do this or we have to do that' – such polarisations inhibit creativity.

One very effective lateral thinking tool for seeking alternatives is the Concept Fan, which, as Peter points out, involves a clear understanding of the difference between a concept and an idea. 'I find it very interesting that even among people who think a lot, there is this unexpected inability to distinguish between concepts and specific ideas. In fact, a major problem for many very professional people is that it never occurred to them that the two are not the same. They would use the words concept and idea interchangeably. And they would use them incorrectly, idea for concept and concept for idea.'

Edward has a simple definition, 'An idea is a concept in action.' Concepts are patterns in the mind, like roundabouts off which alternative ideas flow. They are to do with *processes* rather than things. If you are looking at an idea and want its operating concept, go upstream with a question like, 'This idea is a way of doing what?'

There was a problem with designing a pen for astronauts because in the weightless environment of outer space, traditional biros and pens simply do not work; you need gravity to enable ink feed. So £2 million was spent in R&D by the Fischer organisation to produce a space pen for NASA – a ballpoint with pressurised nitrogen forcing the ink down. The Russian space programme had the same problem, but they went back to the operating concept – 'We want something that writes upside down in a weightless environment' – and delivered it with an idea that cost virtually nothing – a pencil.

'Once you have the concept,' says Edward, 'you can move out and generate many, many ideas. Once you have a concept, go downstream with the question, "How can this be carried through?" The trick is to isolate the concept, clarify it, define it, change it if you want and then find ways of delivering it. The need to find concepts is a very key part of seeking alternatives.'

Years ago, Edward was returning from a skiing trip when a blizzard swept the airport car park. The locks on the cars were frozen over. Others were trying to warm the locks to melt the ice and finding it difficult. Only when he went back to the start-concept of 'raising temperature', and changed it to 'lowering the freezing point' did it occur to him that his duty-free brandy would do the trick. 'A simple change in perception made all the difference,' he recalls. 'There is nothing more useful than a new idea that serves your purpose.' He goes on:

> I was in a smallish town in Australia and the mayor came to me and said the shopkeepers are complaining. The commuters come in the morning and occupy all the parking spaces and no one can do any shopping. Should we put in parking meters? Now what is the operating concept of parking meters? It has been shown that they are not revenue earners because the revenue just about covers the cost of running them. Their purpose is to allow as many people as possible to use a limited parking space. Take that concept and you could have a very much simpler way of delivering it – simply allow people to park for as long as they like within road markings, provided they leave their headlights full on. Now you are not going to stay one minute longer than you need to, because there is now downward pressure on your occupancy of that space. With the meters there was no downward pressure until your time was up. So, once you can identify the concept, very often you can find much much better ways of doing it.

The Concept Fan, which is discussed in detail in *Serious Creativity*, opens out to reveal your objective or purpose at one end and alternative ideas that will deliver your purpose at the other end. In between – by means of a series of questions – you move back from your objective through different concept levels, the concept hierarchy.

I recently attended a four-day seminar of Edward's in Malta. There were eight of us. Two had come from England, myself and a fellow who runs a voluntary organisation in Manchester. There was a mathematician from Omsk, Siberia, to which free thinkers were once consigned by the oppressive Soviet regime; a congenial, wise schoolteacher from Sicily; a young graduate from Silicon Valley in California; a provocative thinker from Thailand; a chap from Poland, whom Edward eyed warily as he may have worked for the Press Association; and finally, a strict, efficient, would-be trainer in Edward's thinking from Denmark. At some point in the proceedings Edward asked us to consider what kind of person would make a good politician. The temptation was to think cynically. But when it was the Thai, Rasmee's, turn, she said, 'A milkman, because a milkman serves the community with something which is good for it, and he sets a good example by getting up early in the morning.'

Edward jumped on the idea, teasing it out: 'That is interesting, very interesting. You might also add that a milkman would make a good politician because we never see him!'

Inspired by the creative pattern that lay behind the suggestion, he traced it back to the highest conceptual level, which he called the 'right wrong answer'. Of course, 'milkman' is the wrong answer. A milkman would not make a good politician, but 'milkman' is also the *right* answer because it reveals what is (or might be) bound up with being a politician. With the concept of milkman, we could cascade a number of ideas about what we want of our politicians.

We had found an operating concept and, as important in the context of the seminar, the idea had emerged as a resonance between two operating concepts – milkman and politician – perfectly consistent within themselves, but up till that moment, hopelessly incompatible. The asymmetric pattern of 'the right wrong answer' also illustrates perfectly how the provocation techniques in lateral thinking work.

The quality in a concept of *movement* towards new ideas became Edward's project obsession. Time and again, he found young children the most naturally ready to join in. In the 1970s, he published a series of things on children designing things as *Children Solve Problems* and *The Dog Exercise Machine*; the latter reproduces drawings by children of the title concept. Once, a class of very young children was asked to tackle the problem of car design for rough terrain. One drew a car with a nozzle at the front, out of which 'smoothstuff' poured onto the rough road below, before being sucked up by a nozzle at the rear after the car's wheels had passed over it.

I set my nine-year-old son the same challenge and he automatically thought of aspects of the four-wheel-drive vehicle, suited to rough terrain, that sat outside in the yard. Had it not been time for school I might have given him the Concept Fan to open his thinking up. Instead, I told him the story of the 'smoothstuff', and after thinking about it for a few moments, he said, 'Yes, that's really good.' It *is* a striking concept, for despite impracticality, it has great *movement* value – it challenges us to consider what 'smoothstuff' might be, in what area of work such a design might be of use, and what, other than 'smoothstuff', might attach to a car to solve the problem. It shifts our perceptions into interesting areas. Kids like to do that a lot, as we will shortly see.

So we come to the nub of lateral thinking, the provocation techniques, for which his self-organising model cries out. These are techniques used to provoke perceptions out of a dominant pattern or rut and into a more productive sidetrack which up to now has been suppressed. There's nothing magical about provocation: it simply relates to the way the self-organising systems of the mind works.

The sequence of events we experience necessarily sets up the main track in the mind and dominates our perceptions, just as the sequence in which you receive a collection of plastic shapes in your hand can determine your perception of how to fit them together. This is why provocation is a necessity, rather than an option. As new shapes arrive to fit into a pattern, there will be a need to go back, disturb and rearrange the pattern to find a new symmetry (or maximum currency and value, what Edward calls 'best use').

As he puts it,

> Time passes and as time passes information comes in. Periodically we have to make the best use of what we have got up to that point. Maybe for policy, project design, whatever. So we have a system with two broad characteristics: 'input over time' and 'periodic best use'. That applies to *all* thinking. What can you say about such a system? Quite a lot. We can model it in a very simple way.
>
> 'Best use' means the best arrangement of the information that is available at the moment and which can most easily be described to someone over the telephone so that that person can reproduce the shape.

2 shapes:

are followed by a 3rd shape:

The shape designed is usually as shown:

Then two further pieces are presented, and there is generally no symmetrical fit with the shape that has so far been designed.

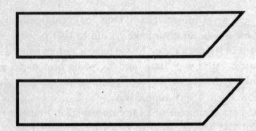

We have been correct at each stage, but in order to go forward we have to go back and change an arrangement which in its day was the best.

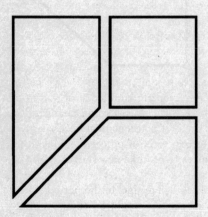

It is only when all the pieces are disturbed and reduced to their original forms that the process to a new idea can begin again.

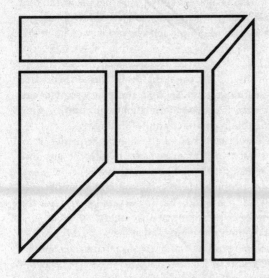

It is a fundamental mathematical principle that any system with an input over time and a period need to maximise for best use is always sub-optimum. Many airline concepts are inappropriate railway concepts because the railway came first. 'Here we have the *underlying* reason why provocation in creativity is essential [and logic won't do]. If we had managed to make the fit, I – in my role as the future – would have produced a different shape which wouldn't fit!' At this point in seminar he drops an impossible plastic shape on the face of his OHP.

So: an arrangement of information making the best possible sense at a particular moment in time is bound, given that time moves on, to require provocation for maximisation at some point. 'It doesn't matter how smart you are, unless you have complete knowledge of the future there is no way you can avoid the need to go back and change ideas which in their day were the best; that is a mathematical necessity.'

Edward is constantly provoking new ways of perceiving something, even welcoming outside disturbances to provoke new starting points:.

When I was doing Out Patients at Cambridge, in the period when I was waiting for a patient to come in, I would be thinking about something, and then the patient would arrive and the fact that I had been interrupted often made me more creative. I found that constant interruption allows you to be more creative. Most people would find that counter-intuitive, but if you are constantly interrupted you rarely start up again exactly where you left off, you may come in at a different angle.

Edward's two lateral thinking provocation tools, the Provocative Operation (PO) and the Random Input, set up a whole new sequence of experience by breaking our minds out from their safe, unified little logic boxes, and bringing totally new ideas out of hiding.

PO means that a *deliberate* leap out of the logical sequence is in prospect. Edward points out that PO can be seen in both the meaning and the spelling of 'hy*po*thesis' (which, like a provocation, brings new possibilities to perception), 'sup*po*se' ('Let's suppose . . .'), '*po*ssible' (the *status quo* is not the only way a situation has to be) and '*po*etry' (for the movement value of its imagery, provoking new thoughts).

PO is placed in front of the provocative (sometimes absurd) proposition which speculates our perceptions out of the dominant track into an as yet unassociated sidetrack. Years ago, a certain Mr Ferguson at Harston County Primary School in Cambridge, one of the schools in an experimental project Edward ran in the 1970s, would hang large paper cut-outs of electric light bulbs across the classroom and greet every new day by asking the children, 'What do I say when you have a new, bright idea?'

'Ah, the light shines!' came the class chorus.

'All those bulbs up there are bright, shining ideas, which I want to get hold of during this lesson,' confirmed Mr Ferguson. 'How am I going to reach them?'

Without waiting for an answer he would jump onto his table and from there step onto a nearby desk, from which he could reach one of the light bulbs. Cutting it loose, he would then hold it up and explain that the desk was a *stepping stone* to reach his new idea.

Edna Copley told me this story. She and her late husband, Bill, were key organisers and teachers in Edward's project, which eventually reached millions of children round the world. It is an amazing story, shortly to be told for the first time (page 128). Ferguson was just one of the teachers swept away by Edward's techniques, and here he makes the point that like a stepping stone for getting to the other side of a river, PO has no value in itself, only in terms of where it leads you. Its purpose is movement. We use it, then forget it.

There are two elements involved in PO – the setting up and the delivering of ideas. POs are set up by the Escape method or the Stepping Stone method (by means of Reversal, Exaggeration, Distortion or Wishful Thinking). While all are well illustrated in *Serious Creativity*, let's look at one or two examples of how they worked for real.

Using the Escape method, list things you take for granted about a situation, then turn one of them around. For example, we take it for granted that restaurants charge for food, so – 'PO, restaurants do not charge for food.' Years ago a similar 'pay later' provocation led to the concept of Diners Club and the first restaurant credit card.

At the 1976 Olympic Games, $1 billion was lost. Not through carelessness, but misguided thinking, as it turned out. The International Olympic Committee approached city after city to find someone to take the next games on and found all unwilling, until finally Moscow reckoned they could make it work. That in itself did little to restore confidence that the games were other than a fiscal gamble, until the state of California agreed to stage the 1984 Games and appointed Peter Ueberroth to organise them. The result was $225 million profit. Why? Lateral thinking, so Ueberroth said in an interview in the *Washington Post* of 30 September 1984.

Edward told me:

> Someone sent me the cutting, so I wrote to him and asked where did you learn your lateral thinking, and he said, 'Don't you remember, I was your host when you talked to a Young Presidents' Association meeting in Boca Raton, Florida, in 1975?' Just a short talk, ninety minutes, but he took the principles and applied them to his company, a travel company called Ask Mr Foster, and built it up into the biggest travel company next to American Express, sold it and applied it systematically up to the Olympic Games. All these tools can be taken and used systematically. It's nothing to do with a right attitude. They are quite deliberate processes in thinking.

The Olympic Games were turned around by some clever Escape thinking. Hitherto it had been taken for granted that huge television coverage vied against audience attendance figures, but in 1984, for the first time, the Olympic Games became a TV Games. Everything was geared to facilitate TV coverage. As far as stadia audiences were concerned, so long as there were enough people to make it a good on-air spectacle, that was OK. The big money came from TV. The story is a good one.

With the media now allegedly threatening the ethos of the Games, perhaps it is time for another provocation.

The Escape method works on more mundane levels, too. The other day, Edward challenged a seminar group I was attending to set up a new sort of restaurant. My PO ran like this. A restaurant must have customers, so – 'PO: Restaurants have no customers.' This led to the idea that the customers were in fact staff, which led to the idea of opening a cabaret restaurant where customers are no longer classifiable as customers because they provide the entertainment. There would be no obligation to do so, but performers would be attracted in the knowledge that if they performed well enough they would eat for free and get noticed. After a performance, everyone would vote (thumbs up, thumbs down, gladiator-style) as to whether the 'entertainer' merited a free meal.

I have been to three of Edward's seminars while researching this book, and I've seen for myself how PO statements emerge and motivate ideas much more outrageous than this one, and which *no one would have thought of otherwise*. It can be an invigorating experience. Once, I invented mouse-shaped cat food via PO and was actually propositioned over lunch by an interested marketing executive!

For Edward, however, it is a gruelling round, hitting the multinationals year after year. He had been 'labouring in the vineyards of corporate consultancy', as *Forbes Magazine* described it, for some fifteen years when David Tanner at DuPont first came upon his work in an article in *Business Week*. At the time, Tanner was a director of research at DuPont, then a company with 125,000 employees and a $45 billion gross. He had responsibility for the Industrial Fibres Division. He recalls,

> It was a $2 billion division, and I had laboratories at six different sites. I read this article about creativity and we had at that time a lot of competition coming on stream and I thought we needed some redirection. The article sparked the idea. Then I received from Diane McQuaig [Edward's manager] a note that Edward would be speaking up in Toronto that spring, the spring of 1986. So I went up there to Toronto. There were two one-day sessions, the first day was all on lateral thinking. I sat at the edge of my seat the whole time. It really was fascinating. There were hundreds of people. Then the second day was a session he doesn't give any more. On this day there were only about twenty or thirty people and it was entitled Opportunity Searching. It was a small session with a lot of interaction. I asked Edward if he had ever been to DuPont and he said, 'No.' So I invited

him, and that was the beginning. After that I must have invited him at least ten or fifteen times.

We had a big R&D budget. There were six businesses that I had responsibility for in R&D. Teflon was one of these. That was relatively small. The major ones were – you know, bullet resistant vests? Kevlar, a fibre [with] five times the strength of steel, with equal weight. In our division we had several growth businesses and we had Edward in many times. I took him down to our different sites. I used to meet with lab directors every month and I was very excited about this creative thinking. I had even laid out some charts using Edward's stuff. The whole idea was to come up with new ideas by instilling a creative environment . . .

The last two years at DuPont I spent as the director of the DuPont Centre for Creativity and Innovation. We had had a lot of successes in my division and the corporate management asked me to do this on a corporate basis . . . When I became involved with the corporate effort on creative thinking I had Edward do a seminar – we had a big theatre that holds about 1,500 people – and it was full to capacity. We had set up a creative thinking network across the company and called it the Oz Group [no connection with the Old Bailey trial]. That seminar by Edward stimulated so much interest that the group grew from 200 up to two or three or four times that amount. I used to leverage Edward whenever he visited to talk to as many groups as I could because it was so stimulating.

Tanner has written a book (*Total Creativity*, 1997), showing some of the day-to-day applications of Edward's work at the company – how, for example, Gene Pontrelli, a research fellow at DuPont trained in lateral thinking techniques, led a group looking for ways to develop Lycra beyond its current limits. The group set about listing all the things that people took for granted about Lycra. The Escape method led to a whole range of provocations. One was 'PO: Applications of Lycra for non-persons' from which sprang the idea to clad dolls in Lycra, even racehorses (during warm-up). And from this there came 'a new product concept unrelated to textile fabrics or clothing', and a programme to develop it.

On another occasion, the Information Systems Division of DuPont needed to reduce costs. Group manager Nancy McDonald led a lateral thinking session to a Reverse provocation: 'PO: costs should be reduced by spending more money.'

'This provocation,' writes Tanner, 'generated the idea that spending more money on fewer vendors would provide leverage to obtain large discounts. The approach was to cut the number of vendors and negotiate better prices on high-volume orders, and led to an annual savings of over $300,000. Applying this concept to maintenace saved a further several hundred thousand dollars annually.'

Again at DuPont, Nomex had designed a new computer system and wanted to minimise the cost and maximise the efficiency of installation. Group manager Ben Jones, trained in lateral thinking, headed the group masterminding the operation. Addressing the problem, they focused on the engineering department, where pre-assembly costs of the equipment were an important element. As things sometimes go even outside a lateral thinking session, a provocation arose by way of the Exaggeration method: 'PO: Eliminate the engineering department!' When the uproar died down, the thinking moved to a decision for engineering to link up with the manufacturing and technical departments to assemble and integrate the equipment actually on site. 'This approach succeeded,' writes Tanner, 'saving well over $1 million in development costs and accelerating installation an estimated one to two years.' The provocation also marked the beginning of a closer relationship between the various departments.

Distortion provocations typically manipulate the relationships between parties and time sequence. At Prudential Insurance Canada, Ron Barbaro's 'PO: you die before you die' led to the hugely successful idea of 'living benefits' – if you contract a terminal illness you benefit from 75 per cent of the insurance money before you die – and catapulted him into the big time. Prudential Insurance USA was the largest insurance group in the world, and partly as a result of this idea, Barbaro became president of it. Later he began using Edward's Six Hats. Today, Barbaro is retired and may occasionally be found whiling away the time on the top floor of the Waldorf Hotel in New York City.

Life insurance premiums, unlike mortgage premiums, are paid prior to benefits. 'PO: you die before you die' came about as a distortion of the hitherto hard-fact identification of death with payout and negative motivational elements, in that no client ever personally benefited from payout. It was a very good idea.

'PO: riverside factories should be sited downstream of themselves' first arose when Edward was talking with people about pollution legislation. 'If you build a factory near water,' Edward reasoned, 'obviously people downstream suffer. From the provocation came the perfectly sensible idea that you legislate so that the factory's input has to be downstream of its output. Then the factory is the first to get a sample of its pollution and has to be more concerned with cleaning it up.' This is a Wishful Thinking provocation. 'Wouldn't it be nice if . . .' Entertain a fantasy wish, knowing it is impossible to achieve.

The systematic methods for delivering ideas from a PO proposition are fully explained in *Serious Creativity*. Peter Low stresses that lateral thinkers 'must recognise the difference between "creating a provocation" and "movement",' by which he means the extracting of an idea from the provocation, and not to try and do the two things at the same time. The most impressive of the 'movement' methods suggested by Edward is the most obvious – Moment-to-Moment. Basically, it means you stick with the provocation and draw it out. (My gladiatorial cabaret restaurant idea did, I have to admit, benefit from a little 'drawing out' by the master.) I like moment-to-moment because it encourages lateral thinkers to remain in the realm of imagination, though not of course with the PO proposition itself.

'PO: cars have square wheels' is one of Edward's classic provocations. Stick with it. Envisage the concept in action, draw it out, moment-to-moment. You are driving this car with square wheels. You move slowly forward, rise up to the first corner and come crashing down, and again, and again, until it dawns on you that if you had to drive a car with square wheels it would be a good idea to develop a system of suspension that would respond to it. You might go on to think, this would be good in any vehicle having to cope with rough terrain. Stick with it. From adjustable suspension enters the notion of a vehicle adapted for rough ground, a jockey wheel travelling in front of the main chassis wheels senses the bumps and hollows and communicates the contours of the terrain so that the suspension adjusts and the car flows over the ground. This is the concept of 'intelligent suspension,' and apparently, Lotus have now developed a similar system.

Practice makes perfect. Fluency, skill and confidence feed off one another. The aim is to come up with a concept or idea of value, a usable idea of benefit. But as you become more skilled you will begin to get other highs along the way. These highs may in themselves have no obvious value, but are made no less enticing by the feeling that there is something there, in prospect. These are seriously interesting moments, signs to slow down and explore.

Should you end up with a concept that you can find no practical way to deliver, store it for another occasion. Should you manage an idea of value, it's time to compare it with what else is around, consider its benefits and consider, too, how else these benefits might be achieved. There is never a time not to think of alternatives.

At this final stage *value* is the focus, not the idea.

The Random Input tool was developed in 1968, a year after publication of *The Use of Lateral Thinking*. It became one of the most popular of Edward's LT techniques, not least because it is so easy to implement. Like PO, it seems illogical, completely unworkable. However, also like PO, it is perfectly logical in a patterning information system, and it brings a high incidence of success. Like the ant on the leaf (page 17), if you start at the periphery you are likely to open up patterns which are not dominated by the central starting point.

Says Edward,

> The analogy I use is, you live in a small town and you always take the same road when you leave by the front door, but one day on the outskirts of the town your car breaks down or for some reason you have to walk home. On the way you find yourself arriving home by a little road you would never have taken on leaving home. Because now you are on the periphery finding your way back (which is different from being in the centre and finding your way out). So the random word is a perfectly logical procedure in a patterning system, but without that universe, in our normal logical world, you say if it is random how could it possibly be of value in this particular case, because it could be just as valuable in any case? That's why understanding the base [the conceptual construct] is so different from just juggling with descriptions, which is what philosophers and psychologists always do.

In the Nobel Prizewinners' Conference hosted by Edward in 1989 in Seoul, Korea, Sheldon Lee Glashow was astonished when there was an impasse and Edward calmly injected a random word into the discussion. 'The problem was quickly resolved,' he recalls.

'At the periphery different possibilities open up,' Edward explains, 'and when these click with something which is associating out of the centre, you work your way down. It is so powerful that one of my trained people, Carol Ferguson, who was working with a company called ISCOR in South Africa, one afternoon set up 130 workshops mixing in senior executives and people on the shop floor, and just using that random entry technique they generated 21,000 ideas. It took them nine months to work through them. Now that's very different from waiting around for inspiration and very different from brainstorming.'

In Edward's 1970s schools thinking project in England, Bill Copley found the random input technique immensely popular with children. Moreover, 'we have found that the more remote it is from the problem, the better, since it stimulates thinking along entirely new lines . . .' He advised aspiring teachers, 'A little word about technique. Avoid comparison. If the practice item is "Design a new kind of window," and the random input is "cheese", the aim is not to compare windows with cheese, but to look hard at cheese and to discover all its qualities to see whether any quality will lead to new ideas about the design of windows.'

Here are some of the ideas that emerged from this juxtaposition:

1. Crumbly: a new safer 'glass' which will crumble on impact instead of splintering.
2. Has a rind on it: a covering for glass to prevent it from shattering in extreme heat or a screen to protect glass activated by rising temperature.
3. Different coloured cheeses: coloured glass to enhance appearance, country scenes to hide ugly views, light-sensitive glass to minimise glare and maximise light on dark days, glass that changes colour in the presence of poisonous fumes.
4. Cheese melts: flexible glass in the gym.
5. Cheese smells: coated glass that emits smell as warning of poisonous fumes.
6. Different shapes: differently shaped windows.

The Random Input begs the question: why sit under a tree and wait for an apple to fall if you can get up and shake the tree for new ideas? Edward's friend Jeremy Bullmore used a tombola tub – a plastic sphere specially made by a Canadian, Savo Bojicic, and known as 'the think-tank' – to throw up words randomly to provoke new ideas. In 1982, at the time of the launch of *De Bono's Thinking Course*, a TV series Edward did for BBC2, Bullmore declared he still made use of it, spinning and shaking the spherical think-tank on his desk packed with 23,000 random-word cards. 'It makes you start somewhere different,' he said, 'and in the process frees you up: all of a sudden you are not thinking along tried-and-tested, conventional lines. You realise you can have ten ideas in ten minutes and it doesn't *matter* if nine of the ideas are rotten.' Bullmore was by then Chairman of J. Walter Thompson, whose annual billings amounted to £96 million.

Edward advises using lateral thinking when there is a focus on *purpose* – distort it, reverse it, exaggerate it, change it – and random entry when there is nothing to challenge, nothing to reverse, and in stagnant situations where you keep coming back to the same ideas. Practise. Like learning to ride a bicycle, once you are practised in the idiom you will be more deliberate, systematic and productive. Creativity will become an expectation.

Looking back over the last thirty years, Edward's mechanism of mind fits in the vanguard of a whole paradigm shift in science towards the self-organising system as a construct for future enquiry. Soon afterwards came the Gaia hypothesis, proposed by James Lovelock and Lynn Margulis, which thrilled New Age people with the concept of the Earth as a live, self-organising system, a system in which man is one provocative element. It galvanised the modern ecology movement with fears of 'what can be'. Few scientists took it seriously at first. Now they do. Lovelock said recently, 'Yes, people have come round to the argument of Gaia, but they don't like the name. They call it Earth Systems Science.'

Again, as we saw on page 18, the interesting thing about particle physics over the last fifty years is the move away from the notion that matter is fundamentally composed of particles. It was quantum physicist Geoffrey Chew's Bootstrap Theory that led the focus away from fundamental particles to the resonances of String Theory. Bootstrap Theory supposes that fundamental particles, quarks and the rest, are not created in a cause and effect way, but trigger one another ... 'particle A would be made from particle B and C, while B was made from A and C, and so forth. Each particle would,' as Chew put it, 'pull itself up by its own bootstraps.'

'Today,' Edward announced in the *Times Educational Supplement* as early as 30 April 1971, 'the emphasis has shifted from static "things" to processes, actions, and interactions. Instead of looking at isolated "things" we now look at "happenings".' Triggering is a key system concept on which Edward's mechanism of mind depends. As John Edwards, adjunct professor of education at the University of Queensland, wrote, 'The key distinction that Edward notes of the biological idiom which he chose to explain thinking is that, except in cases such as genetic information transmission, the biological mechanism is a triggering mechanism.' One state triggers the next state and what then happens depends on 'the existing and previous state and the nature of what is to be changed'. This is classic system interaction.

Once we begin thinking about systems rather than just things, process concepts (such as triggering and feedback loops in the mechanism of mind) come to the fore and tell us so much more about 'what is' with massive implications about 'how' as well as 'what can be'. So that, for example, the bootstrapping of reality is suggestive of a new interpretation of how the universe was created, which echoes Edward's original stable-unstable-stable concept active in the provocation process of the creation of a new idea. 'Gabriele Gasperini and Maurizio Veneziano's work [at the University of Torino] suggests that . . . the universe started out as cold and essentially infinite in spatial extent,' writes Professor Brian Greene in *The Elegant Universe*. 'The equations of string theory then indicate . . . an instability kicked in, driving every point in the universe to rush rapidly away from each other.'

Edward's self-organising, self-maximising system of the mind, with its emphasis on interactions, feedback loops, triggered responses, and so on, his interest in structures, concept roundabouts and interconnectedness, was in the vanguard of this wider, challenging paradigm shift in science away from reductionism (the analysis of things into their constituents), towards system hypothesis and projective thinking, the implications of which man is only now beginning to grasp.

Chapter Seven

A Real-World Fix

'I believe that education currently wastes about two thirds of the talent in society.'

When the moment came to go public in 1967, Edward didn't appear shy at all. Despite his habit of working his heel into the carpet and his dislike of small talk, he came out apparently hugely confident into the fray. Says David Bernstein of his first experience of Edward:

> I thought, 'He's very good and he's almost as good as he thinks he is . . .' Cocksure? Unbelievable! I have never met anybody – to this day! – who has the assurance or arrogance of Edward. He had got onto something and seemed to be able to prove it. But he is a hell of a mixture because I believe he is still shy, although he gives the opposite impression – he is shy and not modest! It is weird.

Jeremy Bullmore adds, with marvellous understatement: 'He *was* breathlessly ready to use assertion, wasn't he? He had an enviable certainty about things. I was uncertain about everything then . . . But the images [of lateral thinking] remain vivid and useful, the metaphors . . . there is no question he was an influence for good, and I liked him a lot. I was always very pleased to see him.'

In the *Oz* trial transcripts, what comes through crystal clear across the intervening years beside Edward's energy is the absolute assuredness with which he delivered his opinions. The judge did not like him for it, that's certain. At one point, Edward described the underground press as 'ego-centric . . . people writing in it use it rather like a soap box on Hyde Park Corner . . . In a sense, they are more interested in saying what they want to say rather than saying something in a way which will affect their readers.' It was a subtle point for the defence, countering the most serious charge facing the *Oz* editors – that they had acted 'with the intention of debauching and corrupting the morals of children and young people'. Having by this time listened to Edward banging on for some hours, Judge Argyll was alive to the possibility that he might be rather egocentric too, and there is little doubt as to the intonation of the lines which followed:

> Judge: What was your last phrase?
> Edward: Ego-centric.
> Judge: Thank you.

During his summing up, Judge Argyll's feelings ooze once more from between the lines:

> Then we had Mr de Bono. This was a Friday, as I remember, and we did have a difficult time, did we not?

Edward's publisher in 1967, Tom Maschler, recalls above all his assertiveness: he was 'very, very good at promoting himself. He promoted himself through telling you how much he's getting, giving lectures, you know. I remember him holding forth about how they were flying him first class everywhere, how they wanted him. This is a form of promotion. Jeffrey Archer is what we are talking about . . .'

The comparison surprised me as Edward is rather naive at publicity, tending to spout his achievements as if on automatic pilot, flying a plane he would rather not be in. Sure, he understands the *need* for publicity, but only when it is bound up with project does he really excel, as he recently did in Australia.

> I was having dinner with Bob Sessions, who is Penguin Australia, and I said, 'I want to do this book, *Why I Want To Be King of Australia,*' and he said, 'Sure, let's do it,' straight off! So it came out in June and it was very well received.
>
> Then two things happened. A town called Geraldton said, 'Come and be King of Geraldton!' This happened because Vicky Buck, a very dynamic mayoress of Christchurch, New Zealand, was on her way to Geraldton when she picked up my book at Sydney airport, and when she got there she suggested they invite me to be king. So they did! And they had processions and the aboriginal community set up a concert and there were other concerts. I talked to prison

officers, I talked to the schools, I talked to the business community, and they took down the Australian flag and invented a flag for me. The shops had signs saying, 'Royal Week!' and so on, and next year I am invited to be king of the best wine-growing district. Then I met the Prime Minister of Australia at an Innovation Summit they have over there, and he said, 'Next time we have a referendum I'll have three choices, Queen of England, a republic or King de Bono.'

The point of my story is that people say, 'Oh no, don't do that, people will think you are arrogant and presumptuous', but my feeling always is, there's usually very little to be gained by not doing anything.

This paradox of assertiveness and shyness marks him out as the committed, preoccupied project-obsessed loner which he undoubtedly is. There is no denying the 'very strong ego-drive,' either, which gifted-child specialist Norah Maier sees as characteristic of his genius: 'Edward is not a team person. He stands alone and goes at it alone totally, but he is very generous with his ideas.'

This ego-drive has helped keep him at the top for thirty-four years. 'Edward wants to be number one, and number one only,' agrees his sometime PA Linda Laird. 'He doesn't like other people speaking on the same platform. If he gets to choose, then it is more acceptable to him. If it is foisted upon him he will decline to be the speaker.' David Tanner of DuPont was in fact ticked off by Edward's manager for making Edward share a platform:

> I got a professor from one of the universities who had spent two years in Japan studying their innovation techniques, and this fellow was an outstanding speaker. Afterwards Edward's manager said to me, 'Edward doesn't want other speakers any more.' He doesn't like to have the attention taken away from him. That's one of his characteristics, it is Edward really.

'This business about not liking to share a platform is a confusion,' counters Edward. 'Whisky is good. So is gin. But a mixture of whisky and gin is not good. Different approaches lead to confusion in the audience. That is all.'

There is, in fact, no lack of awareness of other people's views (which is egocentricity), but there is serious conviction and drive, which some do find intimidating, though, as one associate admitted, it is not really his fault.

Part of the fear is that you think you might be judged, the fear that when I open my mouth he will realise that I am not a great thinker. He quickly dismisses anyone whom he knows is going nowhere, he's a master artist at belittling those who want to prove their intelligence, but if you talk to him on a subject on which you know three things and he knows ten, he will only add two or three. He won't give you the whole ten and make you look stupid, and he is definitely less intimidating to women.

In the right company and away from a project, he will relax completely. Humour and inventive play, the fundamental inspirations of lateral thinking, are two of Edward's greatest delights, and when they are missing from the social recipe, and mundanity intervenes, he will turn off. And why not? As should be expected of a man who comes to lateral thinking naturally, what turns him on is the surprise resonance, the unexpected vibe, not the tedium of the well-travelled rut. I just returned from Ireland, where Linda Laird, who, besides much else, looks after his island off Cork, told me of a recent night out with Edward, when she and her husband Roger took him to a rootsy Irish restaurant where you generally have to share a table – the idea being to mix, mingle and enjoy good *craic*. Doesn't sound like the kind of place a shy, project-obsessed loner would choose. Yet as soon as the threesome walked inside the place, Edward spotted three ladies in their thirties sitting together and obviously having a good time. He said, 'I'll sit over there,' and before they had noticed he had left their side, he was sitting and joking with these ladies who, it emerged, were on a hen night, as their husbands were away fishing.

In 1967, Edward was diving in where no others had gone before. He was the first to take thinking by the horns and steer it directly into the public arena. Up to then, thinking had been the historical, analytical, descriptive province of dusty philosophy and psychology departments. Breaking out of the academic box took courage and conviction, and would need dedication, self-promotion, enormous energy, a certain amount of wariness and a very thick skin.

What is too readily forgotten is that at the start, Edward had marked his card 'anti-academia'. As we've seen, by 1972 he was describing universities as

> irrelevant centres of mental masturbation . . . [where] scholarship has become little more than the triumph of form over content.

You take some tiny part of the field of knowledge and examine it with immense detail and concentration. In the end it is your workmanship which is praised and not the importance of the subject. This was commendable when society was stable and mental virtuosity of this sort had as much validity as exquisite chamber music. At that time the concept of usefulness was ugly and inferior.

His conviction that education should be relevant to and not distinct from life made outlaw status inevitable in Cambridge, and doubly important that he make his case with assurance. There is a comparison to be made in the way academia has treated Craig Venter, an American with a very different educational background but similarly commercial profile. Venter left school at seventeen, became a surfer, and then a maverick scientific entrepreneur who beat the boffins by unravelling the human genome. The venom meted out to Venter by boxed-up academia has been extraordinary. Both he and de Bono are disliked for their go-it-alone philosophy and riches, seen as rank commercialism. Edward's real-world education remains a threat to ivory tower academia in Britain, as does his confidence that sooner or later the case for integrated education will be won.

His position regarding traditional, knowledge-based education is that 'knowing' is not enough. 'The notion that if you know, doing is easy, is not true,' he says, and this is the crucial element of his schools thinking programme, CoRT. His CoRT tools, which he developed shortly after he hit upon lateral thinking, hinge on a 'concept of usefulness' – operacy.

In championing education as an operational, real-world process, he effectively declared war on academia, which responded in two ways. Some hijacked him and made his ideas their own, sometimes without really understanding them. Others wriggled and took pot shots at him for seeking commercial success. Yet Edward succeeded in putting creativity on the agenda of every educationalist's strategy in the world today. He was the first to put creative thinking onto anyone's curriculum, and in virtually every country round the world where thinking is on the curriculum, or is part of future curriculum strategy, Edward first introduced the idea in person to that country. That is, in itself, an extraordinary achievement. Everyone who is involved in creativity and thinking in either the educational or business fields, including Britain, owes Edward a huge debt. For as Dan Sharon, ex-Director General of

Israel's Ministry of Education, said to me: 'Everyone took their basics from Edward. And even today, I don't think Edward has competition. Yes, there are books by David Perkins at Harvard, by Howard Gardner and all these people, but no one has specifically developed the tools, as Edward has.'

What particularly laid him open to criticism in the beginning and got academics' backs up was his deliberate flouting of scholarly traditions. 'Because he was impetuous and in some ways superficial in his scholarship,' says Bullmore, 'I think people were reluctant to give him credit. All the things you are supposed to do to be taken seriously ... He didn't mind being criticised really. He always felt the Establishment didn't take him seriously, but he kind of laid himself open by some of the things that he said.'

I once asked Edward why he never includes a bibliography at the end of his books. (There is often no index either.) I had read a criticism that his system model in *The Mechanism of Mind* has 'strong resemblances' to early work on nerve net modelling (Rosenblatt, 1958; McCulloch, 1965; Minsky & Selfridge, 1961) and certain cellular automata (Holland, 1960), yet Edward does not cite any of this literature. Edward replied, 'Murray Gell-Mann once said the same thing to me and I told him I hadn't read any of these people. He said, "Well, make a list up!" That says it all, don't you think?'

Complaints of plagiarism came from as far afield as North America, where my surprise Deep Throat said:

> Maybe I should tell you – as you are looking for inside information, how some people in the States regard Edward. The Buffalo group, you may not be familiar with them. Scott Isaksen, for example, up there, and Sydney Parnes – these are oldtimers and of course you know this is the home of Alex Osborn, the man who invented brainstorming in the School of Buffalo. Well, their view of Edward – they have expressed this privately – is that he is just a copy cat.

I yawned at the old brainstorming criticism, but my source replied:

> Not because of brainstorming, because of other things that have gone on in the field of thinking. There are books other than by Edward about thinking outside your thinking patterns. For example, in lateral thinking, Edward uses the random word technique. Well, one fellow talks about 'club phrases' – like, titles of books to get

you off track. Metaphoric thinking it's called. There are a lot of techniques described in the literature which people will say, all Edward did was to redress them, repackage them. Of course, I don't have qualms. I am sure he never even read those people. For it is another characteristic of Edward that he is not interested in anybody else's point of view. You must know that!

In *The Use of Lateral Thinking* Edward writes that reading other people's ideas encourages firm acceptance or violent rejection, either of which inhibits the formation of original ideas. He is not a wide reader and never has been, not even at university. 'It wasn't the custom for anybody really to read widely outside set books,' said his undergraduate colleague, Father Peter. He is, however, very well informed, making an unusual (but useful) point of boning up on global surveys of attitudinal shift, frequently drawing on them in preference to distilled opinion. 'I wouldn't class myself as a heavy reader,' he admits. 'I do have a good memory. Even now I often find I will be discussing an article in *Time* magazine with someone who has read it and I will be telling them things they don't remember.'

Don McQuaig, whose business, MICA Management Resources, promotes many different people through the lecture and seminar circuit, concurs with the view that Edward's originality is the whole ticket. 'Most people out there expound other people's ideas. Edward is a true original. He has created all this material and he loves to share it. In this business, we have all sorts of speakers – Covey, Peters, all of them – and yet Edward always stands out as unique, far above the pack.'

Provocation is both the manner of lateral thinking and the mode of his self-promotion, especially if it provokes the academic establishment. His long-time friend, John Edwards, tells me that they were at dinner with Paul MacCready one time in California, and MacCready said to Edward, '*You* are the biggest problem with your material because you continue to upset people. The best thing you could do, Edward, is die! Once you die it'll settle.'

Max Planck, the father of quantum mechanics, prescribed patience rather than provocation when trying to change people's perceptions: 'A new scientific truth does not triumph by convincing its opponents and making them see light, but rather because its opponents eventually die, and a new generation grows up that is familiar with it.'

But upsetting people is the de Bono *modus operandi*, while destabilising and moving forward is the very essence of the system in which, he is convinced, we all reside. And Edward cannot let go. 'He has this energy level which is remarkable,' says Paddy Hills. 'It's a restlessness in him that is not satisfied. The more he moves around the world, the more restless he becomes.'

'From time to time,' said Edward, as he was first making his mark in the 1970s, 'I have a dream in which I am climbing a ladder. Someone is pulling my legs and I kick out. It can be tricky on planes. One fellow got quite angry when I started kicking the back of his seat in my sleep.'

He was superficial in his scholarship deliberately, provocatively, in that sense positively, and not because he was concerned to be thought a cheat – a ludicrous suggestion in the context. His integrity and honesty are two virtues that both friends and foes, who know him, allow. He was pitting his educational programme against the establishment version by highlighting its useability, transferability, and its success in action, but also by flouting what he saw as the irrelevant elements in the establishment version. His interest is in skills that make a difference in life, not in those that attract applause in the rarefied environs of academia. Inevitably, where idiomatic change is taking place, those imbued with the old idiom are approaching the new with the 'mind set' of the old. Edward's style is to put the old idiom down as part of his strategy to depict contrast. It was bound to make him enemies. But he and his work have survived.

Clearly he is capable of the scholarship which his critics would prefer to see in him. His DPhil thesis, *The Control of Blood Pressure in Hypertension*, is exemplary, showing that in 1961 Edward was still working within the traditions. The style is understated, sober. He looks at what scholarly work has gone before, produces his experiments, makes his findings, gives his interpretations, not even gently speculative, and at the end of each section there is endless bibliography. Nothing could be further from the style he adopted when he went public with lateral thinking six years later.

The position he adopted then was, 'Many brilliant minds are wasted in detailed scholarship over trivial matters that lend themselves to [the academic approach – analysis, criticism, judgement, classification], whilst much more important matters are simply neglected because they do not lend themselves to this approach.' His CoRT administrator, Edna Copley, said that when she pointed out grammatical errors in the first publication of the CoRT lessons for schools in the 1970s, Edward objected, calling it academic nitpicking. She went on: 'But I said, "These notes are going to teachers who are grammarians, they will spot the errors and your work will be brought into disrepute." But Edward would not do anything about it.'

If CoRT was going to succeed, the Establishment was going to be perturbed in all sorts of ways. Edward would destabilise the very foundations of the curriculum if he could.

> A lot of these things are taught because they are there. What I would see is the basic skills subjects, language, thinking, basic maths, not all maths that's taught. In the European Union, 25 per cent of school time is spent on maths, of which people use 3 per cent in their life. Then the rest should be taught on an interest basis, a video series on history, a video series on geography, a video series on technology by the best people, not just by the local teacher. They should be taught as background, culture-enriching subjects – not that you have to learn when was the Magna Carta signed and stuff like that. So there's a place for them, but in that way.

Education, he believes, wastes about two-thirds of talent in society. Henceforth it is to be an operational, real-world process – this notion of practicality is endemic to CoRT. He wants operacy to sit next to literacy and numeracy, and, in the meantime, he wants 'lots and lots of steamed-up stuff'.

Not only is he demanding a new curriculum, but also a new approach to learning. Both elements of his strategy rise out of this fundamental concept of *operational value*. 'Throughout school the emphasis is on reactive thinking: sorting out the information given, putting the pieces of the puzzle together in the right way,' he says. 'In real-life situations, very little information is given. The thinker has to think projectively rather than reactively.'

Thinking projectively is the equivalent of seeking movement value in lateral thinking. It is constructive, real-life, design thinking. It is what he wants from the readers of his books, which are a provocation of the stepping-stone variety. 'Go through lightly, stepping on each concept before moving on to the next one . . . use your own thinking . . . do much more than just react to what I have set down,' he exhorts readers of *Future Positive*. 'You may see positive possibilities that escape me. That you may see dangerous implications which I have not set down is very probable. But do not let those pitfalls bring your exploration to an end . . .'

In *Tactics*, he wrote:

> Years ago, I went to see Lord Weinstock [the Managing Director of GEC, at the time Britain's largest industrial group] and these business people were complaining that they weren't getting people with the kind of aptitude they wanted. So I said, 'Why not get together with other big businesses and set a six-month curriculum, and give a preference to applicants who have done this curriculum? Then parents will want it on the curriculum. That is how change will be made.' But they were scared of doing it, said they would be vilified by the educationalists, who would say all they wanted was utilitarian robots, etc. But that is how change will be made.

The false dichotomy between life and education was illustrated when, in the early 1980s, he took his schools programme to Bulgaria. His wife Josephine accompanied him on this trip. She remembers that they were driven around in limousines and treated like royalty. 'I trained twenty-five teachers, who went on to teach my thinking skills in schools,' Edward recalls. 'One time they asked this nine-year-old girl whether she ever used the thinking skills in real life. "Oh yes," she replied, "I use them in life OK, I even use them in school." That summed up what education has become, separated from life.'

Recently I took him up over this challenge to academia, saying that it doesn't square with his non-adversarial, non-judgemental stance in parallel thinking: 'I don't have arguments, I say that the other person is perfectly correct within their perception and then I lay out what their perception is and try to see differences,' he has said specifically. But when it comes to education he is uncompromising: 'To attack the argument idiom is only another example of argument thinking *unless some alternative is offered*,' he replied.

There is a kind of challenge to traditional scholastic priorities in the very act of composition of his books. *Future Positive* was completed in eight days in the summer of 1978. *Teach Your Child How To Think* (a text over 300 pages in length) took ten days to write; some take four or five. One was written on a nonstop flight between London and New Zealand. 'Writing,' he said in an interview with Elizabeth Grice, 'is rather like dancing: it is important to keep the flow.' When I questioned him about this recently, he said:

> I write very fast. *The Mechanism of Mind* took about five weeks. It

varies with each book. I have notes, I write down random notes, and then I go through and condense them into sections – it is a sorting process, then I'll write a framework for each section and then I start writing it, and as I go along the need for other sections or developments may emerge. I found early on that if you try and polish something you throw it out of rhythm. It could have been 10 per cent better but in making it 10 per cent better you simply throw it out of rhythm.

The flow that he manages to maintain in a book as searching as *I Am Right, You Are Wrong*, again completed in a matter of days, is quite extraordinary. It is an ability which Professor Maier witnessed in another context:

I flew down with him to Basle, where he was doing this series, *The Greatest Thinkers* (ITV, 1981). We flew down with some actors, and I think it was in about three days that they taped four shows. Some of these I have been able to show just recently in Singapore, where I have been working for five years. I am still using the one on Columbus – it's very, very good – and the one on Jesus Christ, a very original reading. The point is that I was in the control room with the whole crew and so forth, and Edward was in the studio. At the end of the three days, on the last take, for about one hour they were just taping and he was going straight at it, without any notes, speaking and doing his usual drawings, of course. Later they were going to be inserting various dramatic inserts to do with the concepts he was presenting, but now he was going straight at his speaking part, without any notes! Anyway, at the end of that, spontaneously, the whole crew stood up in the control room and applauded, and said, 'Can you imagine, without any notes, for a whole hour he just delivered!' They were smitten by the brilliance of the man. They had never seen anything like that.

Like self-publicity, this strategy of provocation involves putting your head above the parapet, but unlike self-publicity, it actually directs attention *away* from self to show the workings of the system (of education, of politics, or whatever) being provoked, which is what Edward seeks to do. The tiring downside is when, unable to move beyond the challenge to the focus of the provocation, egos are threatened and people retaliate. This also happens within the more self-conscious sections of the press, who very often fail to look deeply into his project at all.

In the past, as Marjorie Wallace noted, this didn't bother Edward: 'He really couldn't care less what people think. He has got a vision, he has got a mission. Either people believe in it or they don't. The people who do believe in it are good, the people who don't are bad.' And recently Edward said to me, 'I don't bother to try and persuade people,' which put me in mind of something that Professor Mills recalled him saying: 'I'll teach people, but I won't do the nannying'.

Life's too short. I *devise* things, some people pick them up and use them and find they work and that's fine. I do not go knocking on people's doors. I mean, there are a number of people sitting in corners and saying, 'These can't possibly work,' and, you know, good luck to them. It's like this Canadian professor, who looked at the CoRT tools and said, 'These can't possibly work.' And so, well, that's like saying, 'Cheese doesn't exist.' I mean, it does! The kids that use them find they are very useful, make a big difference, and the fact that you sit and say that they can't work really doesn't have any effect on the world.

These days, however, I notice that his ego is less impervious to attack, and he does admit to a certain frustration. 'I am frustrated in the sense that there are people who are using things like CoRT, *showing* it works very well, *showing* it makes a big difference, and you might say, "Well, isn't it so *obvious* that it should be in every school?" So the politics of take-up and acceptance, that is frustrating. Yes.'

Recently his sense of fair play was outraged on publication of a hostile and ill-informed article in the *Guardian* newspaper. This was part of a feud which began in 1998, with Tony Blair's take-up of Edward to advise the Department for Education and Employment and continued across Edward's involvement with the Europe-based multi-national Siemens. The article seemed such a snarl that it had me asking him what he had *done* to the woman who wrote it? 'Nothing,' he claimed, but it led to his setting up a website with a Standard Dishonesty Rating System, a points system for rating inaccuracies and downright lies in the media. Playful? Courageous? Or is he losing touch? Today's paper is tomorrow's fish-and-chips wrapper, after all.

An aide agreed that there were times when there is a danger of losing touch with the day-to-day scene – 'Totally understandable, someone who is moving from A to B at such a high speed.' There are in fact many in sympathy with the unfairness he sees in the ability of the press to publish lies without any comeback other than in the courts. He felt helpless. He likes to be in control. But the website was bound to focus more attention on the venomous *Guardian* piece, and it has.

'Edward was always so convinced of his position, rightly or wrongly,' says half-sister Elizabeth.

> That's like our father was a bit. When he thought he was right, and it was a matter of principle, he could be very sort of unmoving. Edward has a lot of my father in him. My father was convinced in a particular manner and I think a lot of his contemporaries may have wished him somewhere else. There have been other people who were convinced. There have been people very convinced who were wrong. But what would the world be without such people? It is almost a missionary thing.

Perhaps we can talk of mission in relation to Edward's work in politics and in education, and with disadvantaged groups, to which I will come shortly. There are, to be sure, two different sides to his project: 'It was really driven home to me when one year I went down to MIT to hear Edward speak,' recalls his manager Diane McQuaig.

> I had always been involved in the corporate side of things, I am the revenue-generating side; but Edward has a love of education and children, so these are things that he will throw in when he is going places and I am not involved. I went to MIT and I just saw him in such a different light. He was speaking in a room that would probably seat 500 students and there had to be close to 1,000, jammed, wall-to-wall and sitting cross-legged on the floor, right up to his overhead projector. He was absolutely in his element and for me the light bulb went on there. This is what Edward loves to do.

George Gallup, who conducted surveys in education in America and saw firsthand the effect of Edward's work in education, had no hesitation in giving his mission the highest commendation: 'What Edward de Bono is doing to teach people how to think may be the most important thing going on in the world today.' Again, Paul MacCready said recently to me, 'De Bono, more than anyone else, has shown me that you can make huge changes in a very short time by just dealing with the fundamentals and a few little tricks. His great genius is he has been able to make the ideas so simple.'

Father Peter, philosopher, scholar and friend, is more wary when I talk about mission and conviction. 'I think he was convinced that you can teach thinking skills. That was the basis of his conviction,' he says. 'But ... in philosophy we are very convinced that you should doubt everything.'

From the early 1970s, after he had established the conceptual construct for lateral thinking in his mechanism of mind, Edward began to develop his schools programme, which of course flowed from the same fount.

The letters of CoRT stand for **Co**gnitive **R**esearch **T**rust, which Edward set up in Cambridge to administer the project. He was fortunate that his boss at Addenbrookes, Ivor Mills, was supportive, and sensitive, too, to the fight which Edward had on his hands.

Says Mills:

There were plenty in Cambridge antagonistic to him. The concepts were too new. You are an easy target at that level. People can call you a fool. And lots of people will go with you and say, 'I agree he is a fool,' because they couldn't understand what he was driving at. And I must say there were times early on when I wasn't entirely sure. I remember one of the things he brought round was a square bottle and inside it was a pear. It had a round top and the pear was square shaped. How could you get the pear in the bottle? Well, I must admit I failed that test. There is, of course, only one way: you put the pear in the bottle when it is growing and it grows and adapts to the bottle. That was typical of the sort of thing that he brought round ...

There was no doubt that he was way ahead of his time in all that sort of early thinking, but the interesting point was that the general public cottoned on to lateral thinking and the term is now in general use ... The second major contribution he made was that he started to study schoolchildren, because he maintained early on that the teaching methods we use in this country, and which are used in most civilised countries, suppress children's ability to think ... So, for instance, he set problems for them in various papers or journals that were available to either teachers or children, and I remember one of the problems was, 'Devise a means whereby a postman on his round could have help so that he doesn't have to expend so much energy during his round.' Well, they came up with incredible ideas.

One child evolved the concept that the postman would have on his bike a spring device, and as he cycled along he would wind the spring up and when he got half way round, then, instead of him cycling he would switch onto the spring, which then unwound and drove him along! That is quite an idea for a child to evolve.

Edward found that, in general, younger children had more ideas than older children. He reckoned at the age of fifteen their brains had been wrecked by being suppressed, and by formalised views of authority stamped on the children. Once he started teaching children he had experimental work done on a quarter of a million of them in this country. Now, nobody else has *ever* done anything like that. It is a huge number! As a result of that and the publications that came out, people in Australia took it up, people in Venezuela took it up and various countries around the world took it up. Britain never did.

How CoRT began, however, was a sequence of chance, laced with the kind of honest dealing which you can always expect from Edward. 'There was a magazine called *Science Journal*. I knew the editor and he asked me to do some sort of feature . . . think about things and so on,' Edward recalls.

Then there was a fellow who ran an educational journal, who happened to be in a coffee shop, picked up this old copy of *Science Journal* and came to me and said, 'Will you do features like that in my educational journal?' So I did a whole series of things on children designing things, which eventually became my books, *Children Solve Problems* and *Dog Exercise Machine*. Now, because the kids had done the work, I thought it a bit unfair to pocket the money from the book myself. So I put the money into a foundation, and so the Cognitive Trust sort of existed in a very minor way. Then there was an Australian teacher who came to me and said, 'Look, I'm in England for a while and can I come and work for the foundation?' So I said, 'OK.' So then I wrote the CoRT programme to give her something to do in schools. I wrote the first bit, and when the results from testing it came back I wrote more and so on. And so it grew. I think it would be fair to say that if this Australian teacher had not said I'd like to come and work, I probably would not have pushed the education thing so much.

Clare Connell was the Australian teacher who approached Edward, having read one or two of his books. Initially, she was paid out of a grant secured from the Leverhulme Trust in London. Around this time Edward would enjoy telling people that the Schools Council had turned him down on the grounds that no committee existed to discuss a subject called 'thinking', and that anyway, de Bono would go ahead and do it himself, so why pay him? Later there would also be some money from the Social Science Research Council.

On the advice of Connell, a secondary school teacher, experimentation with *CoRT Book 1: Breadth of Perception* began in secondary schools. This was odd, as the children's designs, which Edward was collecting and using in his books, were coming from primary level. However, Connell was the teacher and very enthusiastic, so Edward agreed.

It is, in fact, a defining mark of CoRT, that once the testing was done, the programme finalised and all the books written, its appeal crossed all age groups. In the early 1980s, Edward could write:

> In practice, the CoRT Program has been used with ages as low as four and a half and also by senior executives in such major corporations as IBM and ITT. As a matter of interest the chief executive of the Ford Motor Company in the UK makes use of the CoRT skills in solving his own industrial problems in running a large and very successful company. The same program is used by elementary school children and also by adults (as in the New York School of Thinking). The ability spread ranges from the gifted and schools that only admit pupils with IQs of over 140, to ESN (educationally sub-normal) schools in the UK where the IQ range is 75 to 80. Use across cultures includes rural areas of Venezuela, metropolitan areas such as London, Sydney, Toronto, and also countries like Nigeria.

Later, it would spread far wider and seven of the tools from *Book I: Breadth of Perception* would form the basis of a ten-lesson programme for sharpening perception and focusing thinking, levelled at business executives, and re-labelled DATT (Direct Attention Thinking Tools) – still in wide use today, sometimes incorporating seven rather than ten lessons.

Connell reported on the first CoRT pilot in early 1973. This had been designed to test a prototype programme in fourteen schools: 'A basic lesson format was devised and ten sample lessons were introduced in twelve secondary schools over the period October to December 1972. In the end, two primary classes did also join the project. The lessons were delivered at the rate of one per week, in sessions ranging from forty to sixty minutes.'

Lesson 1 was, in those far-off days, entitled 'Appreciating Ideas as Distinct from Merely Criticising', suspension of judgement being a key principle of what became the first tool, the PMI.

PMI scans alternative ideas for their **p**lus, **m**inus and **i**nteresting points. They must be explored in that order, not with a plus, a minus, a plus, an interesting, a minus, etc. List all the pluses, then all the minuses, then all the interesting points in a timed sequence. Interesting points might include where an idea might lead you.

The difficulty with this tool is that most people believe they use it anyway. It seems simple and obvious because it describes a process which we feel we undertake subconsciously already – that is, until we use it deliberately and the results are seen to be dramatic. In a class of ten- and eleven-year-olds, the suggestion that school kids should be paid might be expected to deluge the teacher with plus points. In Sydney, Australia, Edward himself put the idea to just such a class, suggesting wages of $5 a week:

> All thirty students said it was an excellent idea. I then took *four minutes* to explain the PMI tool, which entailed looking first at the plus points, then the minus points and finally the interesting points. I asked the students to form into groups of five and to go systematically through the PMI. I provided the timing of two minutes for each scan direction.
>
> At the end of the group discussion time, I asked for the output. The plus points were the same as before. But now there were many minus points (older students would beat us up for the money; parents would not give presents; less money for teachers; where would the money come from? etc), as well as interesting points (would the money be used to ensure discipline? etc).
>
> At the end of this exercise, I asked the original question again. Now, twenty-nine of the thirty had completely changed their minds and decided that $5 a week was a bad idea. This was the result of a broader scan.
>
> The point I want to emphasise most strongly is that my intervention was only the four minutes needed to explain the PMI tool. I did not argue with the students. I did not ask them to consider

where the money might come from. I did not remind the students of the behaviour of other students. I simply presented the tool . . .'

There are at least four crucial points in this story. Notice, first, how feelings (judgements) were changed after the PMI had afforded a more complete perceptual exploration. Secondly, the tool's power is apparent in a huge shift of mind which has not been imposed from outside. Thirdly, the PMI is not content-dependent. This characteristic of all the CoRT tools floored an educational establishment, used to knowledge-based subjects like geography, history, etc. But this is CoRT's strength. Because it is a scanning device, it can be *transferred* from situation to situation. Consider the old saying: 'If you give a hungry person a fish, that person eats for a day; if you give a fishing rod, that person may eat forever.'

A similar change of perception occurred when Edward divided a seminar class of 140 senior executives into two random groups. One group was asked to consider the suggestion that currency should be dated and the other was asked to consider whether marriage should be a five-year contract. At the end of a five-minute period, the problems were switched around and this time each group was asked to carry out a formal PMI. Says Edward:

> If they had done this on the first occasion there should have been no difference in the results. Before the PMI, 44 per cent were in favour of a dated currency, after the PMI 11.5 per cent were in favour. Before the PMI 23 per cent were in favour of the five-year marriage contract, after the PMI 38 per cent were in favour. So, asking sophisticated thinkers to do something obvious had a marked effect. This is characteristic of all thinking training. The obvious things are worth doing but do not get done. (The obvious things are also the most difficult to teach.)

So highly motivating was the PMI among kids during Edward's testing in schools that he made it the first CoRT lesson, even though the information-gathering lesson 2, CAF (Consider All Factors), might sit better in pole position.

Lesson 2, CAF. Consider All Factors – the acronym pronounced 'KAF', not 'C. A. F.', as it was found to be more effectively memorised that way. The acronym of each tool has a particular mnemonic value, encouraging *habitual* usage, broadening perception, each in its little way challenging dominant pathways, until 'doing a CAF' or a PMI or any of the tools becomes a thinker's natural frame of mind – exploratory, in the case of a CAF, willing always to look for something else which our thinking should take into account.

The CAF collects information on which other tools go to work: the PMI *rates* factors; First Important Priorities or FIP *prioritises* factors, and so on. You can't be a successful thinker until all the factors are on the table. In the classroom, CAF gets students into the habit of coming up with ideas, but it is really designed to translate a willingness into a deliberate effort to find factors that are not obviously there. For example, the man who said, 'A friend of mine lost his credit cards. Asked by his bank why he hadn't reported them missing, he replied, "I reckoned it likely that the thief would be spending less than my wife does,"' considered all factors.

Lesson 3 is 'Rules'. Not a tool, it is one of two plateau lessons in *Book I*. Public rules (the law, rules of the road, etc) and private rules (club rules, school rules, company rules) provide a neat, well-defined and fundamental thinking situation in which to rehearse the PMI and CAF, CAF being used to set up rules, PMI for exploring existing or proposed rules. In due course, a connection between needs and rules will emerge and exercise a positive effect on class behaviour. During the pilot, a dramatic connection between the use of CoRT tools and class behaviour developed, flowing from increased self-esteem among those students less able to make verbal contributions in the study of traditional, knowledge-based subjects.

Lesson 4, C&S – consequences & sequel – creates a map of where an idea is leading. Immediate, short-term, medium-term and long-term consequences are systematically explored. Getting young children used to the concept of time far into the future did not prove easy. Parents tend to do that for them. In that sense, the C&S introduces an element of self-reliance.

Consequences may change with time and some may be irreversible. In CoRT's early days, teachers' topics included the introduction of rabbits to Australia. The immediate and short-term consequences of this move were good – plenty to shoot at, an additional source of meat, etc. The medium-term consequences were bad, however, because it bred so fast it became a pest, as were the long-term consequences when rabbits spread all over Australia.

There is overlap with other tools. C&S explores the consequences of ideas, which are factors in the future, so there is a relationship with

CAF. C&S evaluates the consequences, too, which must be made from other points of view, so there is a relationship with OPV (Other People's Views, Lesson 10).

This overlap was another problem for academia, with its compulsion for neat classification. Edward responded to an attack along these lines at an international OECD Conference in 1989 (page 280) by replying that overlap was essential:

> It is obvious that C&S and OPV are really part of CAF. In practice, however, when considering all factors, students do not pay sufficient attention to consequences or to other people's views, so these get specific scanning tools of their own. This practical approach to the design of the tools is important . . . Imagine you are walking around a building. Every now and then you pause to describe some particular aspect of the building. At one moment you may describe the whole façade. Next you may concentrate on the porch. It is true that the porch is included in the façade, but nevertheless you can pay attention to it more directly if you wish. When you stand at the corner you may again see the façade, but this time you see the side of the building as well. It is much like that with the CoRT lessons. The lessons are not designed to be separate, watertight boxes but different aspects of thinking. For instance, it is true to say that consequences (C&S) are really part of the factors that have to be considered (CAF). But it is still worth focusing directly on consequences, since otherwise they are easily ignored when there are more immediate factors [such as in the emotionally charged context of the Toronto seminar, page 23]. At other times the lessons may appear to be similar when they are in fact different. The PMI lesson involves subjective judgement but the CAF lesson is neutral and simply lists the factors. You might do a CAF about where to go on vacation, but a PMI on the proposal to go to Mexico.

There are times when CAF and a PMI may be similar. For example, in considering the factors involved in building a highway through the heart of a city, some of the factors have an automatic plus or minus value:

- making people homeless.
- increasing traffic congestion.
- destroying beautiful buildings, etc.

But if a PMI had been done instead of a CAF, then such neutral factors as the following might have been ignored completely:

- the way the decision should be made.
- whose business it is.
- the alternative uses for the money.
- other traffic schemes, etc.

Under certain circumstances two lessons or two operations may be used for the same thing, just as both a hammer and a shoe can be used for knocking in a nail. But their full range of function is different even though there may be an area of overlap. The trouble really arises from our classical method of putting things in separate definition boxes.

Here is the nub of the matter. The function or remit of some tools spills over into other tools. You can see overlap as untidy or you can stop worrying about it and consider the advantages of it *in practice*.

Lesson 5 is AGO, 'aims, goals and objectives', the acronym pronounced as A.G.O., three distinct letters. The AGO explores purpose. What are we trying to do? Spell it out. If you are woolly at this stage, your thinking cannot succeed. In the experimental stage, the AGO was one of the less successful tools, because an attempt was made by teachers to distinguish between aims, goals and objectives, and some students became hopelessly confused. The AGO is concerned with *purposeful action*, real-world thinking, as useful to the physicist as to the manager of the cornershop. Not simply evaluative, the AGO can be an important creative tool in its own right. If you doubt it, do an AGO on your own life.

Lesson 6 is 'Planning', the second plateau lesson. There are all kinds of structures for planning. You might do an AGO, a CAF, a C&S, in that order, then a PMI on each C&S, accept or reject accordingly. You might say that in the perfect plan your C&S delivers your AGO.

The CoRT tools are, above all, practical. The acronyms they're known by make them '*executive* concepts'. Originally they were taught as attitude lessons, without the acronyms, but tests in schools showed that the results simply washed away. I asked Norman Demajo how readily they become second nature after training and he told me an extraordinary story of what happened to him, shortly after he had been trained in CoRT:

I am a delegate for UEFA [the Union of European Football Associations]. Whenever UEFA teams are involved in a match they send a delegate – that's me. What does a delegate do? Basically, he arrives the day before the match, has a quick look around, goes to the stadium, meets the referee, the officials, checks all the security arrangements ... there is a whole book about what you should do.

In April 2000, however, both the UEFA book and his CoRT training manual were set aside. Demajo had been delegated to the UEFA Cup semi-final, first leg: Galatasaray SK v Leeds United AFC.

When I went to Galatasaray I knew it was a high risk match. I had already had a couple of high risk matches, though obviously I had no idea what was going to happen. The evening of the match I went, as is usually done, to the official dinner and met the Chairman of Leeds, Peter Ridsdale, whom I knew from the Roma Leeds match, which Leeds won on their way to Galatasaray. We ate in this very nice restaurant – the Turks were there, the English were there, everyone having a nice good time.

We knew that Leeds supporters were already coming in. I had told the police, 'If there is any problem, call us.' A phone call comes in about nine o'clock. There is some trouble in the town, Leeds supporters are drinking. I say, 'OK, just keep it under control,' nothing much I can do. About half past ten another call comes in. There's been trouble, one guy has been killed. Obviously I left the restaurant immediately. My driver took me to the hospital. I wasn't at this time certain that somebody was dead. In football, people tend to exaggerate a lot. I knew someone was stabbed, but I wasn't absolutely certain that he was dead. When I arrived at the hospital there were scores and scores of photographers, television, the whole thing. The Leeds chairman had also just arrived.

I said, 'Can I see the body?' and was taken down to the morgue, opened this cabinet, and there was this supporter who had just been stabbed. He had had his throat cut, stab wounds everywhere. I came to my senses. The chairman was with me. We got this knot in our throats. I said, 'Do we know who he is?'

Eventually someone said they thought that the man's brother was also in the hospital and was being attended to for some head wound he had. So we got hold of his brother to identify the dead man. Now, this man didn't know his brother was dead. This man was in a wheelchair, attached to some sort of drip, I remember. He had blood coming down from his wound, a youngish boy. Before he went into the room I realised that he was already in a bad state, they had beaten him up, he was expressionless at that stage, and I said, 'This could be your brother in there, but again it might not be,' and we went in and when he saw it was his brother, I tell you . . . I shall never forget it. No one could do anything to console him. It was terrible.

So then I went up and set up a meeting with the chief of police. 'Give me a report. How come this happened, you knew they were in town?' . . . but it was already history, there was nothing I could do about that. So I said, 'Call the Leeds people here, call the Galatasaray people here and we will decide what we are going to do.' The people gathered and it was then that I began to say, 'When you are under pressure like this people don't think, they don't think, they are absolutely gone. I am not saying I am a good thinker, but at least CoRT has taught me to apply some sort of structure,' – the thinking tools. So I began with my objective. What is my objective [AGO]? What is my priority [FIP]? One, my priority is the safety and security of all the rest of the Leeds supporters who are still running around the streets. That seemed to be the thing.

Incidentally, there was another supporter badly stabbed, and when this second chap died, I remember the Leeds people saying, 'We cannot play. The game is off.' Everybody was a mess. I remember telling them that the option to cancel the match was always open between now and nine o'clock tonight, so let's get our priorities right. Give me information [CAF] – 'How many Leeds supporters are already here, how many are on the way and how many Leeds supporters have not yet left England?' Leeds were very organised, saying 'These are the ones that are here.'

'OK,' I said [CAF]: 'Which hotels are they at? Police, get all these people into their hotels and get them to stay there.' Information. 'How many are already in Istanbul? Where are they staying? Police must protect them.' I wasn't sure what state of mind they'd be in having heard their friend is dead. You don't know how they would react.

I was not sure of anything, but at least I had a plan. One, protect the ones who are here. 'Planes that haven't yet left. What are we going to do with them?' Usually fans arrive on the day of the match, go out shopping, sightseeing, whatever, and then they go to the stadium, but I couldn't risk that. So what do I do? Take them for a cruise on the Bosporus? What, for a whole day? Put them in a hotel . . . for a whole day? There were five planes arriving from Manchester. I had all the information. I had all the alternatives. I listed the pluses and minuses [PMI]. I had it all there, and I said, 'Listen, do me a favour, please. Will you please just tell them not to come?' Finish. Picked up the phone: 'Cancel all the flights.'

'What about planes on the way?' British police categorise hooligans, A, B and C. Category C supporters are organised and violent. Any category C supporters would be immediately sent back.

But listen, life is not like CoRT or Six Hats. Life is a very complicated business . . . But CoRT does give you a framework. Slowly, slowly, I managed to sort out people's thinking that night. Being trained to think gave me the edge. Attention-directing tools give you focus. I knew what I was doing and I knew where I was going and I knew what my objective was. We are here to play. Why? C&S – what if we don't play? I could have taken the easy way out. 'OK, match cancelled.' But what would it have done to UEFA? Can you imagine the political implications? When is the game going to be played? Where is it going to be played? It has to be resolved. 'I am going to play it. If UEFA don't want me to play it, they can phone me up, any time. Right now, my focus – that is what I am doing here: I am here to get the match played.'

There was all the to-ing and fro-ing, you think we should play? No, we shouldn't play. You can imagine. Vroom! *Focus.* For me, thanks to the tools, it was obvious. That is what the thinking does for you. We play the match. We sort everything out that needs sorting out and we play the match.

So, priorities again. Police – 2,000 police. 'I need your help. Make sure there are no more incidents.' English police were there. Leeds security officers, etc. 'Make sure the supporters stay there.' The British High Commissioner said, 'Some people are still arrested, please let them out. Let's not create any more trouble.' By about two, half two in the morning we had a plan. I said, 'Right, I am now going to sleep. At half past eight in the morning I am going to phone UEFA, tell them what we have done and tell them as far as we are concerned the match is going to be played, the match is on.'

All I could do was organise my thoughts like this and everybody seemed to tune in and accepted me. It worked because they could see that I wasn't flailing around.

In the morning I gave UEFA the rundown and my recommendation that the game can be played . . . 'And I can assure you that there will not be any more incidents!'

Two hours before the match the Chief of Police phoned me and said, 'We have 150 drunken supporters in the hotel, tell me what to do with them.' Now I knew they had accepted me. The Chief of Police was asking me! *The thinking had given me control.* I contacted the Leeds people and said if it was impossible to separate the drunken supporters from the rest, then all must be kept at the hotel, otherwise keep the drunken supporters there and get the rest to the stadium. Eventually 119 made it to the stadium. Thirty-one or forty-one were absolutely drunk and were kept at the hotel and taken to the airport afterwards.

The match was played, it took place on time. I phoned UEFA at half past four in the afternoon and said, 'Nothing more to report.' No more incidents, not one. After the match I received what I thought was a very very nice letter from Gerhard Aigner, the Chief Executive of UEFA. He spoke to me on the phone for almost an hour as well.

Lesson 7 is FIP – **f**irst **i**mportant **p**riorities. In *Teach Your Child How to Think*, Edward suggests using a FIP immediately after the AGO, 'right at the beginning of the thinking . . . The more strict you are with priorities, the easier decisions become.' It is worth bearing in mind, however, that unlike the other tools, FIP's function is to narrow down, which can run counter to the breadth of purpose of CoRT if used poorly.

APC, **a**lternatives, **p**ossibilities, **c**hoices – Lesson 8 – is, of course, fundamental to all Edward's thinking. As the Jewish proverb has it, 'When faced with two alternatives, always choose the third.' Looking at life through an APC, one is all the time conscious that not only does $4 + 4 = 8$, but so do $5 + 3$, $1 + 7$ and $6 + 2$. Broadening perception by considering alternatives facilitates finding a solution to a problem, or an approach to a problem, or a design for the future, with tools like PMI and C&S finding the best way forward.

How bad we are at seeking alternatives is shown by any number of what have become known as lateral thinking brain teasers. Every day a man takes the elevator to his apartment on the twenty-third floor of a skyscraper, but walks the last six flights. Why?

The examples are endless. Readers who wish to become skilled at these kind of puzzles will benefit also from reading Lesson 3: Clues from CoRT *Book V: Information & Feeling*, which actively explores clues, deduction and implication.

A man was found hanged in a room locked from the inside. There was no other means of entry to or exit from the room. The beam from which he hanged was unreachable from the floor. There was no furniture in the room or means to climb up to the beam. There was a pool of water on the floor. What happened?

Demajo, who now teaches the CoRT lessons and is training in Six Hats, tells me that his hardened students find none of these problems even remotely testing now that they have made APC a habit. For one of his students in particular it had an especially liberating effect. Says Demajo:

> I was reading in a newspaper one day that in our local prison in Malta they had this education programme going. So I found out who was running it, phoned him up and told him I was an accredited trainer with Edward de Bono, and could I come and have a look at what he was doing and see whether he'd be interested in my running a programme. He said, 'OK, sounds great, but we don't have any money.' I said, 'Look, this is not about money. Most important thing is I get receptive people.' So, I went down to the prison. First time I was in prison, thank God! It is not as bad as Turkey, I am told, but it is an old prison in an 'X' shape and it is hot. Nicholas Berry, Edward's friend, son of the man who owned the *Daily Telegraph*, came down with me one time and he couldn't believe the state of the place. 'F . . . ing hell, man,' he said, 'this is a hundred years old,' you know? So I go down there and ask the man to put a sign up – 'Anybody who wants to learn thinking, etc, etc.' And about fifteen people enrolled, which is very strange because the other classes – there was . . . English: one student; Computing: two students; Psychology: two students. And I had fifteen! They told me this is the second largest class we have! The largest is chess.
>
> So, I started the thinking tools and I had the time of my life. I enjoyed it, they enjoyed it. I was using life as the idea bank [examples to work on], not preaching, not 'Told you so,' but life situations. I got such good feedback. People would say, 'If I had had this before, you know, I wouldn't be here,' and so on. I did eight sessions of two hours each, I went through the syllabus and then I said, 'That's it.' And they said, 'Aren't you coming again?' And I told them we had done it, that was all I knew. Then the head of the programme said, 'You have the second most popular class, they are going to miss you. Isn't there something else you can do?' And I said I was going to miss them as well. Bunch of murderers and drug pushers! But it was true. So I said, 'Let me think round the subject. Let me give it until

summer and then by the end of summer we will really have to stop.'

So I went on and began to vary the lessons and introduced what I called the lateral thinking competition, which they used to love. I used to have teams and they became experts, real experts. I would get hold of books of paradoxes and lateral thinking type puzzles and I tell you, they got them all. A man lies dead on the ground with no stab wound or sign of shooting. There is a package intact beside him. What happened?

Then we did a magazine – *Time 2 Think* – which they now do for themselves on the colour printer So, we had begun to get creative. I'd find an article in a newspaper, for instance a big gambling fraud down in South Africa. I'd have them as the board of directors down in this casino, right? There's something wrong with the casino, right? I wanted them to solve the problem – I'd be the one who knows all the answers. We have checked the statistics, we've checked the money, someone is screwing us, we don't know how. And I would see how long it would take them to come up with the answer. They always got there. Applying the techniques, searching, exploring . . .

You want the answer to the dead guy in the field? His parachute failed to open, the unopened package, right? Your mind is a self-organising system, it will screw you! You have to learn to look at things in a different way. Five pieces of coal, a carrot and a scarf are lying on the lawn. Nobody put them on the lawn, but there is a perfectly logical reason for them being there. What is it? Very simple.

In prison, this is mental freedom. They are over the wall! When Gertrude entered the plane she caused her own death and the death of 200 people, yet she was never blamed or criticised for her actions. What happened? Well, I'll tell you the coal, carrot and scarf. It was a melted snowman, of course. The other one? I can't give you all the answers.

Then Peter, Edward's brother, came to Malta and did a course in Six Hats and CoRT *Book IV: Creativity* – that's lateral thinking. So having learned new material, I passed on the new material. I began to teach CoRT *Book IV* in prison.

Now, the story about this one [Norman pointed to a newspaper article] is that he escaped. He was one of my students. He was the one that got away. Hisham Azzabi, a Libyan Arab Airlines engineer, awaiting trial. He had been caught coming in with about twenty kilos of hashish. He was looking at a long sentence and he thought, 'No, I am out of here,' and he really planned it well. He feigned a back injury, kept moaning for a week. He was fat, then started doing weights and running, suddenly got himself very fit, lost weight. Then about one week before he escaped, he missed class.

I said, 'What happened to Hisham?' They told me he strained his back, he is in great pain. I said, 'Serves him right, always playing with those weights.' Doctor examined him, couldn't find anything wrong with him, but he couldn't walk, spent three days in the most awkward position. Eventually they told him they would take him to hospital for an X-ray. He was in such pain and crouched in such a position they couldn't even put manacles on him. They took him to the hospital, he went on to the first flight of stairs. He had two policemen accompanying him, and at one point in time he just turned round and ran like . . .! The guy was gone, never seen again. I am sure he had a plan. He had been a very good student. Edward gave them *Teach Your Child How To Think*, and before Hisham left he used to come to me and say, 'Consider All Factors. You don't know how much you have helped me.'

I remember that Peter de Bono wanted someone to translate CoRT into Arabic, and I asked Hisham, 'Will you do it?' He said only that he would consider it . . . It was very close to his escape.

Lesson 9, 'Decisions', is the third and final plateau of *Book I* and is an opportunity to practise FIP (Priorities) and APC (Alternatives), and, in a general way, the earlier tools. What you find is that the tools have suspended implementation of feelings and emotions, and so rearranged perceptions that they virtually make your decision for you. The PMI and the C&S are both powerful decision-making tools in their own right, but a broader exploration might be as follows:

1. AGO
2. FIP
3. OPV
4. C&S
5. PMI
6. Then, see how you feel.

The final lesson (Lesson 10) in *Book I* is OPV: other people's views. In a sense, an OPV is a refined version of APC (Alternatives), refined because you are not concerned with any old alternative, but the alternative views of a specific person or groups of people. The OPV broadens our minds in a way many feel they do already, until they try it. OPV lies at the heart of one of Edward's boldest attempts to change the way our minds work – parallel thinking (page 242).

There is no best order in which to use the *Book I* tools, nor do they all have to be used on all situations. They are frequently used separately. Habitual use soon instils skill in drawing up utility structures appropriate to certain sorts of situation. In *Teach Your Child How To Think* and *Teach Yourself To Think* (1995), Edward demonstrates a very simple five-stage structure, broadly applicable to a whole host of situations and a good basis for experimentation. It can hold Six Hats (see page 248) and CoRT tools as you wish. For reference later, the appropriate hats from Six Hats thinking are included.

TO – where are you going **to**? Aims, objectives. AGO, blue hat.

LO – as in the archaic '**Lo**!' – Look! What do we know? What information do we have? This is white-hat thinking; use CAF and refer back to your AGO.

PO – sup**po**se. Alternatives, concepts, ideas, possibilities, hypotheses, speculations. APC and green-hat thinking.

SO – **So**? Choice between alternatives. SO leads to choice, decision, conclusion. It is a stage of checks, reviews, choices, a narrowing down: FIP, PMI, C&S, OPV, yellow hat, black hat. Modify input and clearly define the output.

GO – action, where this thinking leads to. If SO fails to produce a choice, decision or conclusion, action may involve more thinking, collecting more information, etc.

The highlight of the 1973 pilot programme, masterminded by Clare Connell, appears to have been Stopsley High School in Luton, 'which broke into spontaneous applause at the end of the first lesson.' There were, however, less favourable reactions. Criticisms included 'the sameness of the lessons from week to week', and some teachers were left 'groping for some fuller explanation of just what the lessons were about'. Some 'proper theoretical framework' was called for, and Connell echoed this in a report which called for more detailed teachers' notes that would put teachers in control and clarify the principles underlying the lessons.

Tape recordings were made of class performances and were assiduously transcribed. Many comparisons were set up between CoRT groups and control groups (groups not taught CoRT). Once in the habit of tackling subjects with CoRT, be they essays or group discussions with artificial content, the CoRT groups sailed away.

For instance, when individual English essays were commissioned at a grammar school (girls aged twelve to thirteen) on the subject of whether there should be special weekend prisons for minor offenders, the CoRT group put forward 200 arguments while the control group came up with only 105. Arguments put forward against the proposal as a per cent of arguments put forward in support: CoRT, 59 per cent, control group, 21 per cent. That CoRT influenced outcome can, at least in this instance, be in no doubt.

Eight groups of nine- to ten-year-olds were given the following as a discussion topic: 'A schoolgirl wants to train to be a teacher. Her father has to live abroad for five years because of his work, and her mother is going with him. Should the girl go with them or stay with relatives or friends so that she can finish school and do the training?' You might think this a testing subject for such an age group, but this was an army school, so it had some special relevance. Four of the groups had done ten CoRT lessons; the other four groups had not done any. The results, scored to number of aspects of the problem considered, were as follows: CoRT and control groups respectively – 17/3, 17/5, 19/5, 13/5. And in a group of pupils aged thirteen to fourteen at 'a village college' discussing what can be done to stop prices rising, more aspects were always considered by the groups experienced in CoRT.

There are many such examples, and anyone actually using the CoRT tools knows that they provide a framework that organises the effective tackling of all kinds of problems. In that sense, the control groups were at an unfair disadvantage because they had nothing to organise or guide their thoughts. They had nothing actually *to do*. Moreover, what is notable in Connell's report of this first pilot is that 'boys who were normally behaviour problems (the sort of boy one teacher called "hellions") often responded well . . . [and] pupils of quite low IQ seemed interested and were able to recall the content of lessons given some weeks previously.'

However, this was not always the case, and some children couldn't get hold of the idea that CoRT is a set of tools to apply rather than a knowledge-based subject (like history, geography, science) to learn.

Lister Comprehensive School in 'a very depressed area of East London' attempted to give CoRT to 'classes of average and below average ability and some remedial groups.' David Tripp, who succeeded Connell as Leverhulme Research Fellow, reported that:

> Mr Pidgeon [the teacher] confessed himself astonished by the pupils' reaction to the lessons ... They could not understand that the lessons *produced* anything. Where the teacher steps down [group working, etc] from his position of authority and invites their co-operation to initiate ideas, he places such pupils – and himself – in an ambiguous situation ... On a visit to the school late in the Spring Term, the Leverhulme Research Fellow was given the impression that more careful consideration would have to be given to the content in which these lessons might be conducted in future, if they were not to cause too much disruption. Mr Pidgeon described the material as 'literally revolutionary'!

It is one of the fundamental principles of CoRT that thinking skills are not dependent on the prior acquisition of a knowledge base. At the time, Edward was at pains to point out that 'all pupils start equal in the CoRT thinking lessons. This is very important because certain youngsters, on account of their background, interest or opportunity, do acquire a better knowledge base than others.' In general, this went down very well. A teacher is quoted as saying, 'Everybody has a chance because they all begin at the same point, and they're not handicapped by the fact that they're slow readers, find writing difficult or can't spell. Everybody has something to say and they're all encouraged and have the opportunity to say it.'

Early in 1973 there was a revision of the CoRT material in the light of experience and, in particular, of teachers' comments. Henceforth, there was to be a clearer, simpler format; lessons were to deal with distinct questions; there was to be clarification about how an operation or process should be applied; the operations or processes were to be given the mnemonic 'carriers' (PMI, etc), which had not appeared in the original version, specifically to aid transference to other contexts, inside and outside school. Finally, there was much discussion about testing. The system of scoring to show how successful kids had been in tackling a problem or topic seemed to run counter to the emancipating, non-judgemental character of CoRT, the great thing being that everyone in the class wanted to contribute at whatever level. The idea of then testing the kids wasn't sympathetic to this, it seemed to belong to the traditional knowledge-base lesson format and became something of an issue. First the method of testing was simplified, then it was dropped. Evaluations were still made by the teachers, however.

The revised CoRT lessons were the ten we have now in CoRT I. A new standard lesson format was included to help teachers present them.

Introduction: explains the particular aspect of thinking covered in that lesson and gives an example.

Practice: short, timed application of the tool to simple situations.

Process: a discussion about the tool's use.

Principles: from the foregoing, certain principles arise. For example, the earliest principles derived from use of the PMI were, a. the PMI is important because without it you may reject a valuable idea that seems bad at first sight; b. without a PMI you are very unlikely to see the disadvantages of an idea that you like very much; c. the PMI can show that ideas are not just good or bad but can also be interesting if they lead on to other ideas; d. without a PMI, most judgements are based not on the value of the idea itself but on your emotions at that time; e. with a PMI you decide whether or not you like the idea after you have explored it, instead of before.

Project: discussion groups, using real-world problems and thinking situations on which to rehearse the tools. For example, one of the earliest PMI projects was, 'People should be allowed to work ten hours a day for four days and have the rest of the week free instead of working eight hours a day for five days.' There were many ideas in these idea banks, and teachers would build up their own, not always with as much understanding as Edward's original ones, though sometimes with more relevance.

The job of publishing the six CoRT books (undertaken between June 1973 and March 1975) became that of Edward's younger brother Peter.

The death of our father in 1974 coincided with my retirement from the army – I had been Senior Systems Analyst and Chief of Programming at Defence ADP Training Centre – and Edward suggested that I might look at the CoRT lessons. I taught myself to print, taught myself to set the stuff and got on with it and advertised in *The Times Educational Supplement*. I didn't leave the publishing altogether until about 1981 and then it was taken over by Maxwell, Pergamon and SRA [Science Research Associates, who published the CoRT Workcards and Teachers' Notes in Chicago].

In fact, Robert Maxwell's daughter, Christine, took personal charge of it at that time and sales soared. 'She was really fighting for CoRT,' recalls Professor Maier. Robert Maxwell, as we shall see, had earlier introduced an influential South American politician to Edward, which would lead to more than a million Venezuelan children studying CoRT.

When David Tripp replaced Clare Connell, who had returned to Australia unwell, he reported to the Leverhulme Trust on the use of CoRT in more than 300 British schools. 'Younger pupils approach the lessons with spontaneous vigour and enthusiasm,' he wrote. 'Older pupils often need to be convinced that they are learning new skills.' Edna Copley arrived on the scene at the moment that a resistance to CoRT among older children became an issue. She had given up her lectureship in business studies and her husband, Bill, had taken early retirement due to a heart attack. He had been headmaster of a grammar school in Lancashire. 'David Tripp was testing the system in secondary schools,' she recalls.

> I remember saying to Bill, 'You know, I think he has got this in the wrong age group,' because he was getting such resistance from the secondary school pupils in the first couple of years. It took them some time to realise you really have to get the skill in top primary so that they are used to doing these things. Edward resisted that no end.
>
> We had arrived in Cambridge around 1968 ... Bill made me promise that if he had another heart attack, which we were expecting, I would get myself a job, be independent. I promised. Well, he had his second heart attack, and I was sitting in Addenbrookes Hospital waiting for the third. I was beside myself with worry and my eyes fell on a newspaper. I picked it up and saw an advertisement – 'Edward de Bono requires an intelligent person to run his Cognitive Research Trust.' Believing, fearing that if anything happened to Bill I would not keep my promise to him, right there and then I begged some paper and an envelope and wrote out an application. And I got the job, basically, I think, because I had lecturing experience and knew bookkeeping and how to run an office. Bill did survive, however; the third attack never came and I found myself with a job.

In spite of an apparent blip in progress in some secondary schools, CoRT was gaining considerable ground, as Tripp's 1973 report shows:

Pupils acquire a more deliberate approach to problems and situations. They are able to focus their attention on a substantially greater range of aspects involved, and to generate ideas with which they are not themselves in sympathy. There seems to be less irrelevant discussion, particularly among younger children. Pupils' willingness to listen to and respect views of others is reported by several teachers to have improved considerably and backward pupils become more confident in their own ideas, and in their ability to voice them. Some teachers have reported that the structure and maturity of their pupils' written work has shown marked improvement. Pupils' approach to problems seems to be less egocentric . . .

His study indicates broader perception among CoRT thinkers, which was of course the aim. For instance, when thirteen-year-old girls were asked to consider the suggestion that everyone should do a year's work on leaving school, the result showed many more ideas generated by the CoRT groups. Edward noted, 'The difference between the CoRT trainees and control groups increases as one moves away from the egocentric points (which tend to be considered anyway) towards the practical points. With younger children the differences are even more striking. In a 1977 study in New Zealand Dr Shallcross investigated six classes that had had CoRT lessons and found that the pre- and post-test performance showed a significant difference at the 1 per cent level in all cases.

In 1974 Tripp issued another report on the effect of the programme in some fifty more schools, including anecdotes which suggest that the tools were being transferred beyond the classroom. At Carmel College, Wallingford, an independent preparatory school, two boys came to the headmaster to settle their quarrel about a broken cricket bat. 'He found that the argument was resolved when he asked one of the students to do an OPV [Other People's Views] on the other student's position . . . this "gave clarity and emotional detachment that would otherwise have been impossible to achieve".'

Edward described this as a most important element. 'Thinking is of little use if it remains a game played only during that class period,' he wrote at the time. 'To be of any use a thinking skills programme must provide skills that are transferred right out of the classroom and out of the school itself into life outside and after school.'

In 1976, there was a further 'carefully controlled trial with 300 pupils,' recalls Edward, 'which showed a huge shift in a test of innate ability (the

Alice Heim number 4).' Later still, Tripp refers to a study of 'the effect on grades and performance in other skill areas,' by one Sidney Tyler, who carried out a study at a US Defense Department elementary school in Britain. Tyler showed that after CoRT training, 58 per cent were working above their grade level, 87.5 per cent were reading at or above their grade level, and 63.5 per cent rated above their chronological age. Tyler subsequently returned to America, where she is still teaching CoRT today.

With all this activity, an extraordinary amount of evaluation data was becoming available, which Edward summarised as follows:

> A readiness of pupils to consider themselves as thinkers and thinking as a familiar skill. This leads to confidence, speed of response, breadth of view, willingness to consider alternatives and other points of view. Respect for the thinking of others is also important. There is a spread effect into other subject areas. The most obvious of these is English language and such thinking tasks as essay writing. There can be effects on grades and such matters as spelling. Other subject areas like social studies, geography and history can also benefit. There is an effect on the behaviour of children both in general terms of discipline and application and also in terms of problem-solving and conflict resolution. There is evidence also of an increased use of thinking and particularly the CoRT process outside school and at home.

At the Perse Girls' School in Cambridge, pupils began writing more original essays. For example, in history, instead of simply churning out facts, the girls were looking at 'what would have happened *if*'. 'They were applying the thinking skills, looking at alternatives, possible consequences, etc,' recalls Edna Copley. Jennifer O'Sullivan, a remedial teacher in Australia who is using CoRT today, has found the same benefit:

> I had a girl who was having difficulties. She brought an essay along to me and it had written on the bottom, 'Needs more work. Not enough points.' And she said to me, 'I have written everything I can think of. What am I supposed to do?' So I taught her the CoRT lessons, really because they offer what she needed, a whole range of questions. This girl's problem was not that she didn't have the ideas, it was that she couldn't access them. She wasn't asking the questions. CoRT gives the person the questions . . . If you are doing an essay on

Shakespeare and you go into an OPV and say, 'Well, how did Shylock think? How did Portia feel?' you have got another paragraph. Now, this girl was not expected even to attempt Level 12, which is the final year before university, but she started to have successes where she had failed before. She had gained confidence, she gained motivation. She did Year 12, passed her BCE and she is now doing further studies. So that is how I use it, to train people to ask questions.

Edward's view on the evaluation of CoRT was that 'in general the CoRT lessons train the thinking required in real-life situations. Therefore, the most appropriate tests are performance tests. In a performance test, pupils are asked to apply their thinking to a typical real-life situation. When this was done on an individual basis the output was either written or tape recorded. When it was done on a group basis the output was taped. This output constitutes the performance. The performance was then analysed.'

By 1979, Tripp had developed an elaborate evaluation system of his own. His paper, *Changes in Children's Corporate Thinking*, was delivered at the symposium on Language, Communication and Thinking at the 49th Congress of the Australian and New Zealand Association for the Advancement of Science, held in Auckland.

However, Edward clearly favoured the simple point-count of aspects considered during a lesson. This, he wrote, 'can, with experience, be subdivided into broad categories such as Concern for Consequences, Realisation of Other Points of View, Balance of Argument, Considera- tion of Alternatives, Sense of Objective, etc.' However, these studies were usually conducted by the class teacher and usually involved samples of less than twenty pupils per group, and later Edward admitted that '[they] do not succeed in proving anything, because in each case it is always possible that a special set of circumstances biased the results.'

Edna Copley thought this was a critical failure on Edward's part. How could he expect academia to take on CoRT officially as part of the national curriculum if he did not deliver the necessary evaluation results? 'Edward fell down on this one thing – he will not test. Now, look at this material about Singapore. There they did test. They got very good results from it.'

Edna had herself gone to Singapore, following initial contact in London by the Singapore High Commission. By this time she carried the title of Deputy Director of the Cognitive Research Trust. She stayed for three weeks and trained thirty-nine teachers from sixteen different schools, including the prestigious Raffles Institution and Raffles Girls' Schools. The ages of the children ranged from nine to over sixteen. Members of the Secondary Schools' Inspectorate were present at all the training sessions and accompanied her to all the participating schools to observe and assess teachers in action. The inspectorate then saw the programme through the sixteen schools, undertaking a pre-test and a post-programme test, and comparing the two results.

The results, back by detailed tables, were as follows: 'An evaluation of the pre- and post-tests was done for both the experimental and control groups . . . all the experimental groups [CoRT taught] showed significant mean gains.' Where there were mean gains by both the experimental and control groups, the gains made by the former were significantly higher than those of the latter.

As a result of the testing, *Book IV: Creativity* and *Book V: Information & Feeling* were also taught. (*Book IV* is lateral thinking, *Book V* we will look at briefly later, see page 199.) Mrs Lim Soon Tze, Director of Curriculum Planning, and Dr Tan Bee Geok, Director of Gifted Education, prepared an evaluation stating: 'Results have indicated that the programme has benefited all the pupils concerned.' And in 1992, ninety-three secondary schools and twenty primary schools were teaching CoRT.

Through all this Edna proved invaluable to CoRT. In her, Edward found the administrative arm that he needed, someone to put his ideas into action. She was willing to work all hours, was extremely efficient, and she and Bill were soon directly involved with the CoRT project in-school. She says now:

I was a good foil for him. Edward had the ideas and I went and did them and gave the back-up. Responsibility never lay heavily on my shoulders. I enjoyed the challenges because there were so many, a lot of very hard work, but I enjoyed it. Edward and I just got on. We haven't been that close. We just clicked. People used to say to me, 'How on earth do you manage to talk with him?' Well, we never stopped. I never had to pause and think, what shall I say?

She was also meticulous in her testing. In selecting an experimental group and a control group to compare, she rigorously minimised the variables. One area proved a particularly rich seam for testing.

Invariably, we found the CoRT group far more *disciplined* than the control group, where there was much more of a free-for-all, and they jumped from plus to minus, and if anything of interest came up, it was almost always an accident. After trying for some time, I finally persuaded St Andrew's School, a state school in a poor area of Cambridge, to take part. The number of ideas generated by [public schools such as] the Perse was high, and you might expect St Andrew's to perform a lot lower. But they were not in fact abysmally lower, they turned out to be quite good thinkers. The quality of ideas in the Perse was better, but in terms of quantity, St Andrew's performed well. But the main point we discovered was that *behavioural* changes were taking place in St Andrew's, in the CoRT group. Now, this is soft data, as opposed to the hard data we were getting from the recordings, but it proved to be important. We had a boy called Johnny, and when Bill came home I'd debrief him.

'Talk to me,' I'd say, 'Tell me what you saw.'

'Oh, Johnny was off this week.'

'Oh, right.' Numbers made a difference to the testing, and we had been told that Johnny very often went missing. Then, the following week –

'Oh, Johnny is back, cut and bleeding.'

Why? Because he was a fighter, very unruly, very disruptive, you really had to sit on him to stop him being disruptive. But the following week he was there again. Unusual! . . . He just missed the once. And his fighting lessened. And instead of shouting the others down, he listened more, and made contributions. Edward actually published one of Johnny's contributions in a book.

Then we had another pupil, called Tina. The teachers thought that she was being abused. She was certainly undernourished, the wind would have blown her away. Sometimes she would have cuts and bruises on her. And nobody, absolutely nobody listened to Tina. Then one day, after school, when the class had gone, Bill was at his table in the classroom and Tina, with another girl, walked up and threw a sweet at him. And walked away.

The next week Tina walked up on her own, and put a sweet on Bill's table. At the end of the course she said – I shall never forget this – 'When you didn't used not to come here, I didn't know nothing, but now I know quite a lot.'

And what was more important, Tina was getting peer group recognition.

So there were behavioural changes. I remember there was a place,

Picturesque Marsamxett Harbour in Ta'Xbiex, Malta, where the de Bonos lived from 1937.

Edward as a boy. The car became a metaphor for thinking: 'If we regard innate intelligence as comparable to the engineering of a car – the horsepower and so on – and thinking as a driving skill, then you may get a powerful car driven badly, or a humble car driven well. Thinking is the operating skill that makes the difference.'

Edward at eight years of age, a boarder at St Edward's College, Malta: 'I only saw my parents during the holidays, even though they didn't live very far away.'

St Edward's College, which Edward attended between seven and fifteen, used to be the military hospital at Cottonera, across the Grand Harbour from Valletta. It was modelled on a British public school.

During the war, after the school was evacuated to what is now the Cathedral Museum in the ancient city of Mdina, Edward pioneered an escape route into the town, going down through the cellars.

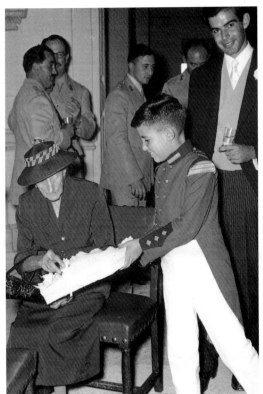

September 1955, Edward's sister Elizabeth's wedding. Nanny, with Edward at her shoulder. Formidable Nanny Porter served the family for sixty-seven years, bringing up twenty-four children, 'all of whom were highly creative... and very self-disciplined'.

The entire de Bono family in August 1974, a week before Edward's father, Joseph de Bono died. Seated on the ground, left, is Edward. Joseph is sitting centre stage with, on his left, his wife, Josephine. Behind them stands Mary de Bono. Edward's wife, Josephine, is standing far right. Behind her is Edward's brother Peter. Farthest back stands Edward's older brother Antony. In front of him is the youngest of the four brothers, David, who is talking to Elizabeth.

Edward with his manager, Diane McQuaig, and Diane's husband, Don, who first brought Edward to Canada.

Palazzo Marnisi, the de Bonos' sometime summer retreat in Malta's eastern, wine-growing region of Marsaxlokk, where some of Edward's most successful books were written.

Linda Low, who with her husband Peter deploys the de Bono thinking methods along the Pacific Rim, presents a copy of Edward's *Six Thinking Hats* to the Pope in the Vatican.

The Seoul Symposium of Nobel Laureates, organised by Tom Farrell, which Edward chaired in Seoul, Korea, in 1989. Laureates left to right: Herbert C. Brown, Wole Soyinka, Ivar Giaever, Walter Gilbert, a Korean guide, Rita Levi-Montalcini, Burton Richter, Dudley R. Herschbach, Sheldon Lee Glashow, Brian David Josephson, Daniel Carleton Gajdusek.

One of Edward's four islands – Tessera in the Venice lagoon. The island, seen here from the wooden jetty (where the author was stranded), is small and contains just three attractive villas, one with bell tower.

People who attend de Bono seminars remember, above all, his drawings, his visual language of thought. 'It is mesmerising to watch it. He's thinking aloud.'

Simon Batchelor with his team on the Six Thinking Hats aid mission to Cambodia. Twenty-two thousand people, more than fifty Khmer villages, benefited over a seven-year period. The mission tackled everything from contraception through to education, to water supplies, to starting small businesses – 'the whole culture thing'.

Edward with miners and staff of the Lonplat Platinum Mines in South Africa, where in a project masterminded by Susan Mackie, his thinking programmes have had a dramatic effect on miners' own lives as well as profitability at the mines.

Is Edward's performance, then, the ultimate 'Svengali' schema? 'He is fantastic at holding an audience,' says Tom Farrell. 'Whether it is 10,000, 1,000 or 100, it doesn't matter. He is hypnotic.' (*Jane Bown, Camera Press*)

a holding place for young men awaiting trial by the courts – not on the way to prison but on the way to borstal. We had a volunteer in there, who was trying CoRT, but she didn't have the expertise. Because we were beginning to notice behavioural changes elsewhere, it gave me an idea, and Bill and I went to a Community Home with Education on the premises.

Now, these were children out of control. They were taken away from their parents and put in this place because of bad behaviour. We are talking primary school age. Bill was training the staff in how to use this material and one of the housemasters came to him and said, 'I have a boy here and he is just so disruptive. His mother hated him and he couldn't live with this because he adored her.' The mother was supposed to come and see him, but she wouldn't turn up or she would turn up the worse for wear, and whenever she went away the boy became far worse.

So, this boy was being taken through the CoRT training by his housemaster, who was aiming the tools at his particular problem. And he spoke to Bill about it. With CoRT *Book I* (*Breadth of Perception*) the boy had come to realise that there was nothing he could do to change his mother's feelings for him, but he could learn to live with it. And this brought about a huge change in his behaviour. A housemaster can talk through problems with such a boy, but that is quite different to what happened here. That is discussion, but he was (and we were) creating better thinking and so actually changing the boy's perceptions.

We had so many examples of this at the time that Bill and I decided to go further. We became interested in testing CoRT on the problem of borstal recidivism, habitual relapse into crime. So Bill went to the borstal. In fact we did write something on this, *CoRT and Conflict* . . . The problem was that we had a high turnover of boys, we didn't have the stability we had in the schools.

First of all we had to get Home Office permission and the borstal didn't want to let us in – I think it was a power thing: 'We are in power and we don't want any do-gooders along here.' But it turned out the best work Bill and I ever did.

We had had problems with the authorities over recording because the boys had to be left on *their* own in their group discussion. That was essential. It had to be their group thing. But the authorities said that the boys wouldn't talk into a tape recorder anyway or they'd nick it or smash it to bits. And Bill said, 'What do I do?'

I told him to go in there and leave it. 'It's a risk we have to take.' Anyway, he got on well with them. The first thing I told him to tell them was that he was not a god-botherer. 'You are teaching them the same lessons as you taught to Beecham's and other top companies. You are going from there.' He did. Then he said to them, 'You are going to have to have the discussion on your own, which is what the primary kids did, and you are going to have to control yourself.' They did.

In fact, later one of the kids said he didn't abscond on account of Bill doing 'a C&S last week' – Consequences of Action. 'I knew if I absconded the first consequence would be a plus – I'd be free of this place – but the long-term consequence I knew would be that they would find me and it would go on my record . . . Not worth it, mate.'

Edna then showed me a letter written to Bill by one of the boys at the end of the ten-week project, thanking him for what he'd done.

They were allowed to write one letter a month, and Bill got it. The lad was just borstal, about eighteen. Bill was ten weeks up there, everything was taped and I had to transcribe them all. We sent the lot to the Department of Criminology at Cambridge, and they were so impressed that they sent for us. The professor said he couldn't believe that after such a short time we could get a group of borstal boys to sit down and actually discuss themselves. One of the discussions they had was, 'Should there be special treatment for social misfits?' Aha, significant! Because they have got to recognise that they are the social misfits, which they did – no emotion: 'That's us, isn't it?' they said. And they sat there and discussed it, and we sent it to the professor. He had the tape and the transcript. We said we needed some funding, but we couldn't get any.

Pointing at the mounds of research material between us, Edna said, 'That's all we have left – just bits of paper gathering dust.'

The upshot of this extraordinary programme of experimentation was that by the end of the 1970s, Edward could boast that the CoRT programme was being used in more than 5,000 schools in England, Scotland, Wales, Eire, Australia, New Zealand, Canada, Spain, Malta and Nigeria.

Singly the most significant research on schools programme at this time was undertaken in Australia under the auspices of Professor John Edwards. In 1978, when he first started working with CoRT, he was head of the Science Department at Canberra Grammar School.

The headmaster was not happy with the exam results, and he knew that earlier I had been in Malaysia doing research on concept development in children. So, he asked me to do something. We had able students but weren't getting the results we should be getting. I had read some of Edward's books, including *The Mechanism of Mind*. I looked around and there was a small range of programmes about teaching thinking, but Edward's absolutely stood out. The thing I like about Edward's stuff is that it is so applicable to everyday life. It is not just schooly stuff. Some of the other programmes were teaching students how to do IQ tests, almost. I could see that Edward's material would work in the real world, as much as in the school. So, I threw out part of the science curriculum and replaced it with CoRT *Book I*.

We had a programme in year 10, which is our fifteen-year-olds – it was the end of their junior high school years and they were having to make decisions about what to do in their senior high school years. We used to rotate them through introductions to the academic disciplines. So, [we have an] introduction to physics, to chemistry as an academic study, not as an integrated study as they had done in the junior high school, and I decided to give them a whole section on thinking as well.

We had a lot of complaints, to be honest. Some of the parents worked for CSIRO, which is our scientific organisation in Australia, and I remember one of them came in and said, 'What do you mean, throwing out part of the science curriculum?'

I said that I thought it was very important that they learned how to think directly, and he said, 'What's thinking got to do with . . .', and then he stopped himself. He was going to say, '. . . with science.' The kids would cycle off from me to physics or whatever subject it was – and the teachers down the line said, 'What's happening? I can't believe the difference in them.' And I realised I was on to something. Then parents started ringing up and saying, 'It's wonderful,' and the exam results started to go up, and I started to do research on what was happening in my own classroom.

This research was first made public at an inaugural educational conference in 1982. This, the first of what is now the annual International Conference in Thinking, convened annually in a different country, was altogether an extraordinary event. It was organised by the academic Bill Maxwell, who had first heard of the de Bono phenomenon as it broke:

> I was finishing my doctorate at Harvard, and the Learning Institute of North Carolina, the first state-supported think tank in education in America, sent an emissary to Harvard, saying, 'We need a black on the staff.' So they nominated me for that exalted post and I accepted it. When I went to work for them, they had a staff of only three other people, one of whom had heard of Edward de Bono. This is 1967 . . . We couldn't get him to come to America, but there was the will and the desire to get him there.

Time passed and Maxwell found himself in the enviable role of head of the School of Education at the University of the South Pacific in Suva, Fiji. Bill said,

> The university is/was the national university for the eleven nations of the South Pacific, all former colonies of Britain. It was originally established by New Zealand, who gave them their navy air base on the condition they establish a university there. I arrived in 1977, and there was only one Pacific islander with a PhD. There was nothing intellectual happening, so I went to the university and said, why don't we have a conference? They said OK, here's $2,000.
>
> So, first I called Edward. I don't know how I got in touch, because I had had no contact with him. He said he would come. He also said he would pay his own way, do his own hotel, which was an incredible thing. So, then I called the British Council in London and they said I was in luck, they had some extra money and I could have three of their people too. I said I'd have the biologist Richard Dawkins at Oxford, who was then regarded as a kind of successor to Darwin and is now a professor at Oxford. After that I didn't know who else to ask for, but they suggested Margaret Boden (the expert on Artificial Intelligence) and Don McKay at Keele, who established the first brain science department in Britain.
>
> They all came and as soon as I announced to the world that we had all these top British scholars, everyone wanted to come, including David Perkins. Perkins was/is co-director of Project Zero

at The Harvard Graduate School of Education, better known as the home of Howard Gardner, the author of *Frames of Mind* (1983), about multiple intelligences.

It was a magnificent setting for a conference and we had more parties than you can imagine. Let me give you the scene on the closing night. We were outside the dining hall, standing right next to a *bouré*, the traditional Fijian thatched roof structure, waiting for dinner. Normally in Fiji at this time of year it would have been raining cats and dogs, but there was not a cloud in the sky, and just before the bell rang to invite us all in, up comes a full moon over Lol Bala Bay. It was enough to give everybody a full orgasm!

John Edwards also recalls that night.

I remember that they had a superb Fijian feast and that the after-dinner entertainment was to offer a 'dare' to any one of the plenary presenters to take off his shirt without taking off his jacket. Edward took the dare and proceeded to do so in front of the whole gathering. Superb! The price to pay was a five-minute leapfrog line of all the Australian participants – quite challenging also.

Memories differ as to whether Edward actually managed the feat, but the conference was, as a result of both the spirit in which it was carried out and the high-profile gathering, a big enough success for it to have been carried over even until today. 'Later I simply asked everyone, "Would you like to do this again?"' said Maxwell. 'And David Perkins stood up and invited us all to Harvard. De Bono was again the keynote speaker, and when it came round, it was so popular that they had to turn 300 people away.'

'Now it is very big,' Edward tells me. 'It attracts about 2,500 people. It will be in Auckland in 2001, then in England the following year. Sadly, Bill Maxwell, who launched it, got eased out. So, whenever I give my speech I say, "What about Bill Maxwell, who set this whole thing up?" I mean, he should have an emeritus position. It is most unfortunate.'

By the time of the inaugural conference in Fiji, John Edwards had left school teaching:

I had joined James Cook University and I went over to Fiji to present a paper on this research I had done in the school. I said to Bill Maxwell, 'Look, there's a guy called John McPeck who is doing a philosophical critique of Edward's work and I am doing a paper on the practical value of it. Why don't you put us on together? It'll be interesting.' So that is what happened, and McPeck had a bit of a tough time! Edward will remember him, he was his whipping boy for a number of years. McPeck was one of these classic guys who would say in theory this guy's stuff just doesn't work. But there I was, standing next to him and saying in practice it does.

The full text is available in *Thinking: The Expanded Frontier* (1983), edited by Bill Maxwell. It was the first occasion on which the de Bono CoRT programme was independently assessed in scholarly literature. John Edwards's published report on tests at Canberra Grammar School (Edwards & Baldauf, 1983) concerns a five-week exposure to CoRT on seventy-two fifteen-year-old male students as part of their Grade 10 Science programme. Using pre- and post-essays on familiar and unfamiliar topics, there were 'educationally significant improvements on both essays ... significant correlations between achievement on CoRT and on the end-of-year science exam, even after controlling for the effect of IQ.'

In another, much more scientific study by John Edwards, a CoRT group of 108 Grade 7 pupils and a control group of 82 Grade 7 pupils were taken from two schools – mixed sex, mixed ability, state and Roman Catholic primaries in North Queensland – and compared. Significant gains were recorded on a number of counts: IQ, as measured by the Otis-Lennon School Ability Test (OLSAT), Intermediate Form R; and creativity, as measured by the flexibility and originality scales of the Torrance Test of Creative Thinking. Significant gains were also recorded on the Thinking Approaches Questionnaire (TAQ) and on overall academic achievement as measured by teacher-designed tests, particularly in the areas of language, arts and social studies.

One of the tests Edwards used, the Torrance Test of Creative Thinking (1966), includes forty-five-minute tests involving questions about a situation shown in a drawing, making guesses about possible causes and consequences of a situation, producing ideas for improving a toy, thinking of unusual uses for objects and suggesting ramifications of an improbable event. They're serious testing. Edwards also records a 1977 test on ninety university students by Rosenthal, Morrison and Perry. Half the students were given two CoRT lessons and the other half a lecture on the same topic. The CoRT group performed significantly better on three of the four subscales of the Torrance Test subsequently.

Says Edwards:

A major study begun in 1987 aimed to look at the effects of teaching a group of twelve-year-olds in their last year of primary school all sixty lessons of the CoRT programme – two lessons a week for thirty weeks. The teacher was helped to infuse the CoRT thinking skills, once learned by the students, through all disciplines of the curriculum. Once again the students showed improved scores on a range of quantitative measures. In addition, the teacher showed growth on a range of measures. Both the teacher and the headmaster, who also regularly took the class, reported impressive benefits. The teacher noted that her teaching style had become much more interactive; she now used group work more; she had gotten to know her students and their thinking at a much deeper level than ever before in thirteen years of teaching; the students had achieved outstanding and unexpected results on a set of standardised national tests; and the students now contributed many more ideas of a far higher quality than they had done before CoRT instruction . . .

When the results on the standardised national test arrived near the end of the school year he reported: 'I was thrilled . . . they were certainly startling and outstanding'. The test consisted of five sub-tests, each designed to produce a standard distribution with Australian students. This meant that 31 per cent of the students tested would normally fall one or two standard deviations above the mean. The results for the CoRT trained group, and for the mean scores from the previous six years at this school were, in relation to proportion of students above the mean, as follows:

Test of learning abilities

National Norm	31%
School Mean	39.5%
CoRT Group	52%

Study skills

National Norm	31%
School Mean	31.2%
CoRT Group	48%

Mathematics skills

| National Norm | 31% |

School Mean	24.8%
CoRT Group	52%

Language vocabulary

National Norm	31%
School Mean	42.8%
CoRT Group	62.4%

Language comprehension

National Norm	31%
School Mean	35.8%
CoRT Group	50%

Feedback from the children themselves was also positive, with the majority reporting seeing big improvements in their thinking and self-confidence, and many reporting wide use of the CoRT skills across the curriculum and in their everyday life. These students completed their secondary schooling in 1992. In the state of Queensland all students are given an overall level of achievement based on school ratings moderated through a state-wide set of standardised tests. The scores allocated to students range from a high of 1 to a low of 25. The CoRT-trained group had had a few hours of CoRT reinforcement outside school hours in their second and third years of secondary school, but nothing in the other three years, and no reinforcement from their teachers in secondary school. Their scores had a mean of 10, compared with a mean of 15 for the other students in the school. (It should be noted that the mean IQ scores for the two groups were not significantly different when they were tested in their third year of secondary school.) These results reinforce the obvious potential of programmes such as CoRT for improving the thinking of students, particularly if the skills are infused broadly through the curriculum and reinforced once learned.

Our most recent results come from comparing students trained in CoRT skills during their last year of primary school (approximately twelve years old) with an equivalent group of untrained students in the same two schools. On completing high school the tertiary entrance results for the two groups were compared. Scores on four measures determined by the State Board of Senior Secondary School Studies, based on moderated school academic results, were available:

The treatment group consisted of twenty-four students, all of whom had undergone CoRT training. They had received only brief refresher training in CoRT during their five years of high school, following their grade 7 training. Ten of the students had received training in all sixty CoRT lessons, fourteen had been trained in CoRT *Book I* only, but introduced to CoRT *Books III* and *VI* during refresher training. The control group of twenty-four consisted of a random selection from all 136 students in the two schools who had received no intervention.

All scores are inverse, so a lower value indicates better performance.

MEAN SCORES

	OP	FP A	FP B	FP C
Trained	10.92	5.00	4.92	5.35
Control	15.21	6.52	6.63	7.26

OP – Overall position is a measure of the student's overall achievement at school. This has a range of 1–25.

Also three field position (FP) scores were available, with range 1–10. These are measures of student skills in specific fields of study at school:

FP A – Extended written expression involving complex analysis and synthesis of ideas.

FP B – Short written communication involving reading comprehension and expression in English or a foreign language.

FP C – Basic numeracy involving simple calculations and graphical and tabular interpretation.

Differences on OP, FP A and FP B were significant at the 0.05 level, for FP C it was significant at the 0.01 level . . . Most parents in Queensland would kill for such shifts. They represent a difference between getting into university and missing out altogether. (See Bibliography: Edwards, John.)

Elsewhere in Australia, CoRT was found to be useful in remedial work, as Edna Copley had found in Britain. Jennifer O'Sullivan first came across Edward's books when she was working as a speech and language pathologist for the Commonwealth Rehabilitation Centre with brain-damaged (stroke, car accident, etc) victims and dyslexics, both adults and children. 'I was working with people of working age – between fifteen and fifty-five. I searched out the CoRT lessons and read up on them and just began using them,' she said.

The brain-damaged people were mostly young people who had been in a motor car accident and suffered head injury and the effects on language, thinking and memory that this causes. A serious loss affects every facet of language – grammar, spelling, word-finding, reading, comprehension, time-telling, talking, writing, memory, thinking. It is a loss of word. A minimal loss can cause havoc at work. Doctors would hold up four fingers and if the patients could say, 'Four,' they passed the test. But you need rather more than that if you are going back to work. Some were sent back to work and failed because of this level of loss, which is not obvious in the doctor's surgery. They could not concentrate, or cope with interruptions, or cope with decisions or prioritise.

Some are unable to appreciate humour or form an original thought. Some had had strokes in young middle-age, which has similar effects. My work with them was at a tertiary level of therapy and they were wanting to get back to work or study or university and, as part of my therapy, I used the thinking lessons. These were valuable for several reasons. They demand concentration for only two or three minutes at a time, but repeatedly. They give a means of working on abstract thinking, which is a higher level of therapy. They give an opportunity to judge ability for new learning. They do not depend on memory. They offer a strong framework for anyone returning to study after a break. They also offer an edge in that this needful person has a skill which others may not have. They offer an opportunity for success and for building self-esteem. They are fun!

I am not a teacher, I am a therapist. My work was to enable people to *think* again. If they had had a stroke or had been in a motor car accident and suffered brain damage they had lost the ability to think. CoRT does not help in the very early stages. You have got to relearn to count and name the days of the week first. All your basic names like shoes and socks, the ability to write your own name and dress. They have lost numbers, the ability to tell the time. It was later in therapy that I brought in CoRT, and among those who wanted to move on to that kind of abstract thinking. With CoRT they were not being confronted by something they had learned once before and forgotten, so that was important.

Then O'Sullivan took CoRT to job clubs for the unemployed.

The Australian government has for several years now run these. They run for three weeks, generally with ten members and a leader. They work on their résumés, their interview skills, on extending their work possibilities, what they would like to do and what else they could do, and make a concerted effort to find work. Success rate was 40 to 45 per cent in general, 50 per cent was considered excellent. The two with which I was involved were for unemployed deaf, and that was an Australian first. Their ages varied, a few school leavers who had never worked, most semi-skilled workers, a few with work experience and some qualification. I remember a bookbinder, cleaners, an accountant, many had worked in noisy jobs because the noise did not worry them. Their hearing loss also varied. Most were severely deaf and communicated through sign language, some could lipread.

I was allowed a total of six hours and I worked with two sign interpreters, who alternated between themselves every fifteen or twenty minutes, and who had to translate both ways – my words into sign language and any communication from the group into speech for me.

I could do what I wanted with them but I knew that in six hours I could make no difference to the clarity of their speech. So, it wasn't a matter of doing routine speech therapy. I really wanted to offer them something that would make a difference in the six hours. . . . So, I spent the time teaching them the seven tools from CoRT Book I. Beyond that, it was a matter of me having a cup of coffee with the leader Bill and saying, 'What's different, what's happening? Did he notice anything?' And he said he would want to have the thinking lessons with any job club he ran after that. He said they didn't start thinking until after the lessons, they communicated much more with him and with each other. They thought of more possibilities – well, you could do this or what about if you did that – and solved the problems. The results were that eventually 90 per cent of one of my groups found employment and 75 per cent (which later became 80 per cent) of the other. These figures had never been heard of before. The highest had been 50 per cent.

After that, I gave a paper at the Australia–New Zealand Conference on Communication, entitled *Giving the Deaf a Thinking Advantage*. It was seeing that paper and seeing those results that led to groups for unemployed people [New Deal, page 286] being taught CoRT in England.

Just how helpful the tools can be in remedial work was brought home to me when I visited a school for children with autism and Down's syndrome. Charmaine Agius Ferrante is an expressive woman, a performance artist as much as a teacher, who has a school bubbling with life. Susan Mackie, a remedial therapist and de Bono master trainer from South Africa, first brought Edward's CoRT tools into the classroom here a couple of years ago, and they are now part of the daily routine.

I sat on the sidelines in a great hall where the children were gathered. Mackie, on her first visit for more than a year, was greeted by the children like a mother. She and Ferrante calmed the children and sat them cross-legged on the floor; some thirty were interspersed with a handful of adult helpers. The children had already been told that today was a *big day*. 'The professor is coming! The man who invented the PMI!' Hand signs are key with these kids. Ferrante and Mackie never mention a tool without issuing an accompanying hand sign, which the children then use back to them. Hand sign and acronym – PMI, CAF – are signals which switch on the brain in these children. It was extraordinary to watch. Edward sat on a chair in front of the group. Mackie gathered up one of the children in her arms and plumped down on the floor among the rest.

Amazingly, she immediately managed to elicit CAFs on the proposal, 'You don't have to go to school,' and I saw how the tools establish discipline, structure and motivation in a class. There was only one set-to during the hour or more I was there, which called for independent action by a helper and ended up with two children being separated from the group. Generally, there was just this buzz, a cadence of excitement and communication. With these children the whole thrust of a teacher's day is *how to connect*, and the CoRT tools provided the perfect responsive format, and more: 'We have proved that there *is* development,' Ferrante said to me afterwards, 'for now they actually think about the thinking they are doing. As a result, they have learned more about themselves. People with autism don't have a sense of themselves. The tools are giving them that and now we can say, "We value them and they value themselves."'

She and Mackie are naturals, but what about Edward, sitting quietly on his chair and so far not involved at all? I had been told that he wasn't especially good with children, but I had also heard this from John Edwards, which had struck me forcefully:

One year the International Conference on Thinking was in Hawaii, and Edward asked his personal assistant there – Alexandra Ahrens – to arrange to take me and my four children, who I had with me, out to dinner. I said, 'Where are we going?' She said, 'Well, Edward has asked me to find a place a fair distance away because he wants you to sit in the front with me and he wants me to put the top down so that he can sit in the back with your kids and have the wind blow their hair around!' I thought that was great. How many would do that? There was my young son Luke and as we are getting to dinner Edward is calling him Spook and Luke is calling him Dreadwood! Luke's about nine and Edward is absolutely warm, charming, thoughtful.

I had remembered the story on this day in Malta, as it wasn't until just before we climbed into the car to get to the school that Mackie had sprung it on Edward that he was expected to talk to the children. His response had been surprise. I connected it with his 'I'll teach people, but won't do the nannying' approach. Today, quite clearly, a bit of nannying was expected of him. How would he cope?

In the event, on the word, Edward switched at once into magician mode, removing his tie, asking the children what it was and informing them that, 'No, this is not a tie. In fact, it is a snake!' There, before our very eyes, his colourful tie did indeed *become* a snake, not only a snake but a snake 'with two heads! So let's do a PMI on a snake with two heads.'

It worked a treat. Plus points offered by the children included, 'A snake with two heads could go into a hole and come out without turning round.' 'It could be awake and asleep at the same time!' 'It could see danger coming up behind it when it was climbing a tree'. Minus points included, 'The two heads would fight,' and offered as an interesting point – 'It'd eat twice as much.' The session went on until Edward brought it to a close with, 'How many of *you* would like two heads?' And a kid in the front shouted, 'I want three!'

Watching this, I found it extraordinary that the same thinking programme can be used by top executives in multinationals, by schoolchildren, by the hearing impaired and brain-damaged in Australia, and by autistic and Down's syndrome children in Malta. Back in the 1970s, CoRT found an audience in a yet more diverse area. Bill Copley had presented a week's course to a group of gifted children in Norfolk, by arrangement with the county council. 'I think he did five of the CoRT lessons in one lesson time, they were that bright!' Edna recalls. The lessons were the same as for others, only the effect was different. 'Gifted children can think too fast and need to slow down,' Edward says, 'whereas for remedial, CoRT gives them something to do, helps organise and discipline the class. Gives self-esteem too. Socially, gifted children operate very differently in exclusive schools incidentally.'

'For the better?' I ask.

'Yes,' he replies. 'I had to become a monster to survive!'

So when, in 1975, Edward travelled to the University of Toronto School for the Very Able, he was not breaking new ground for CoRT. Nevertheless, the impact of this particular visit was to be decisive in one sense. 'My area of specialism is gifted children,' admitted Norah Maier, 'but it became thinking after Edward's influence.

> Edward came to speak at the University of Toronto in 1975 and that was the first time that I heard him. I knew of his work, but did not delve deeply into it. He actually spoke in the auditorium of the University of Toronto School for the Very Able, to the academically gifted, from the age of eleven to seventeen. They are specially selected by very high profile tests – 900 people going for seventy places. I was head of the English department there at the time. When I heard Edward speak of the Intelligence Trap and the Ego Trap and highly gifted people looking too narrowly, I of course immediately recognised my students.

Norah came to know and use CoRT, using it 'all the way up to grade 12 by 1979 – even the principal was teaching thinking skills'. When Edward heard about her work, he invited Maier to do some research analysis for him. 'Edward at that time was giving dinners with people like C.P. Snow and Lord Mountbatten and Sir Keith Joseph. He recorded them and asked me to do a reading and analysis.'

These dinners were conducted at an exclusive apartment in Albany in central London, a house designed by Sir William Chambers and built between 1770 and 1774 for the first Viscount Melbourne. In 1802 it had been converted into chambers for young single men, with two large blocks added on either side of the garden, leaving a cloister walk between Piccadilly and Burlington Gardens. It is one of the most exclusive addresses in London. Aldous Huxley, Terence Rattigan, J.B. Priestley, Graham Greene and four prime ministers – Lord Palmerston, George

Canning, William Gladstone and Sir Edward Heath – have had apartments there. Edward entertained in, and still to this day retains, Gladstone's old apartment on the ground floor.

The dinners were to be a significant element in the development of Edward's enterprise. By the late 1970s, this encompassed much: besides his work at Addenbrookes Hospital, there was the CoRT schools project; the books – he had published eighteen by 1979 – invitations to speak from media and industry; thinking retreats at his country house, Cranmer Hall, where he lived with his wife Josephine and their two sons Caspar and Charlie; and of course his lectures and seminars abroad.

'An excellent way to find out what people really think,' Edward says, 'is to invite them to dinner,' which is exactly what he and an obscure Greek millionaire called Demetrius Comino did. C.P. Snow, Lord Mountbatten and Sir Keith Joseph were only the start. There were captains of industry – Sir Terence Becket, Director General of the Confederation of British Industry; Nigel Broackes, Chairman of Trafalgar House; Sir Monty Finniston, British Steel; Sir Kenneth Corfield, Standard Telephones & Cables. There were assorted politicians, ambassadors and political figures – Enoch Powell, Dennis Healey, John Pinder, Director of the Policy Studies Institute, Sir Kenneth Berrill, Head of Central Policy Review Staff. There were academics – Sir Max Beloff, Sir Hugh Ford (Imperial College), Sir A.J. Ayer. There were figures from the arts and inventors – Sir Christopher Cockerell, inventor of the hovercraft, Dr Alex Moulton, innovator in bicycle design and vehicle suspension, Eduardo Paolozzi, the sculptor, Sir Hugh Casson of the Royal Academy. And it goes on. It was the most incredible exercise in networking that could have been devised, this series of little dinner parties for the powerful and successful, in which, no doubt, Edward would suggest the odd lateral shift towards a more designed way of thinking.

'It's quite remarkable how rarely a conscious method *is* employed by these people,' Comino said at the time. 'It is also fascinating to understand the way they tackle problems, though we do try and keep away from particular problems.' In his invitations, Edward's declared purpose was –

> to try to gain some insight into the thinking processes used by individuals in a variety of situations and for that reason the people attending the dinners come from a wide variety of backgrounds ... I would like to emphasise that we are essentially concerned with the thinking involved in 'getting things done' ... The usual practice at

the dinners is for a guest to have some time in which he puts forward his own insights and reflections. Apart from this, the guest is invited to enter the discussion at any point with his own agreements, disagreements, comments, questions and any other noises that can be transcribed.

To outsiders, the discreet enterprise had an intriguing, even *Magus*-like, ring to it. 'From what I hear,' ran a short diary piece in *The London Evening Standard*,

the dinners have verged on confessionals ... Recently the likes of Robert Maxwell, Sir Charles Villiers of British Steel, Sir William Pile, chairman of the Inland Revenue, Mark Weinberg, managing director of Hambro Life, and Sir Huw Weldon [then Chairman of the BBC] have attended. Wives, significantly, are not invited ... I understand that the informal think tanks have become so popular that one guest flew from Canada for the evening.

As Norah Maier rightly recalled, these dinners were all tape recorded, and then painstakingly transcribed by Edna.

Edward says today,

Some of it could never be published ... very sensitive stuff, but I remember that Mountbatten was at the first dinner and told a story, which I am sure is not classified, about when he was Commander in Chief in Burma during the war. They had surrounded this Japanese division one morning on the bank of a river or in the bay, and through the binoculars they saw all these guys get up and arrange themselves in parade formation and then their Commander in Chief gave the order to march into the water and then, when it was up to their necks, 'Sit down!' And the whole division committed suicide! They didn't want to surrender.

The late Demetrius Comino held a BSc in engineering from Sydney University and came to London in the 1930s, where, at Imperial College, he took an MSc and later invented and developed that amazing 'adult Meccano Set' – Dexion Slotted Angle, thereby making his fortune. Dexion was hugely popular. People couldn't get enough of it, and once the company was up and running Comino turned his attention to 'his real love in life', which ex-colleague Mike Chapman told me was 'training people to sort out problems. Any half-intelligent person, Comino believed, could be trained to any job. University degrees were not required. He put that into practice in his own company.' It was the self-same level playing field, promised by Edward's thinking programmes. It led to the bankrolling of the dinner parties for some three years.

The money went into the Centre for the Study of Thinking, situated, like its sibling the Cognitive Research Trust, at Warkworth Street in Cambridge. Comino put up the initial money for the lease and funded the dinners (thirty-three of them). Edward paid the rent. 'Oh, and how he loved those dinners,' recalls Copley. 'He was absolutely in his element with them. The guests were intellectuals or very successful people. It was seriously done. We had a great time, but it *was* serious.'

When, in 1982, as an independent publisher, I approached Edward with the idea of *Tactics* – hatched on a squash court during a particularly testing series of games with a psychiatrist from the Maudsley – I had no idea just how timely my approach would be. The book was intended as a comparison of tactics and strategy in as wide a variety of fields as possible – business, sport, personal relationships, and so on. Edward invited me to Albany and we went across the road for breakfast at his favourite café. There he told me the good news: that he liked the idea, but gently suggested a refinement, that we run the themes of the book through interviews with people successful in these various fields. It was a winning modification, born out of those Albany dinners. The book went on to become a bestseller.

In the course of my research for *Tactics* I went along to the ACC (Associated Communications Corporation) offices in London to inter-view the late millionaire Australian entrepreneur, Robert Holmes à Court (TV, newspapers, transport, oil). He had just ousted Lord Grade as chairman of the company, much to the annoyance of Gerald Ronson, whose rival Heron Corporation asked the Takeover Panel to censure Holmes à Court for alleged breaches of the Takeover Code. Holmes à Court came through the whole very public affair with exactly what he wanted, which didn't surprise me. It was clear when we spoke that his style as negotiator was that of a cold realist, the chess player who made every move count, and, for whom any complicated mating dance or subterfuge was anathema.

It was a good interview. Edward picked him to exemplify the predator for the section on entrepreneurial style in *Tactics*. As a result, he and Holmes à Court met, and Edward remains a close friend of Janet, Robert's widow, to this day. It is symptomatic of just how well Robert and Edward connected that the former surprised everyone by uprooting in the midst of his subsequent headlining bid for BHP to chill out for a week with Edward in Malta. They became closely involved – 'there were discussions,' as an aide said to me. Edward's Little Green island in Queensland, Australia, came to him via Holmes à Court's Heytesbury Holdings, though Edward did not find that out until after he had bought it. By then, in the mid-1990s, he had become a very rich man indeed.

Edward accommodated the variety of interest in his programmes, but organisation was never his strong point. 'His life in actual fact was a successful mess,' sighs Edna about their association in the 1970s. 'He would have twenty, thirty, forty things on the go at any one time, trying to divide his time and his thoughts and his efforts among all of them. Even he couldn't possibly do that and do it well.'

Early on in the research for this book I asked him for his itinerary for the six months from April 2000. It took in Hanover, Prague, Argentina, Australia, London, Paris, Buffalo (New York), Ireland, and Istanbul, then India, Hong Kong, Singapore and Malaysia (where he is as I write). 'Yes,' said his manager, when I expressed amazement,

> it does sound incredible and I have never known anyone like Edward, who comes up with an idea and goes ahead and actually implements it. One after another. We have started so many things over the years, trademarked so much over the years, because Edward has always said, 'Let's do it!' And if it captures him enough he'll stick with it, and if not he'll move on. He never felt constrained by implementation!

Energies and ideas were flowing fast in the mid- to late 1970s, and although it would be a few years yet before his international itinerary meant two or three global trips a year, the effect of the Albany dinners, the relentless worldwide spread of CoRT through Malaysia, Singapore, Hong Kong, Indonesia, Bulgaria, the Middle East, Canada, Mexico, the US, Venezuela, South Africa, Botswana, India, China, Russia, Japan and the Philippines, plus the effects of a correspondence course which Edward had designed for Wolsey Hall in Oxford – 'We used to have governments from all over the place sending dignitaries to Edward for training in London,' Edna recalls – meant that there was hardly pause to draw breath.

All was grist to the mill as far as Edna was concerned. She may rue the fact that Edward did not single-mindedly pursue her dream to get CoRT on the National Curriculum in Britain, but she readily admits that she has earned a very nice living on account of it.

> As a result of my working for the Singapore government with CoRT, Singapore Airlines got in touch. So I came to write a training programme based on Edward's concepts for them. Then I went to Turkey. I was training the Prime Minister's advisers. I used to go to Ankara. I went for many, many years until there was a change of government. Then I did the most magnificent training I ever did in Brunei. . . .

The fast and furious flow ensured that pretty soon some additional organisational help would be needed.

When Paddy Hills came into the picture in early 1976, she built a much-needed bridge between Edward's business and family. 'I think it would be safe to say that I am the only one that has been close to his family and his home life,' Paddy said to me when we met. 'And I guard it for him.'

She is, indeed, protective. I ask whether she thinks that Edward and biography make a good combination. 'He doesn't like reminders. He doesn't like yesterday to be brought in front of him too often,' she warns. 'He prefers it just to be what is *going* to happen.' I agree that that is his whole nature. 'So,' she concludes, 'if one drags it out . . . This is a creative book . . . There's no standing still. He has got so much more to do.'

I do not for one moment doubt that Paddy Hills has been a crucial element in the build-up of Edward's enterprise. She is the reason why making an appointment to see him is something of an art. Warm, chatty, an apparently very helpful person, Paddy operates from her London home and, when he is in town, sees Edward for briefings at Albany. When you speak to her, she somehow manages, in the most polite and pleasing way, to eradicate from the proposal you make anything which she feels that Edward will not countenance. This can be helpful, but it's not always what you want to hear. Then, on something you propose which she feels will advance his position, she is almost conspiratorially encouraging, even offering a nugget of advice about presentation, which will meet with Edward's approval. Once you realise how many people are vying for his attention, this is helpfulness indeed. Typically, Edward needs to assimilate information quickly. Anything longer than one side of A4 is out. He has a strong sense of 'the right time' and a mistrust of pushiness. Lack of preparation – background knowledge – ensures a negative response ('unless you are a journalist, in which case he expects it'). The time *has to be* right. The purpose *has to have* positive value. Forward momentum. That is the de Bono style. It is what characterises his thinking.

Paddy Hills finished my briefing with the words: 'I think that what you are going to find through your research is a great sense of warmth from various people and energy, but they are not going to be able to hold the butterfly for you or pin things down. When you try to get a neat order around him you won't be able to.'

The day we meet, Paddy makes me feel honoured. 'Do you realise how many people have met me since I have been doing this? I would say about ten. I am what he wishes me to be, I am behind the scenes. He used to refer to me as PH. I would have PH in a little circle put on things. When he writes to me, he writes in this extraordinary clipped way. "Dear Paddy," signed "Edward" via fax modem, and in the middle this string of clipped instructions. Absolutely no emotion whatsoever.

We met actually in Albany itself, when he was coming to take over the lease of the chambers from the uncle of a girlfriend of mine, who was taking up a diplomatic posting in Kenya. He was a widower and needed someone to help him move out. My girlfriend, thinking it rather amusing, suggested I give him a hand. No sooner had I got there, but her uncle said, 'Someone wants to meet you. He has heard that you work at Imperial College.' I was working as a secretary there in the mechanical engineering department.

So, we came together really by accident. He asked me to do a little work with him in the beginning. I was not really working too much, because my daughter had been rather seriously ill. He is very relaxed . . . but very particular, very precise – when the work is done he wants it to be good. His comment to me at the beginning, when I was doing some letters or some small manuscript, was, 'You can spell?' I said, 'Yes, of course!' and I continued from there. I think he was watching to see how I would function. He said that I had to be the letter 'D' in the alphabet, and now I had to find out what the letter 'D' was. This is very much Edward. So I worked out, 'Devoted', but, no, I couldn't come round to it, and finally he said, 'Dependable. That is the key point, because it means wherever I am, whatever I am doing, I know I can depend on you to do things.'

When I very first spoke to Edward, we were sitting having a cup of coffee and he said, 'Maybe one day you will be doing work for me and you will know where I am and nobody else will. I will be on an island somewhere.' It is curious that he made that comment to me all those years ago, when here I am now quite often the one who is the key holder of the telephone number to an island. I always say I am there to look after his moorings . . . it is nice to protect him from anything that comes flying his way that is going to grind him into the ground and be of no use whatsoever. I can stop that, protect him to some extent. But as for inner happiness . . .

At Paddy's suggestion, we walk over Piccadilly to Albany. She remarks on the quiet, the peace of the place as she leads me from the lobby through the cloisters. We pause outside the door of his apartment with its quirky sign, 'Please knock *and* ring.'

Inside the main room, the drawing room, about fourteen feet square with a glass chandelier, wing-back chairs (one beneath a large portrait of the man), a sofa, a low table, a large fireplace, there is unlived-in elegance and the prospect of enormous work to be done in countless piles of paper, marked with words like Action, Future Action. A few fresher piles cluster on the floor beside chairs, which Paddy knows he'll use, in the hope that a hand will drop idly on some amusing invention that has been sent in by a fan.

The mantelshelf, I notice, is massed with tiny objects – gifts, prized toy-shop purchases. She picks up a pair of false teeth which join our chatter, and I reassure myself that they are far too small to be his. She points out various gadgets invented by him to increase efficiency, but the handmade filing system, pen holder and other paraphernalia look to me more an expression of a playfully inventive mind than a serious attempt at making order out of this magpie clutter.

Next door is the dining room, where the famous dinner parties took place. Paddy mentions that the apartment is not actually well designed for entertaining as the kitchen is in the basement, and today, with the large round dining table piled with yet more global gifts, electronic bits and pieces, junk and jars of currency from around the world, destined for BA's charity fund, it seems sadly uninviting. There is now so much stuff littering the room that Paddy recently insisted on introducing some shelving (not Dexion Slotted Angle, fortunately). Edward reluctantly agreed so long as she did not have it fixed to the wall. Typically, he wants to keep his options open. As we left, I quizzed Paddy about the bed. 'There *must* be a bed!' Had we somehow missed a room?

'*That's* the bed,' she said flatly, pointing at the sofa. 'It pulls out, he'll use it when he flies in and has to rearrange his night and day...'

My abiding memory of the months we worked on *Tactics* in the mid-1980s is of us arriving simultaneously at the front door of Albany around 8.30 am, me fresh from a night's sleep, him dishevelled, struggling from an airport taxi under the weight of his luggage, the shoulders of his black corduroy jacket peppered with dandruff following an all-night flight from the Far East. Yet there would be no hint of stress. There is time allotted for a meeting, and that is how long it will take. It will not be hastened to fit the time span; it will be conducted calmly. He has an extraordinary ability to slow down time, like an expert batsman who appears to have all the time in the world to deal with the fastest of bowlers. Most impressively, you watch his theories take shape for real, perhaps for the first time consciously realising that his system is not some good idea to make a killing, but something that is a part of him, something he lives. You make a proposal, he does a PMI on it. You present him with a problem, he offers an apparently absurd statement – it's quite embarrassing when it first happens – before using it to work our way together to a solution via a concept neither of us had thought of.

His punctuality is legendary and he claims only to have missed one appointment over the years – 'when I developed a dentiferous cyst that had to be removed in hospital overnight.' Paddy recalls only one other health crisis, which almost led to cancellation: 'Edward had been doing one of his seminars at the SAS Portman Hotel in London, when halfway through the morning he discovered that he couldn't see through one eye – suddenly, while holding forth about clarity of perception, it was like looking through the cloudy bottom of a bottle! During an interval he called me and calmly told me to make him an appointment with a specialist during the lunchtime break.' Paddy did so, drove to the hotel with some lunch for him, and transported him to the specialist, who diagnosed a cataract. Edward then returned to the hotel and completed his afternoon performance without even the organisers knowing what was up. It was while recuperating from the ensuing operation on his eye, unable to read, that he learned Italian. Paddy went out and bought him the *Reader's Digest* tapes. 'He sat up in bed with his headphones and dark glasses on, looking for all the world like a member of the mafia,' she recalls.

Around the same time as the Albany dinners, Edward made a move into Canada that was to become a regular, twice-a-year event, and would eventually make that country his third largest market after Australia and Singapore. Here's how it came about: 'In 1976,' recalls Don McQuaig of MICA Management Resources in Toronto, 'we had a client, the Institute of Association Executives, and the executive director had seen Edward speak in London.' Don's father had started MICA after the war with a psychometric assessment/personality profiling system, still known as 'the McQuaig system' and based on work he had done with the Canadian Airforce. In 1976, Don had been on the business consultancy scene only about four years, and felt relatively inexperienced.

So, this guy gave me Edward's number. I phoned him, we chatted. I got hold of his book and said, 'This is good stuff,' and we organised a visit for that fall. From then on, we promoted his workshops and conference appearances and seminars in the Canadian market. Edward had firms like ours in different parts of the world. He would come here typically twice a year and he would do a tour, Toronto, Vancouver, Montreal, that sort of thing. He developed quite a following in the Canadian market.

I asked Don about the initial response.

I don't think Edward had been to Canada before, but when we sent out a brochure we got a phenomenally good response. I remember being quite surprised, because I hadn't heard of him before and maybe most of the people who responded hadn't heard of him either, but the notion of creativity that you can learn is pretty provocative.

I then asked him what he had thought of Edward's presentation at that first seminar.

Well, that's the other thing. His presentation is unlike anyone else's. Just sitting there doodling on his overhead projector. I have to admit this worried me at first, because we had had this huge response and I didn't know what he was up to. I mean, I was relying totally on the references of these clients who had seen him (which made me nervous to begin with).

I shouldn't have worried, within fifteen minutes he had just captured the attention of the audience. Six or eight weeks ago I saw him – that is, a quarter of a century later – and though the material has changed, the basic message remains the same. I think people like it because he is different and also he maximises the learning because he is illustrating it as he is talking.

Says Diane, Don's wife: 'He is not an entertainer, but Don and I think the same way about this. We love Edward the way he is. Tony Robbins came on the scene. Edward used to kid me about him. We walked on a pit of burning coals with him. Robbins is a motivational speaker, he came on the scene in 1988, 1989. He was a blockbuster success, sold zillions of videos, on TV all the time. People loved him because he was so high energy, larger than life, about six-foot-five, massive hands, would just yell at the crowds. Now, Edward is not that. Will never be. He has a very distinct following of individuals who are interested in something different. I would never want to change Edward's style. There is just something about the way he is. Yes, that overhead projector is out of date, but he is not interested in changing his methods. For him his method is timeless. And he is right. Unlike others on the circuit he *is* timeless.'

I have seen Edward lecture and run seminars on a number of occasions, and I have had the opportunity to attend a four-day seminar with only a handful of others. I have also spoken to a number of people who saw him perform in the early days, when he was young and building a following, and then, just recently, I read a criticism of a 3M-sponsored seminar in England, in which his delivery was described as a 'ponderous monologue, sounding like a war-time newsreel.' Before researching this book I had not been to any of Edward's seminars, but I had seen his BBC TV *De Bono's Thinking Course* in 1982, and on seeing it had wondered at his sedentary, low-key performance.

So, here we have a man who is paid huge sums for performing, is very popular, and employs none of the usual performing skills. How does it work?

Early in my research for this book I was invited by a slick group of management, communication and technology experts called Business-Lab to watch Edward on the same platform as John Kao. Dubbed a 'serial innovator' by the *Economist*, Kao runs a post-Warholian creativity centre in San Francisco called The Idea Factory. I sat between a director of Cisco Systems, one of the most successful companies in the world, and a fellow from Oracle. Nice guys, living a life in which top executives own their own helicopters. Expectations at the seminar were high. When we assembled for drinks on the evening of our arrival, each of us was photographed digitally and fitted with a tag, which could be swiped *en passant* by anyone interested in getting to know you. It struck me as the basis for a late-night, hi-tech party game, and it might have become one, but the champagne flowed and by nine o'clock it was all I could do to get my swiper to work.

At dinner, Edward sat at the top table with key helicopter passengers. No sign of John Kao. Rumours spread through the Oscar-style maze of tables that the principal players had been jockeying for top billing and Edward had won. Apparently, the California agent who put the deal together had managed to secure £40,000 for Edward and a mere £35,000 for Kao. When I put the figures to Edward in the general context of his rates, he allowed it – 'Yup, can be, can be . . .' To illustrate his drawing power today, he'll ask you to imagine a theatre audience paying £1,600 a ticket to witness a fourteen-hour one-man performance. That is what businessmen normally pay for the lateral thinker's two-day seminars, though this was one day. It seems plausible enough when one hears from Massachusetts-based International Data Corporation that the total spent on consulting is expected to grow nearly 15 per cent per year, to reach $55 billion by 2003.

Whatever. The point that evening was that Edward had landed the preferred slot and the only relevant question was, Would John Kao show up, or was he skiving off in a fit of pique?

With thirty-five grand on the table and the organisers paying a first-class air fare from California, we should not perhaps have shown surprise when a mini-tornado suddenly swept in, and the buzz through the dining room was that Kao had arrived. As one, we craned our necks towards top table to see how the great men would greet one another, but BusinessLab screened the scene more effectively than a hospital bed bath and the floor settled into mundane things, such as how many millions I would now be worth if I had invested £1,000 in Cisco at start-up.

Next day, on the way to the conference centre, I asked my taxi driver whether he'd heard of de Bono. He had, but wasn't impressed: 'I think they're looking for something that's not there.' Moments later, as Kao strutted his stuff on stage, promoting jamming (the jazz variety) and how to locate 'the sweet spot' as the means to creativity in business, I made the taxi driver's comment the first note on my pad.

Nevertheless, the process demonstrated that besides his academic qualifications (a PhD – he lectured at Harvard Business School for fourteen years), Kao merited applause for his performing skills. How would Edward, with that Pathé News voice, match up?

When his turn came, the set revealed his low-tech overhead projector, the roll of acetate on which he doodles his concept art, the sock (a recent innovation) which rubs the art away and the dapper figure of Edward himself, perched on his high chair, with half-moon dark glasses to protect his eyes from any more cataracts, and his pockets stuffed with assorted pens, ballbearings and other oddball props.

No pop star antics. Nothing, except the glasses and the sock and what he refers to (to his closest) as his Mediterranean tummy, had changed since the TV series in 1982.

I asked the guy sitting next to me whether he'd seen him perform before. He hadn't. I gave Edward a slim chance at following the first act, but eyes were already directed away from the figure on the stage towards the bright light screen and the concept squiggles he was throwing up at it from the acetate below.

I remember Edward's son, Caspar, saying that before the sock, when Caspar was a boy, he used to clean his father's acetates after seminars. 'It was incredible, 50, 100 foot of acetate, all arrows, little men running around, boxes, a few words here and there. It is mesmerising to watch it. He's thinking aloud.'

I glanced at my neighbour. 'Mesmerised' was indeed the word.

Since then, I have been to more seminars, watched the same thing happen and listened to his audience laugh at jokes, some of which they might not give the time of day to outside. Journalists are in a difficult position, as I was at first, because nine times out of ten they remain too judgemental. To benefit from the de Bono technique you have to be prepared to give yourself to it. As Edward himself has written in respect of reading *The Mechanism of Mind*, 'It is best not to have any pre-occupations and to let the intangible subject of thinking gel into something definite and usable.'

Writes John Edwards in a PhD thesis: 'Welwood (cited in Wilber, 1982) defines intuition as "direct access to the implicit, which operates by scanning a holographic-type blur with a diffuse attention that does not impose preconceived notions on it." Welwood argues that much scientific and philosophical argumentation and reasoning is often a working back from a conclusion arrived at intuitively, adding the logic or proof steps afterwards.'

There are similar elements in how the de Bono performance works on us. Edward's presentation technique, like the overlapping images in *Mechanism of Mind*, is not to build up our thought patterns point upon point in a linear, logical, tell-him fashion, but in gently delivered overlapping conceptual layers. He encourages a diffuse attention, interspersed adroitly with 'aha' moments and the surprise of humour.

By chance or design, this is, in its effect, hypnotic.

The recent venomous *Guardian* article mentioned earlier describes Edward's delivery – and this was one-to-one in Albany, not in a seminar – as 'a lilting intonation that ... is tempting to read as a device to minimise the chances of interruption'. The journalist, it would seem, so nearly got there, so nearly fell under the spell! 'Whether he is writing, talking or thinking, de Bono's fluency is mesmerising,' wrote another journalist, Elizabeth Grice, in the *Daily Telegraph* seven years earlier.

Now, the interesting thing is that when Edward was involved in medical research, in the early days, he was experimenting with treatment by hypnosis. 'My understanding was,' I was told by an associate of those days, 'that he was doing research using hypnosis. I certainly know that he became a very, very powerful hypnotist, to the extent that he could hypnotise without realising it. And he had some rather unfortunate experiences. For about three years, he would never look you in the eyes when he was talking.'

On one occasion, in the CoRT offices, Edward suggested that Edna Copley might like to participate. 'They were running experiments at Addenbrookes at the time and he said to me once, "Would you like to become one of the people taking part?" I jokingly said, "Yes, why not?" And he said, "No, it's dangerous." They were hypnosis experiments, but he didn't go into details. He said, "No, no, I was only joking."'

Readers of *The Use of Lateral Thinking* will recall the description of a patient carrying out bizarre instructions after being awakened from trance, like putting up an umbrella indoors, handing everyone a glass of milk, or getting down on all fours and barking like a dog. 'When asked why he is behaving in the odd way the subject immediately provides a perfectly reasonable explanation ... an unforgettable demonstration of the powers of rationalization.'

What about 'of manipulation'?!

Elsewhere Edward described what happened when a patient was told that on a given signal he would see a friend come into the room. The subject was then awoken and the signal given. The patient got up, shook hands with the friend, who wasn't of course there, and even introduced him to other people in the room. Another unforgettable example was when Edward suggested to a patient that he draw the image of a square circle. The patient woke up, the signal was given, and he tried again and again to reproduce the impossible image on paper, even while acknowledging that it was quite illogical.

Time and again you will hear Edward say, 'Change a person's perception and you will change their behaviour. Rarely can you change a person's behaviour by logic alone.'

Is Edward, in performance at least, the ultimate Svengali? Svengali was the mesmerist in George du Maurier's artful, melodramatic novel of exploitation and possession, *Trilby* (1894). He fashioned artist's model Trilby O'Ferrall into a superstar singer. When Svengali died, such was the power he held over Trilby that her voice died with him.

'With a book you can get away with a lot,' Edward says, 'but the notion that in person you could fool so many people is pretty absurd.'

But, in fact, since the 19th century, when stage hypnotists caught the public imagination, we have been awed and, at the same time, have hated ourselves for being susceptible to charismatic figures. Those new to these kinds of cerebral acrobatics may be especially susceptible: 'People are quite frightened because they are worried that [the seminar situation] is going to expose the fact that they are not a good thinker,' said Caspar de Bono to me in another context. 'They are uncomfortable with it because they haven't done it before. They are possibly suspicious. So in that kind of environment, putting someone at their ease can be especially rewarding.' Which is precisely what Edward's performance does.

Said one of Edward's key associates, about first meeting him face to face,

I had a fifteen-minute meeting over coffee. I thought he was riveting. If you track the flow of concepts that come out of him, it is just like calisthenics, it is just so rapid-pace intellectually. I could catch it all because I had lived it – this whole story that he was telling, the difference that these concepts can make – I had already seen that happen. I was both exhilarated and terrified. I just thought he was everything you wished things could be, if you were describing a world that behaved in a way that you wished things could be, so the anticipation and fear that it was all going to crumble, that it would not be real ... He was *wonderful*, he was *so* kind. Just the fact that he remembered my name and remembered that we had an appointment was surprising to me because he has so many things going. Anyway we had our coffee and he was just very inviting in terms of

'Gee, you could do stuff, we could do stuff, and here are some things I have been thinking of doing.' And he is consistently like that with people who present themselves in front of him who have energy and seem to have some desire to get connected.

Tom Farrell agrees. 'He is fantastic at holding an audience. Whether it is 10,000, 1000 or 100, it doesn't matter. He is hypnotic.'

'Hypnosis? There is no doubt about it,' says David Bernstein. 'When he is talking and when he is doodling you are paying attention to what he says because you have got nothing to look at. All the books on presentation talk about the relationship of the picture to the word. I think you get to a stage where you are sort of lulled.'

'He is so charismatic and delightful, people are drawn to him in droves,' says Diane McQuaig. 'People, no matter where he goes, are mesmerised by him and want to be a part of what he does.'

As noted above, however, you have to have an interest, as Linda Laird once discovered:

> He has this lovely lilting voice – if you are tired, and lose concentration, Goodnight! I remember once in South Africa we were at a seminar and this girl, quite a pretty girl, who seemed to have attached herself to Edward because of his wealth and intellectual capacity (she wasn't particularly intelligent herself), sat up on the stage. He was doing his normal talk in the middle with his little projector and she was over on the right-hand side, and she started to nod off in the middle of it! So, her head's bopping up and down on the stage as she's falling asleep, and Edward can't see her because she was behind him, but everybody else sees nothing else! There are 250 people in the theatre, watching her nodding, waiting for her to fall asleep. When she does, her head dips forward and she wakes herself up, realises where she is and runs off the stage!
>
> He tends to take these butterflies under his wing a bit and say, 'Now, I'll set you on the right road, love,' and when he realises it is not quite happening, he can't get rid of them, y'know? Over the latter years with Edward, we have learned of a lot of these people, some who are still good to him and some who are not.

According to one of Edward's early secretaries, he had girls chasing him the length and breadth of the world. 'I dealt with those. Put them off! Put them off!' she said. 'I think I'd back him against Clinton. I think

Edward would have the edge. No, I am not giving you names. We would be here till next year!'

In a sense, all teachers, doctors, politicians are in the seduction business. Some are better at it than others, and the talent for it does not invalidate the content. 'You can propel a heavy ball across a sponge surface by pushing the ball,' says Edward, 'or by depressing the surface just ahead of the ball, thus leading it forward.'

'He *is* the complete manipulator,' said Edna Copley, 'but then he manipulates the *best* out of you.' He understands how the mind works and how ultimately effectively to communicate and alter his audience's perceptions. With that understanding comes a responsibility, which he discharges to the full in both public and private life. 'He has great respect,' one of his closest female associates since the late 1980s said to me.

> Edward is always a gentleman. He would never harm or push or demand anything from any woman. If there is ever a man you want to be safe with, he is the one. He has respect for you as a person, as an independent person. Whatever most men think they're doing when they are respectful, they don't really understand it. Edward does. The problem for some people is that respect, independence, while it does masses for your self-esteem, sort of puts him out of reach of your emotions. Everything is fine until he leaves. Suddenly he has gone and the emotions come roaring into play. That is where Edward's problems can start.

Chapter Eight

The Venezuelan Experiment

'What Edward de Bono is doing to teach people how to think may be the most important thing going on in the world today.' Professor George Gallup

The place is Maracaibo, the second largest city in Venezuela. This is a meeting of about twenty people – doctors, parents, government officials – to discuss the setting up of a new medical centre. For some time the arguments flow back and forth. Then, a ten-year-old boy who has been sitting at the back of the room waiting for his mother approaches the table and says, 'Why don't you do an AGO, then an APC and a FIP, and finish off with an OPV?'

The boy wasn't being a smartarse. He had participated in the routine thinking skills programme compulsory for all schoolchildren in Venezuela, and the skills were second nature to him. The group followed his advice and in a short while the meeting had a plan.

Edward used to tell this story. Whether it happened exactly like that I cannot say, but it attaches to an educational revolution in Venezuela which happened in 1979. It was the brainchild of one Luis Alberto Machado, and the reverberations of it may still be felt today.

Says Edward, 'The story of Machado is an interesting one. He was professor of philosophy at the University of Caracas. He read my book *The Mechanism of Mind*, and became interested.'

In 1979, the Social Christian Party of Luis Hererra came to power in Venezuela, and through a longstanding friendship with Hererra, Machado was given a ministry in the new government.

'They said, what ministry do you want?' Edward recalls. 'And he said, "I want a Ministry for the Development of Intelligence." There were all sorts of roars of laughter and, "What about a Ministry of Stupidity?"'

Nevertheless, the ministry went forward and Machado set out to deliver his project: 'to increase the level of personal and social self-fulfilment of Venezuelans, so that they may act with paramount intelligence, skill, ability, sensitivity, and creativity.'

Edward continues:

> Then Machado was at a Club of Rome meeting in Austria, either in Salzburg or Vienna, and he said, 'Does anyone know de Bono?' Whereupon Robert Maxwell, who was at the meeting, said, 'Oh yes, a great friend of mine,' though we had never met before. So it was that Maxwell invited Machado and me for dinner at Headington Hall in Oxford, and Machado said to me, 'I have got this new ministry and I don't know what to do.' So he translated CoRT and invited me over, and first I trained fifty local teachers, then I trained another 200 teachers in the public and technical institutes, and the Venezuelans then set up their own seminars and in four years had trained 105,000 teachers. And it then became compulsory in all schools. The Venezuelan project was the impetus for the current interest in teaching thinking in the United States.

After he had established the programme in Venezuela, Edward could announce that –

> Venezuela has become the first country in the world, and in history, to put the teaching of thinking skills directly on to the school curriculum as a subject in its own right. The programme being used is the CoRT Thinking Program, adapted to local use by Dr Sanchez, who is also in charge of the project. The Cognitive Research Trust provided initial training and continued training during the pilot stage. So successful was the pilot project that the Minister of Education, Dr Rafael Fernandez Heres, decided to put the programme into all schools at grades 4, 5 and 6. The project will involve the training of 42,000 teachers and the teaching of thinking skills to 1.5 million schoolchildren . . .

Machado is a man of passion. Besides being a professor of philosophy and a politician, he is a poet. As Edward puts it, 'He is a very driven fellow.' What fired Machado was his own conviction that intelligence is not inherited and that the myth that it *is* has enslaved whole portions of the population. In 1978, his beliefs were set out in his book, *The Right to be Intelligent*. He sees the existence of social classes as dependent on –

and membership of them determined by – 'the degree of development of intelligence,' and he set out to reverse that process in Venezuela.

We are dealing with an important context here. Fourteen years earlier, in London, tests claiming to show that intelligence was in fact hereditary, which had been carried out by Sir Cyril Burt, the daddy of educational psychology in Britain and the Commonwealth and first Chair in Educational Psychology at the University of London, were put in the dock. Their validity was challenged and found wanting. In a sense, as the educationalist Bill Maxwell suggested to me, 'You could see the whole de Bono phenomenon, which kicked off a year later, as a response to this. Now, Machado was definitely batting on the new wicket.'

Matt Ridley's recent bestseller, *Genome: The Autobiography of a Species in 23 Chapters* (1999), picks one newly discovered gene from each of the twenty-three pairs of human chromosomes in an attempt to tell us who we are. Chapter 6 tackles chromosome 6, which, following work done by Robert Plomin and published in 1997, we are to believe is the home of the 'intelligence gene'. This, however, turned out to be an uncertain description because Plomin's work was based on a study of kids with very high IQs, and pre-empted what IQ tests actually measure.

When one reads books like this, it is easy to see why Edward shies away from arguments of description. No one even seems able to agree what 'intelligence' means. Ridley fails to come up with any startlingly new evidence, but his final thrust is a nice twist on the nature/nurture argument, suggesting that 'the environment that a child experiences is as much a consequence of the child's genes as it is of external factors: the child [my italics] *seeks out and creates his or her own environment*,' which is more or less the conclusion I came to in the case of the child Edward. Overall, Ridley sides with those who hold that 'the genes may create an appetite, not an aptitude,' which he calls 'a richly satisfying end' to a century of argument.

Despite what Bill Maxwell suggests about the overthrow of Sir Cyril Burt and the way being left open for Edward's skills-based programmes, Edward avoids being sucked into nature/nurture arguments. One evaluation of CoRT, published by a university in Bulgaria, claimed that CoRT increased IQ ratings (whatever they show), but Edward's focus was elsewhere. Intelligence is the potential of the mind, probably determined by the speed of transmission along the neurons, while thinking is a skill anyone can learn. 'Many people regard thinking as if it were no more than intelligence in action, in the same way that bounce is a rubber ball in action,' he says. 'We do better if we regard innate intelligence as comparable to the engineering of a car – the horsepower and so on – and thinking as a driving skill. Then you may get a powerful car driven badly. Or you may get a humble car driven well. Thinking is the *operating skill* that makes the difference.'

He had found a use for that boyhood interest in cars after all. CoRT was like new software for the brain. Who has what measure of intelligence to begin with, how or why, is not Edward's point. The CoRT tools aim to apply native intelligence more effectively. They do *not* seek to develop the learner's intelligence as such. How deeply Machado understood this about Edward's programme, when he paid him $40,000 to change the education of a country, is, as later events would show, open to question. It is not easy to escape the IQ culture, as sometime editor of the *Times Educational Supplement*, Stuart Maclure, once noted. Still, there was certainly nothing in Edward's storecupboard to prejudice Machado's venture. On the contrary, as Machado's assistant all those years ago, Beatricz Capdeville, told me, CoRT was precisely what was needed in Venezuelan schools.

Said Capdeville:

> The way we worked that time was that there was the Minister, which was Luis Alberto Machado, and then there were three directors. I was there also as the assistant of the Minister. I was like a co-ordinator at the level of the office of the Minister. I co-ordinated the relationships and the communications between the three directors. I became a friend of de Bono and still am. I was trained by him.
>
> I was in my twenties at the time of the Venezuela project. De Bono's part of it was very successful. The director in charge of the de Bono project was Dr Marguerita Sanchez. She was in charge of all the projects in the school system. We used the Venezuelan version of CoRT, which was called *Learning How to Think*. We used it in the primary levels, and in that project we trained more or less 100,000 teachers in four years. That was our goal and we did meet that goal. I met Bill Copley once but he only came at the beginning. After that we used de Bono directly to finish training the facilitators. Actually we called them multiplicators, multipliers – they were the ones, a small group, who then trained the teachers.

Dr Sanchez later reported on Edward's project – 'After the course, not only did the volume of these children's ideas increase by 50 per cent, but 98 per cent of their contributions were relevant to the subject.'

Aware of the revolutionary nature of what was going on, Edward fired the interest of Marjorie Wallace, who by now was a member of the award-winning, investigative *Sunday Times* Insight Team. She said,

> I go out to the Montreal Conference [a conference in 1981 organised by Norah Maier] and meet Machado. I remember Machado very, very well. He wrote me the most romantic letters. Very amusing story – of him coming through my bedroom window in the Hilton Hotel. All quite jolly. Machado wrote the most beautiful poems. He used to write poems to me. Don't ask me why, I was prettier then. I had an extraordinary time with him, absolutely bizarre time. He was a very eccentric man, very eccentric. Machado believes love is even more essential to increasing intelligence than the techniques he is teaching.

Says Maier of the Montreal Conference: 'I was one of the founders of the World Council for the Gifted and Talented and we have this biennial conference. We had a conference in 1979 in Israel, where I spoke about Edward's work and insisted he be invited to Montreal in 1981. I was part of the organising committee. So I brought him there, and I have a wonderful picture of him, Machado and myself, where he gives the keynote address, and Machado talks about how important his work was to Venezuela.'

Machado then invited Wallace to Venezuela. 'I arrived at Caracas and nobody had told me that I needed a visa.' Although her eventual article, which ran to many pages, appeared in the *Sunday Times Magazine*, they hadn't actually commissioned it, so Wallace was very much on her own.

> I had pushed it on the *Sunday Times* by saying I was going anyway and I think Edward got my fare paid – Economy! – through the Cognitive Trust. The *Sunday Times* didn't pay for me. I was a young thrusting journalist, I was finding my own stories everywhere. What I tried to sell to the magazine was that if I went under my own steam, would they accept a story? They said, No, because they were the most arrogant group of journalists that you have ever met in your life.
>
> So, I arrive at Caracas, and they won't let me in. No visa. And I sat at the airport and didn't know what to do. They wouldn't let me in. I didn't want to go back. Finally, I got hold of Machado at the government building and he sent a car for me. I still didn't have

permission to get in, so I went to see Luis Machado. By this time I am really knackered and I think I am going to get some wine and some food. This was serious, high, Venezuelan rich country! I am shown into this room on Government Hill or whatever and I sit looking at this aesthete, who offers me a glass of water, *warm* water! He then talks to me about life, love, poetry, the cosmos, while I am dying of misery. And then he says, 'Do you mind if I have my supper?' And I say, 'No,' thinking, 'No, no, anything rather than be thrown out of the country on a plane.' I was so tired. So he sits in this dusty office, with this little bit of mashed potato, while I sip the warm water. That was my dinner in the wealthy centre of Caracas. However, he managed to fix it so that I got into the country.

I went to the Hilton having not eaten anything. He said he'd come with his poems later on, which he did, through the window because he was a minister. Anyway, nothing happened. He was very nice and his poems were very sweet. He was just a bit difficult to take when you have had all these problems getting into the country and you haven't eaten and you are quite worn out. The whole philosophy of enlightenment is a bit remote when you just want a shower and a good bed. I stayed a week.

The sheer scale of this project, which Wallace then went to investigate, was extraordinary, and Edward's programme was but one of the elements. Said Capdeville:

Altogether it was a dramatic enterprise. We were reaching different levels. At that time we had the Family Project up from birth to six years, and that was like pre-school but not only pre-school, even family life. Then we had the whole educational system – primary level, secondary level and pre-university, and at various stages we used de Bono. Then we also had Feuerstein materials, which we used at the higher levels of primary school. Then we had the whole adult formal educational world, where we were addressing different occupations. For example, labourers in the different public companies, like aluminium, electricity, we also used the de Bono method in the army for about two years. And then we had a whole group of programmes through the media, through TV. But what was really successful was the application of de Bono in the schools system.

Reuven Feuerstein, an Israeli psychologist-educator, derived his Instrumental Enrichment programmes in response to post-war immigration into Israel of large numbers of people deemed to be socially or economically disadvantaged. His method faces the student with complicated problem-solving tasks and exercises, grouped in fourteen specific areas of cognitive development, and requires a 'mediator' (a teacher) always to be present to prompt responses. Much is said to depend on the quality of mediation. Like Edward's CoRT tools, Feuerstein's exercises are devoid of curriculum subject matter.

The so-called Family Project sets, more dramatically, the wider context in which Machado's revolution was taking place. It took a lot from Glenn Doman's methods at the Institutes for the Achievement of Human Potential. The institutes seek to enhance 'brain growth', which sounds quite alarming in itself, through visual, auditory and tactile stimulation.

Marjorie Wallace recalled:

> When I went to investigate Glenn Doman, I went to just south of Chicago, where they had a whole village, a whole commune dedicated to turning their babies into geniuses. I spent a week there. They would spend their days and nights collecting bits of information. You took your baby of about three months and you showed them a Manet and a Monet and the baby could tell the difference. Parents would come for a week and learn to turn their baby into a genius. He used to take brain-damaged children and make them walk and talk. This was part of this scenario of the 1980s, that you can take a brain-injured child, as they call it, take it from that state to blinking, or you could take an ordinary child and turn it into an Einstein or a Mozart. That was the theory.
>
> In Venezuela, I went round to all the people – some of them were really delightful and really good people – [whom] Machado had arranged to do the programme. Venezuelan grandees, aristocrats. And I looked at the babies [in the Family Project]. I was going into the tiny little squats, where they would have $E=MC^2$ and a tiny baby looking at this, and there is no bedroom or kitchen.
>
> I went to the hospitals, where all these babies were being born and were all on trolleys – you know, Third World medicine.

She saw the mothers in maternity units stimulating their babies, bathing them alternately in hot and cold water, squeezing a drop of lemon juice onto their tongues, playing them music, and so on. She described the scene at the Concepción Palacios (the main maternity hospital in

Caracas) – the reality of Machado's wild enthusiasms – as crammed with mothers from the shanty towns on the fringe of the city, 'with battered, exhausted faces [lying] on sheets stained with blood.' Poor hygiene, few drugs, women screaming their way through labour, and suddenly a TV set appears on five-foot legs and someone plugs in a video to 'teach the often illiterate mothers how to improve their babies' minds'.

Wallace's judgement of this extraordinary experiment was naturally affected by the dire poverty and deprivation, the hopeless housing, the garbage-infested conditions, which she saw all around: 'My immediate view, as a cynical journalist, was that this was an amazing delusion, but the article was supportive because what I said was, "Better to do something than nothing."'

All of it was justified in the context, she says today, but *only* in that context. And she insists that I place Edward's project in the same context, because Machado had: 'We are talking about a whole movement. Machado scoured every possible hot housing scheme round the world, from Suzuki to Glenn Doman. He looked at all these accelerating intelligence programmes and chose Edward for one part of it. It was a sweeping exercise and they came up with a patchwork of all the best of the programmes at every level.'

Wallace's article, 'Elite Babies, Weapons for the Future', was sensitive to the situation in Venezuela, but there was a science fiction dash to it that encouraged readers to question the ethics of such wholesale social intervention. The perception of a link between the cognitive education movement – thinking as part of the school curriculum – and the more bizarre developmental intervention programmes, however, unfairly tars Edward's CoRT with the desperate eccentricity of the Family Project.

In my opinion, this link never existed, except perhaps in Machado's driven mind. Glenn Doman had established his methods as early as 1955; there was nothing new about them, and outside (even inside) Venezuela, people directing the schools thinking programmes were not connected to Glenn Doman or to any of the programmes in Venezuela that taught illiterate mothers how to turn their babies into geniuses. Moreover, the concept of elitism was precisely what Edward's mission eschewed. CoRT is about levelling the playing field. It is a practical, pragmatic method, designed to give every individual control. It does not turn out geniuses, nor was it designed to. It is concerned with raising self-esteem at remedial level and slowing genius down – 'Gifted children need to slow down,' he has said. So, the charge of elitism is badly misplaced.

The following extract from Wallace's article, which deals specifically with the de Bono project, is not, indeed, at odds with my view:

> An exuberant young instructor wades through the excited children. 'We have a problem,' she announces. 'What shall we do about all the rubbish which surrounds our homes?' The children talk excitedly and there is a rash of raised hands. 'We should do a CAF,' says one girl. 'Why don't we do an APC?' says another child. Each group suggests a different thinking tool. Soon solutions emerge.
>
> 'We should ask the government to clear it up. We should make a deputation to the president,' says the spokesman for one group. Another group objects. 'The president is irrelevant,' they shout. An important part of the 'learning to think' philosophy is that whatever happens is the individual's responsibility and should be under his control.
>
> Other children put forward ideas of forming a community policing system. Fining offenders is suggested, but later rejected as impossible to enforce. The children then apply a C&S, listing all possible short, medium and long-term results of any proposed action.
>
> Should it be a crime to drop litter? If that involved a prison sentence, then the prisons which are already full would be overcrowded. Should a democratic country like Venezuela limit freedom by creating more rules? What if they just left the garbage? 'People would get sick and die,' the children reply. Should they look at it from other people's point of view (an OPV)? 'It would be negative for all the flies.' 'If the garbage were all cleared away they would have nothing left to stand on.'

And the age of these children? They were boys and girls aged nine. Suddenly the story that Edward used to tell about the ten-year-old who intervened at that meeting in Maracaibo seems wholly plausible. Edward's dearest memory from these days, however, is of a class in which a disturbed Venezuelan girl spent most lessons sitting under a piano. 'Her teachers had given up on her. Then, now and again in my thinking lessons, from under the piano would come a suggestion, then another. Eventually she came out of hiding and became the star of the class.'

In North American schools, the real groundswell of interest in teaching thinking began in the 1980s and was sparked by Edward, greatly boosted by the Venezuelan experiment. 'Maybe the most important impact [of our project in 1979] was not inside Venezuela but outside,'

Capdeville said to me. 'I think the movement that took place at that time in Venezuela – this is not said only by me but by David Perkins at Harvard, for example – pushed forward the issue about thinking skills. That really made an impact. The fact that Venezuela at that time took it so seriously made a big effect outside.'

Certainly, both in North and South America, cognitive education and creativity have, since then, featured on the educational map. Also, in 1980, the time was ripe for thinking to come onto the curriculum. In that year, Professor George Gallup wrote:

> In the annual surveys of the public's attitudes toward the schools in the United States, conducted by the Gallup Poll, we find that of all the goals of education, teaching students to think is always rated as the very most important by the public. And yet, in the United States and elsewhere, one finds little or nothing being done on a systematic basis to teach students to think.

Maier records how high energies were running at a conference in North America soon after leaving Edward in Europe in 1979/1980:

> I was supposed to deliver at a conference here in the States on creativity. I had planned to deliver on make-me-feel-good-inspire-me-creativity, which was the North American approach, and through the Cognitive Research Trust, and in particular through lateral thinking, I saw there was a deliberate, structured and very logical way of teaching creativity. At the end of that lecture, a man rushed up to me – he was the principal of a high school here, a high school of 1,500 pupils. 'Norah,' he said, 'I want to grab you while you are still cheap!' So I mentally put my price up, and he said, 'I want you to bring about change in my whole staff. I want you to do a three-day seminar at a hotel and introduce lateral thinking and the tools.' He was particularly interested in Alternatives, Possibilities, Choices (APC). He said, 'My staff are so anti-change and don't look at alternatives . . . I would like to do something with that.' So, I drove out in a snowstorm for a meeting with their planning committee, and there was one woman who cried, 'I will never forgive my educational system for not teaching me how to think.' That moved me deeply . . .

What Machado's combining of the various programmes also did, which was extremely useful, was to bring to the forefront the question of what we mean by intelligence, and the thought that perhaps IQ tests only examine one element of it. One project in particular, which was going on outside the classroom experimentation, developed this more than any other, and concerned the Suzuki methodology.

In May 1979 Machado took a group of thirty-five Pemones Indians from the Amazon basin and said that in two months they would have learned how to play the violin with sufficient talent to give a gala concert at the Caracas Concert Hall. These Indians had never even seen a violin before, and come the night of the concert there was some nailbiting about whether Machado would deliver to an auditorium packed to capacity. In came the thirty-five Pemones Indians with violins tucked under their chins. Up stood a conductor and the players let rip with . . . *Twinkle, Twinkle, Little Star.* There followed some simple pieces by their teacher, Takeshi Kobaskaya, then Haydn's Tenth Symphony, and finally, to a standing ovation, Beethoven's Ninth Symphony: *Ode to Joy.* It was a triumph not only for Machado and Hererra's new government, but for the teachers of the Indians who had used a special adaptation of the Japanese Suzuki method.

Five hundred miles from the city at La Puerta in the mountain foothills another project was in full swing. In a music school made out of an old Spanish monastery, a troupe of youngsters with every instrument under the sun – 'the noise was indescribable,' wrote Wallace, 'a cacophany of scraping and squeaking and banging' – were part of the Integral Creativity Programme, which went hand-in-hand with a pilot scheme teaching 'integral creativity' to eighty fourth-graders selected at random from Venezuela's poor. Wallace was amazed at the bizarre scenes that she saw and the mechanistic notion of talent that was implicit, but she was also knocked out by some of the responses she witnessed, like the child in the playground, clutching his violin, then 'playing his latest composition', while his headmaster told her how little Hugo had only recently had 'severe behavioural problems . . . We could scarcely cope with him. When he got his violin he seemed to identify with it and treat it as a friend.'

The whole idea of treating musical talent as a form of intelligence was later developed by Harvard University's Howard Gardner, one of the first people to be awarded the MacArthur Foundation scholarship. His book *Frames of Mind*, which I have already mentioned, was published in 1983. Gardner's 'Seven Intelligences' are Linguistic, Musical, Logical-mathematical, Spatial (art, architecture), Bodily-kinesthetic (dance, sport), Interpersonal (relationships with others) and Intrapersonal (handling oneself, awareness). It is an attempt to redefine intelligence, take it out of the straightjacket of IQ, give it to everyone, irrespective of genes. Which is precisely where Machado began.

When, in 1984, the Social Christian Party ceded power in Venezuela to the Democratic Action Party of Dr Jaime Lusinchi, one of Lusinchi's first acts was to abolish the Ministry for the Development of Intelligence. However, thinking lessons were by then compulsory in all schools, and though the ministry was closed, the programme became part of the Ministry of Education. Machado, though no longer in government, and Capdeville are both still involved today.

'Machado is less than 65 and is very well,' Beatricz reassured me.

He looks older because he is bald. But he is very healthy. He continues to be part of our Board of Directors. He is Director of the Board. He was written three books in the last two years, and he is an adviser to businessmen here.

For me what was really successful at the time was the application of de Bono in the schools system because even now, which is almost sixteen years afterwards ... many of the teachers I work with were trained at that time. And they have said that even though the government did not continue, they used the same strategies to teach, because they really thought they helped and the children responded well. Sadly, there was no follow-up at the time. We did massive training, and I think the training itself was quite good, but there was no way of reaching the teachers again to follow up, because there were so many. Today we are going in at a much slower pace but we are doing things more thoroughly. I am not talking about the method itself, but how it was applied in Venezuela.

Today, we are doing it specifically in two states in Venezuela. We are not doing it through the Ministry of Education, as we did the first time. We are doing it more at the regional level, in Miranda and Zulia, through our foundation, a trust, the Foundation for Educational Excellence. I think it is much better this way.

Since the early 1980s, Edward has introduced the Six Hats programme, which, as we will see, is a thinking structure designed to give a comprehensive exploration of a subject, rather than a programme of separate tools like CoRT. Often the CoRT tools are used within the Six Hats framework, as, for example, they are used in the TOLOPOSOGO structure (page 143). Beatricz Capdeville told me that one of her Foundation's international advisers, Arthur Costa of the University of California, recently returned from a survey of the Venezuelan schools to report that 'in every classroom, and we have more than 3,000 classrooms with our programme, he saw posters of Six Hats. It is something that has become a normal language here. I am not sure Edward is aware of that.'

As we have seen, by 1980, Edward, through Machado, had not only put thinking on the curriculum map in Venezuela, but had made it an issue beyond that country. Crucially, in that very same year in North America, the Association for the Supervision of Curriculum Development (ASCD) Conference – the big United States conference on the school curriculum – for the first time put up 'thinking' as its theme, and Edward and Machado were the focus. As Professor Maier, who attended the conference, recalls: 'They were so obviously taken with Edward's work and with the whole movement, because Machado was there, the Project Zero people were there . . .'

The significance of this should not be understated. The ASCD had the power to bring thinking on to the curriculum of the most powerful country in the world. Says Maier: 'That was really the beginning of an American breakthrough. They then organised a weekend for top people – there were about thirty people from the States and myself from Canada – it was the Wingspread Conference, whereby they discussed how to put thinking onto the map in North America. I was amazed at how quickly things moved, considering how large, complex and varied is the United States. But once the ASCD picked something up, it went forward.

'So, they adopted it and they decided to create materials and make it a big force, and ever after that of course it was on their conference agenda as well. When you are talking about a big movement that's what it was all about.'

So, why did Edward not attend these conferences? If, as Maier suggests, he was truly the toast of the town, why wasn't he there? 'Edward couldn't make it,' she said to me, 'and I was asked to take his place.'

This is euphemism. Edward's project in Venezuela was the first anywhere in the world to include thinking on the curriculum nationally. According to Beatricz Capdeville and David Perkins of Harvard's Project Zero, it had been such a success that it had 'pushed foward the issue about thinking skills' in North America. But the sad truth is that Edward did not even receive an invitation to these crucial conferences to design a way forward in the US. Said Bill Maxwell: 'The establishment lot hijacked everything.' The academic establishment closed ranks, it would seem, and squeezed out the maverick innovator.

Relationships that persist to this day in this field of teaching thinking in schools were forged at this time. Through the 1980s, in the United States, the strong push for a focus on teaching thinking came through ASCD under the presidency of Arthur Costa, professor emeritus at California State University, Sacramento, the man who is, according to Beatricz Capdeville, an adviser to the Foundation for Educational Excellence, which has Machado as board director and is implementing Edward's programmes in Venezuela today.

Back in 1980, however, others were looking to replace Edward's work. Within two years there was a rival thinking programme in Venezuela, commissioned by Machado – this despite the success of Edward's programmes, still acclaimed even by his rivals. Politically, a link with the US educational establishment made sense for the Venezuelan government. De Bono – brilliant stuff, but a bit of a wild card and no organisation behind him. Project Zero, on the other hand, had the backing of Harvard. They were institutional people, whereas Edward had no institution – he was not representing Cambridge University in this – he was a one-man show and would always remain a one-man show. It is not difficult to see why, following the 1980 conference, an alliance between Harvard and the Venezuelan government looked promising. But it was a bit tough, given his contribution, for Edward to have been excluded from the party.

One evening in Malta, when I was having dinner with a de Bono master trainer who knows Edward well, I asked about the legendary Maltese *shrug*, which Edward had described to me as 'a disconnection from compulsions'. Without hesitation she called over our waiter and said, 'If I were to give you a problem and you couldn't sort it out, what would you do?' The waiter shrugged. There and then he disconnected. 'See!' shrieked my guest. 'The shrug!'

Whether, back in 1980, Edward had simply shrugged as the entire North American education market was snatched from under his nose, I do not know, but Linda Laird has a fundamental grasp of Edward's attitude to those who have supplanted him: 'He is nonplussed by a lot of it – "If that's what they do, that's what they do," y'know? What he hates is when they *change* his work, or add to it. And he is right because if his work gets shuffled around then it becomes weak and loose and there is no substance to it at all.'

Project Zero/Intelligence did not change Edward's work. Nor, in the end, did it replace Edward's work.

In his book, *Outsmarting IQ: The Emerging Science of Learnable Intelligence* (1995), co-director David Perkins writes: 'Project Intelligence emerged from a remarkable national commitment by the government of Venezuela for six years commencing in 1978.' This is unfortunate phraseology, for he would not mean to imply that it was originally responsible for fulfilling the government's remarkable national commitment to teaching thinking in schools, which was Edward's achievement.

The facts are that a course, called, in its English version, Odyssey, was commissioned from Harvard University and the Massachusetts consulting firm of Bolt, Beranek and Newman. But it did not come into play in Venezuela until after Edward had established thinking on the school curriculum nationally. Not until the academic year 1982/3, shortly before a new government put the brakes on Machado's revolution, was the Harvard project even evaluated in Venezuela. Only 'about 900 students were trained in [it], compared to 1.5 million in the CoRT project,' Edward wrote at the time, adding: 'I mention this only because the impression given in the United States is somewhat different.' Moreover, it is Edward's work that has survived.

Project Intelligence, originally Project Zero, had been around since 1971, concerning itself broadly with the psychology and philosophy of education in the arts – good safe descriptive stuff. That its thinking course, Odyssey, should be so utterly traditional was not surprising, but in the context of the strides that had been taken by CoRT, it was the big disappointment. There was an emphasis on critical thinking – traditional observation, classification, analysis and judgement, what Edward used to refer to as 'lawyer-type thinking'. Analysis – the division of something into its constituent parts – is useless for creating anything, such as a new hypothesis, without a crucial element of design, but yet more fundamental was this programme's failure to take cognisance of the crucial priority in any kind of thinking, namely to foster the habit of suspending judgement. It must have seemed to Edward as if those adopting the new programme had failed to understand what his own revolutionary system had been about. The success of CoRT was its simplicity, its practicality, its appeal across ages, abilities and cultures, its training in thinking skills required in real life, its independence of a knowledge base and its ready transferability to real-life situations, which represented a complete paradigm shift in education.

'To be of any use a thinking skills programme must provide skills that are transferred right out of the classroom and out of the school itself into life outside and after school,' Edward wrote. His point was that otherwise you are just giving kids a simple descriptive course in psychology. 'That is why I consider the Harvard case-study method rather inadequate as a teaching device. The more interesting the case the more difficult it is for any attention to be paid directly to the thinking process that is being used. It is excellent for motivation, but the thinking skills acquired in tackling one information-rich problem are not easily transferred to other, different problems. Nor should we suppose that skills acquired in abstract mental processes carry over into real-life situations.'

Edward questioned Harvard's traditional 'analytical classification' approach in deciding on what topics (or abstract mental processes) to teach. They had failed to appreciate the essential difference between the old analytical (reductionist) approach and Edward's new system-based operational approach. 'We can analyse what we perceive to be the components of the thinking process and then we can attempt to train each of these components ... Alternatively we can analyse what people seem to be doing when asked to think about some laboratory task and then dissect the process into trainable segments. In both these cases we produce a functional classification and then attempt to train that classification. The weakness of the method is that description is quite distinct from operation.' Edward's alternative had been to teach the mental processes by doing them.

To Edward, teaching 'observation' *per se*, which is part of Odyssey's Topic 1, *Foundations of Reasoning*, is not useful. Even if observation is a key part of the thinking process, it can only be described and classified in a philosophically tidy sort of way, which has no *operational value*. To be of any use, we should ask, for example, 'What do you like and what do you not like about X?' So, instead of describing an abstract process we rehearse pupils in *declaring a preference*, which entails observation. Observation then becomes a by-product of something that is, in practical terms, trainable.

'It is on considerations such as these that the CoRT method is based,' says Edward. 'The tools are not derived from description but from *operational ease*. We can analyse a square by saying that it is made up of four corners and four sides – but in practice we do not draw it like that.'

That Machado took on Odyssey shows that he failed to realise this vital distinction, that he had not understood what in Edward's CoRT tools he had lucked into.

A few years later, in 1982, at the aforementioned first International Conference on Thinking in Fiji, John McPeck criticised CoRT for failing to recognise that there are many more types of thinking than the practical, constructive, design thinking of CoRT I. In fact, there are five other books of lessons that go to make up CoRT, but these are often overlooked because CoRT I is so useable, popular and practical. These books cover such traditional abstract mental processes as analysis, comparison, and selection, but they are dealt with by Edward in practical, constructive, design-thinking mode.

For example, when discussing analysis and comparison, the lessons demand active examination of an object or of situations. 'This is how analysis works, let's see if we can *apply* that process on this situation.' Two methods of analysis emerge – analysing into parts that can be seen (wheels, brakes, handlebars of a bike), and into aspects that can be perceived (the bike's cost, comfort, safety). Similarly, in comparison, attention is directed through application to aspects that two situations have in common and features that they do not share. Again, the emphasis is on examining these aspects and features rather than categorising them, so that the situation is kept free of conceptual category bias until after the true, broad perceptual work can be done.

Always retaining the possibility to move forward in perception is paramount. To illustrate this style of analytical thinking, Edward tells of a farmer who instructs his son to divide apples into two boxes, sorting the small from the big. The son does so, examining each carefully to judge which might be reckoned small and which big, naturally enough discarding a number of bad apples along the way. The farmer returns and praises the boy for his efforts, then puts big and small apples together into one container. The boy is furious at the waste of his time, but the farmer explains that the boxing task was merely a device to ensure that each apple would be examined carefully and any bad ones discarded. The process of analysis, compare, select is a useful device by which we can get close to information before organising perception. That is all.

CoRT *Book III: Interaction* looks at argument and discussion, picking up on a fundamental willingness to look at alternatives and at other people's views. Here is the basis for his later concept of parallel thinking, and the Six Hats programme. It is grounded in the escape and movement values of lateral thinking and in the breadth of perception engendered in CoRT *Book I*.

Underlying the Books and CoRT *Book V: Information & Feeling* is the essential dichotomy between judgement and movement. Judgement recognises, identifies, locates and keeps us within the pattern in which we are thinking, which is fine – we need to do it. Movement is an idiomatic change of gear, used to skip across patterns and find alternatives, realise other people's views, new possibilities, the undreamt-of ideas of CoRT *Book IV: Creativity*.

Everything flows from this concept of design thinking. There is no right or wrong, only *ways* to be right and *ways* to be wrong. There are no automatic value-labels for fact and opinion, which would ignore circumstance; only constant allegiance to real-world thinking, and an aversion to absolutist, fundamentalist, boxed-up thinking, which inhibits opportunity and has led, on a global scale, to all sorts of conflict.

CoRT is disinterested, controlled, unemotional, inventive, provocative, projective and emancipating. As, indeed, is Edward. But how he remained controlled when Perkins defined his Topic 6 as 'Inventive Thinking, highlighting the concept of design as a way of developing students' awareness of the inventions all around them and introducing strategies for creative design,' I cannot imagine. This was Edward's central concept.

Edward's whole *modus operandi* is outside the establishment system, and it looks like he made the right choice. CoRT likewise transcends the self-organising system of the mind as meta-system. It provides an active organising framework for thinking. In teaching thinking, describing what the mind does is not enough, even if, like Perkins, you exemplify what it does in case studies. Edward's design concept is all about skills, action and operacy. This fundamental point about the revolution in thinking Machado and Perkins failed fully to grasp, retreating safely into description with Project Intelligence and Odyssey.

Edward shrugged, sniffed the air, and in design mode moved on, narrowing his focus for a while, rearranging his diary and leaving the rest to preen themselves at conferences and win jealous plaudits from campus colleagues.

Chapter Nine

Expansion

'De Bono stands alone totally and goes at it alone totally.'
Professor Norah Maier

'Imagine a planet going about its proper business. It is constantly passing through different relationships, transitions, phases and temporary states.' This, or something like it, is Edward's 'out-of-this-world' self-image. So it was perfectly appropriate that when the European Creativity Association canvassed its members as to who had most influenced them in terms of their thinking, Edward came out far ahead of the rest of the field. They wrote to the Naming Committee of the International Astronomical Union. They said, 'We think de Bono should have a heavenly body named after him.' The IAU agreed and had a planet, up till then called DE73, renamed EdeBono.

Edward showed me the certificate. 'Who,' I asked, 'are the European Creativity Association?' Was I spoiling a joke? 'They were in existence, went out of existence and came back into existence again,' he said, as if that was all that could be said with certainty. And the Naming Committee of the IAU? 'The thing is that whenever anyone discovers a heavenly body they have ten years to choose to put their own name on it and if they don't, it goes to the Naming Committee. It is absolutely official. This is the official naming committee of the International Astronomical Union, which is part of the Smithsonian in America.'

'Will the planet be your ultimate destination, perhaps?' I ask.

'Well, if you get a little bored with the Starship Enterprise, perhaps you can come to tea.'

It was a wet day in late spring, 2000, that I set off for Edward's island, Tessera, to the north of Venice. This was to be our first interview. You can't miss Tessera, it's the first island you come across by water taxi from

Marco Polo Airport. You sweep right past it on the main track to Venice. As I had been told that I had a slot from 2 pm – 'not a moment before' – to 4 pm or possibly 5 pm ('if all goes well'), I had bought a cheap day return from Stansted, London, and caught a plane which actually landed not at Marco Polo, but at Treviso, 30 kilometres inland. So it was that, as midday approached, I found myself on a bus, in torrential rain, travelling to Piazzale Roma in Venice herself, where I was advised to take a water bus to San Marco, the main Venetian tourist trap. I couldn't have gone more dreadfully wrong.

The isle of Tessera did not figure on my map and no one in San Marco, least of all the taxi drivers, would admit to knowing its whereabouts, confused possibly by my English Italian or because, as I soon discovered, there's another place called Tessera out by the airport. It was only by luck that I chanced upon the wife of the local air traffic controller in a bar and, with the controller's help over the phone, she eventually discovered how to get me there.

A water taxi dropped me, mercifully just a few minutes before 2 pm, on Edward's jetty, a short wooden affair. The rain had stopped, the sun was out, the lagoon was blue and I turned from watching the taxi speed off back to Venice to face a truly beautiful sight. The island is packed up to the shore with plants and pinkish hacienda-style masonry, being very small and containing just three 18th-century villas, one with a bell tower. It was inhabited when Venice was still a swamp, before the decline of the Roman empire, and there remain a number of ancient columns from that era. At the far end of the jetty stand iron gates and a sign, which warned me of a pair of rottweilers, plus a smaller sign saying Fondazione Edward de Bono – which at least reassured me that I was in the right place. On walking up to and trying the gates, however, I discovered that they were locked. I pressed a bell nearby. Nothing.

Paddy Hills had told me that I would be arriving as Edward's son, Caspar, was leaving, which was why I should not be early, so I assumed that Edward had taken him by boat to the airport and would be back at any moment. I had a camera, so I started using it. Looking about, my eye was caught by a rose garden, which stretches beyond the gates across to the farthest building. Time passed, five, ten, fifteen minutes, and it occurred to me that if Edward had been called away, or perhaps forgotten that I was coming, no one would have been able to let me know. I was surrounded on three sides by water. I had Edward's schedule and knew that it would be two or three months before anyone returned to the island. I had packed no telephone and signalling by semaphore across the 4 kilometres to Venice, or at the speedboat surf of a passing water taxi, seemed a rather hopeless prospect.

I tried the gates again. They were definitely shut fast. Then, on peering through them, I noticed in the distance a figure shuffling slowly, even painfully, towards the farthest building. I called 'Hello!' The figure stopped, as if it had heard me, but then moved on. It didn't seem to be Edward, the gait was too slow, too shuffling. I called again, louder, 'Hello! Hi!' The figure stopped again, and this time cocked its head as if having heard something, though not from my direction. And then disappeared into the house.

With a growing sense of absurdity and indignation I became more determined, pressing the bell and shouting at the same time. Almost at once a face appeared at the window of the villa to my left. It was a large, male, Venetian face, which seemed almost to fill the window. I gesticulated wildly and shook the gates. The Venetian began struggling with his window, but couldn't get it open. A few more minutes passed, with both of us trapped, and then this giant of a man emerged from behind the house and came over. We managed to communicate not at all, but he unlocked the gates and led me up a path towards the building with the bell tower, whence, as we approached, emerged an Italian matron dressed in traditional black. Paddy Hills may have mentioned her. Certainly, I hadn't been expecting her. Nor was her name close to conscious recollection, but it came to me in a flash.

'Giuliana!' I exclaimed, as if I had expected her all along. She and I also understood little of what the other said, but communication was eased by the spontaneity of my greeting and her excited cries of 'Il Professori!' each time I mentioned de Bono's name.

So it was, disturbed by the commotion, that Edward, who had completely forgotten I was coming, emerged from the far house, for it *was* he whom I had surprised, shuffling through the rose garden earlier. Now, he looked more alert, more as I remembered him in London, and I followed him back into the far house. We did the interview and drank pots of tea and ate delicious chocolates and cakes made by Giuliana, who, with her husband Bruno, I now know, attends on Edward when he is in residence.

'The advantage of an island is that it is good for thinking. It induces that feeling of being outside the world and yet still of the world . . . It's a special atmosphere,' said Edward. My first impressions of him that day led me to agree. He had certainly seemed 'outside the world', and how appropriate, indeed, that he should have decided to buy himself an island, given that the story of his life is one of independence, self-reliance and autonomy.

He has himself been an island since childhood and when he left Malta he became yet more cut off. 'Essentially he abandoned the convictions in which he was brought up,' as Father Peter put it. Finally, he broke out of the traditional 'medical' de Bono mould altogether and was further isolated for doing so. Certainly, there was disapproval. Edward recalls, 'My father said, "Stick to medicine. That stuff's nonsense."' Father Peter claims that there was no desperate unhappiness, 'but I remember in those early days meeting his father . . . clearly very disappointed that Edward had not followed the orthodox medical line . . .'

When, in 1982, Edward cut all ties with Cambridge University and Addenbrookes Hospital, there were few raised eyebrows. 'His colleagues would no longer tolerate the absences,' I was told. 'If Edward didn't turn up, somebody had to do the work. It got a bit messy in the end.' His boss, Professor Mills, disagrees, recalling that any hassle was down to the fact that Edward's ideas were far ahead of their time, which attracted antagonism from colleagues. 'He always found it difficult that so much of the academic environment here was against his ideas.'

At the time Edward wrote, 'I am leaving Cambridge University precisely because it is no longer possible to fit "thinking" into the Department of Medicine. Curiously this has been a suitable home because thinking depends on the system behaviour of one part of the body, and I believe that the biological idiom is a more useful entry point than either mathematics or philosophy or computer science. It is not surprising, however, that a medical department should see its role as the practical care of patients rather than broader conceptual issues.'

Cutting loose takes courage of a sort, but not because it made him more alone. Edward was always comfortable with being alone. The 'D' for dependable which he wanted Paddy to allow him was very unusual and, she says, in reality it was limited: 'I don't think he likes *anyone* to feel that they are the ones that he is going to have to be dependent on completely. Hence the islands. It probably goes back to childhood, when he had to learn to be self-sufficient.'

It is *the* most noticeable aspect of his character. He demands the same self-reliance in people with whom he works. 'He gets weary of people expecting him to make things happen once it has been started,' Paddy points out. 'He says, "I do like people to work independently, not depend on me to further the situation."'

When Edward and I had finished the interview that day on Tessera, we stood for a while together on the jetty, waiting for a taxi. It took longer to arrive than expected, so we passed back onto the island and into the building with the bell tower, where a large baize-covered table dominated one room reserved for conferences and occasional thinking retreats. I remembered his manager, Diane McQuaig, telling me about the conference they had convened to launch the island ten years earlier, something like $2 billion in assets sitting around that table. The idea had been to raise funds for educational projects from various charitable foundations shipped in from the United States. All had been fine until 'we discovered too late that the charities they give to have to be local in the United States!' Tom Farrell had told me.

But that is not the point of Tessera. Mainly Edward tends to use it for writing or getting away. 'For me,' he said, 'Tessera is simply the most beautiful place in the world.'

He has a surprising sense of beauty – surprising because it is rarely given public expression. He will extol the sunny beauty of one of his Tessera roses, and can appreciate a more sublime beauty too. Linda Laird told me: 'I looked at an island in Nova Scotia for him. I was going to go over and do it up, but he decided against it. My goodness, Nova Scotia is beautiful. He relates to beauty. Now, the island off West Cork, that is *very* rural, windswept, interesting but wild. That's why I thought he wouldn't want it, but he did.'

On West Skeam, in Rushing Water Bay, he puts his denim jacket on, rolls up his trousers and might not shave for three days. Here, completely untroubled by the world, he can stand on the cliff and, like Caspar David Friedrich's *Traveller*, look out over the great Atlantic sea of fog and indulge Nietzschean thoughts on a more terrible beauty...

He bought Tessera in 1989. 'It was the beginning of a pseudo-obsession with real estate,' says McQuaig, ever in practical mode. 'Actually, [Tessera] came after the New York apartment, which was very exciting because at last he had somewhere in the US to call home. It gave him a lift to be on Central Park South and a part of the hub of the city and having a place to entertain, because he is very gracious and loves his friends. He also has an apartment in Venice on the mainland, an apartment in Australia, and an apartment in London.' And the mews house in South Kensington, I thought. And Cranmer Hall in Norfolk, and of course the other three islands, one in the Bahamas, West Skeam and Little Green Island in Australia, each one reflecting and reinforcing his favourite self-image of autonomy. 'The island is a contained universe,' he says. 'I would rather have a small island than a big estate. It's contained, it is your universe, it is not competitive, you do not have to show off, all these things ... I often say islands are cheaper and less trouble than women. They don't chase after you, they don't mind being neglected, they don't get jealous, they age beautifully.'

So, where is home? One is bound to wonder. Perhaps the answer is that, like Baudelaire's 'passionate spectator', Edward, liking to be 'outside the world', is 'everywhere at home; to see the world, to be at the centre of the world, and yet to remain hidden from the world.'

We walk slowly out of the conference chamber and through the rose garden, mulling over the hundreds of thousands of miles he travels each year. I mention that McQuaig had said, 'He just loves to be on the road.' Edward smiled.

> My work is international. I travel a lot, so I feel international too ... I ought to point out that my idea of 'roots' isn't what I did, where I lived, where I went to school. I don't feel I have to hark back to that for my inspiration. I consider my roots are the things which led up to the work I am doing now, but instead of imagining them like the roots of a tree, I imagine them as tributaries of a river. They don't anchor the river down: they've flowed together to make it what it is. My study of medicine was one of those tributaries ...

The metaphor is exactly the model of the dominant track and sidetracks which he uses to explain lateral thinking, but the itinerancy is genetic, a throwback perhaps to Great-grandpapa Agius, shooting the rapids of the Nile: 'Tony says we are like Arabs and Bedouins,' his sister would say to me. 'We roll our tents up and move. Of course, it is true that this desire has made Edward *totally* without roots. He doesn't even go to Norfolk. It is the children, Caspar, Charlie, who love it there. He just goes for Christmas.'

When I came to speak to son Caspar, I wondered what childhood without a father had been like, and he remembered the times when they were together:

> We used to invent things. I used to ask him for a challenge for something I could make with my Lego set. He'd tell me, you know, to design a car that could climb up that. I remember once it was to design a fly-catching machine, which involved a plastic bottle with

the bottom cut off it, and a balloon that would suck the target fly into it as it inflated, but I don't think it worked. We would do things like that. He'd invent games and we'd play the games. We built an igloo one year at Norfolk, packing all this snow into boxes. That was successful, lit a fire inside so that it would all melt together . . . we invented this game of sticks, various board games, like the 3 Spot game [a board game, three pieces, two players, in which the winner can be the loser], so he tried those out on us, and also we'd help him put together a game to entertain people at adult drinks parties.

Had he, as a child, understood what his father did?

He had thinking weekends at Cranmer Hall and we'd be involved with those and I had been to seminars, and clearly it had come up in conversations all the time. I mean, building with Lego there'd be some kind of, 'Why don't you think about it this way? Why don't you think about it that way?' But in terms of the formal techniques, yes, I think preparation for the Oxford Entrance exam was the first time we had gone through it in detail. I illustrated one of his books recently, *Parallel Thinking*. We had been watching *Life in the Freezer* together and he likes penguins so I said I would illustrate one of his books with them. I think that what he does is quite different . . . [but] he's always been very concerned to emphasise that novelty is only one value.

I think of my childhood in Norfolk, but I liked Malta and it was always an opportunity to see my grandmother. The whole family saw her as the head of the family and rightly so, because she was a strong character, but also very protective as well. I think my father was very fond of her. When she wasn't well, he organised a nurse twenty-four hours a day for her and would go to see her. And he can be quite a private person so that was the best true indicator that he did care. He was never physical with his emotions, but it was always clear that there was a bond there. I think when they were both in good form they enjoyed each other's sense of humour. From our perspective he had quite a respecting relationship as opposed to a peer sort of relationship with her.

What surprised me was the very closeness of the relationship between son and itinerant father, an understanding that Edward would not have given away. Caspar's upbringing has been such that it will never inhibit his confident exploration of the world, but family friends suggest that his mother must take credit for that. 'The boys have done rather well, thanks to Jo-Jo,' Marjorie Wallace said. Caspar attended Harrow, Charlie Eton and on to Edinburgh University to read architecture. Following a 2:1 at Oxford, Caspar took an MBA and works for the *Financial Times*.

'Jo-Jo is carrying this whole thing,' Marjorie went on. 'And Edward is visiting about once a year. Jo-Jo went to all the school days, the prizewinnings . . . You just don't know what that was. Huge! She set up a school for dyslexics in Fakenham.' Caspar had dyslexia as a child. Mrs de Bono denies setting up the school, but agrees that she was supportive of the venture. She is extremely wary of interviewers, complaining of misreporting over the years. She is annoyed in particular by a report that she had lost huge sums of money in the Lloyd's Insurance crash, which I had certainly heard from several sources in great detail. Recently, the press focus shifted her business problems on to Edward, such that a hitch over planning permission on the Norfolk estate was misreported as a case of English Heritage out-manoeuvring the master of lateral thinking, when in fact it has nothing whatever to do with him.

Mrs de Bono is a strong character, sociable, with a good sense of humour. She likes to maintain a certain level of style at Cranmer Hall, where dressing for dinner is expected. She also has a reputation as a gifted designer and is planning to write a book now on the gardens of Malta.

Edward has been quoted as laying the blame for having seen 'relatively little of his own wife and his children' on an upbringing that made him feel less troubled than he might about it. But as Caspar recalled, in the early years Cranmer Hall was a venue for seminars, his parents have been hosts together both in Palazzo Marnisi and Cranmer Hall, and, as in Bulgaria and Scandinavia, Josephine did on occasions participate in Edward's peripatetic lifestyle before it became impractical.

Tom Farrell points out that separation goes with the job: 'My marriage suffered. Even now, the girl I am going to marry, she reminded me the other day that I hadn't been around for a long weekend in eighteen months.'

Had there been a price to pay? I asked Diane McQuaig. 'I don't think for Edward there has. I think Edward is doing exactly what he wants to do. He is really a bit of a chameleon, he takes on the family of where he is.'

Work and play know few boundaries. 'Edward is our friend too,' agrees Linda Low, Singapore distributor.

He comes to our house. I have stayed in his Norfolk home, Cranmer Hall, and we know his wife and his children. In fact the house that we just bought in London, Josephine actually looked at the place before we bought it. When Caspar was in Singapore, on attachment from the *Financial Times*, he worshipped at our church every Sunday to hear Peter's choir. And his younger son stayed with us as well in Singapore. Edward is a boss, a mentor, someone who makes things happen in our life, but he is a personal friend. He is like a grandfather to my children.

But when all's said, what sticks in mind is Norah Maier's incisive comment: 'He stands alone totally and goes at it alone totally.'

After I left Tessera I would begin to pick up on the global scene, where he has 'gone at it' more or less alone for the past thirty years. As he did in the Philippines, in the early days with Tom Farrell. Farrell recalls:

I went up there in 1979 to work with Louis Villafurtea, the Minister for Trade and Industry brought in by President Marcos. I had been there for about six months and decided to bring out Edward. So he met Imelda Marcos and we went to Malacanang, to the palace, and she had a whole evening with all her generals, the public servants and all her friends and the ladies – the blue brigade as we called them. They all wore blue dresses, like a uniform. Anyhow, we went there and then she decided to fly down to Leyte on her BAC 111, and her enormous palace down there. She had her own bedroom in this BAC 111, and on the way down she plays the L Game with Edward and she beat him! He always says he let her win. I always say, 'Edward, I watched the perspiration on the top of your lip!'

We were supposed to be back up two days later for a seminar with some company in Manila, so she decided she would call them and say, 'Dr de Bono is not coming up today. Transfer the seminar to the next day,' and we had an extra day in Leyte. And we danced and we dined and she had him dance this famous dance in the Philippines – they have these two long poles with two guys holding them who keep clacking them together and you have to dance in and out. He has fantastic co-ordination. I couldn't do it, but here he was, the great de Bono dancing in and out of the poles. So back we go and we have a huge dinner for all her friends in the Japanese restaurant that is built within Malacanang.

Today, New York is one of his favourite places. 'He has a lot of very nice friends there,' says Linda Laird, who would travel with him to the States in the mid-1990s, 'some fabulous, really interesting people.' From Australia, Julia Pomirska now runs a global party circuit for her boss in a kind of modern equivalent of the Albany dinners. She says:

It is the part of my work I really enjoy immensely. The parties I have organised for him outside Australia have been in Los Angeles and New York. I do one in LA for him every year. We have a great mix of people, some from the film industry, people like Pat and Michael York, who have become very close friends. I introduced him to Buzz Aldrin so he and his wife, Lois, are always present at the dinners. On the last occasion we also had Eric Idle, Herbie Hancock, Mark Rydell – he's a regular, a film director (*On Golden Pond*, etc). The LA ones are always great fun and we try and loop in new people each time round. Edward plays games, he invents them on the day. People love it, it's not daunting at all. It's a great switch into the fun stuff in his life and it's when he really comes alive. I just see a really happy, relaxed Edward, a man, a human being with his mates.

We just had a brilliant one a week ago in Sydney. We had former prime minister Gough Whitlam, we had Bryce Courtenay, Harry Seidler, one of our acclaimed architects, Harry and his wife Penelope, who is also an architect in her own right. It was held at an Italian restaurant called Lucio's. Lucio was given a special award in Rome for his contribution to Italian food in Australia. It is a great establishment, all the artists used to hang out there in the 1970s. One of my great friends is Tim Olsen, the son of John Olsen, the artist, so Tim came.

Though it is not the main purpose, occasionally there will be a direct spin-off into business. For example, Ron Jones, composer and conductor of the theme music to *Star Trek: The Next Generation*, was called to have lunch with Edward in Los Angeles and ended up contributing the score to Edward's movie, *2040*, an 'unusual' look at the year, with radical ideas how our lives may change. 'I had been reading Edward de Bono's books on lateral thinking as a hobby to increase my ability to understand what's going on here in Hollywood . . . through a friend I was invited to have lunch,' said Jones. 'I am very much into creative processes and use a lot of the techniques he's put out.'

Networking is Julia's speciality.

> Peter Gabriel I met through one of his musicians, Tony Levin, who gave me a call when Peter was in town. After the show, someone came up and said that Peter was interested in Edward's work. So I met him and set up a meeting in LA, a lunch between myself, Peter and Edward. They hit it off. Then Edward invited Peter and some of his staff to a lecture he was giving in Bath [where Peter Gabriel is based] a couple of years ago. So Peter brought some of the guys down, which was pretty cool, to sit there with the rest of the students.

I asked Edward whether there was much take-up in the music scene. 'Interestingly, I was talking to Harvey Goldsmith, and he said, "You would be surprised how many rock groups use your stuff deliberately," – the Eurythmics, the Pet Shop Boys, I have heard.' Peter Gabriel and Edward, I learn, have a mutual friend in the software designer, Kai Krause. 'We met Kai at one of those amazing TED [Technology Entertainment & Design] conferences in America,' Pomirska tells me.

> TED is the best of what's going on in these fields. That's how we met Herbie Hancock also. Kai has just bought a castle in Germany. He lives between Los Angeles and Germany, where he is setting up this incubator for new ideas, bringing people with ideas together (and together with people's money, I guess). Making things happen. Then, in England, I put Edward together with Malcolm McLaren. They seemed to get on quite well, a couple of quirks together, bouncing ideas. Malcolm is such a wild guy, design orientated, designing the future!

But is the circuit – up to 250,000 miles travelling a year – so energising all of the time? I asked Linda Laird, whose experiences with Edward's travelling-suits-for-travelling-people seem a far cry from this cutting-edge rock music, sci-fan, software design scene. 'After a while, most people who travel with Edward find it intensely boring,' she assures me.

> You end up going to the same places continuously, same places, same hotels. For him that's understandable because it is home away from home. But after my tenth trip to Toronto I was fed up with the place. I had no home there, but I seemed to be going there an awful lot. It is unsettling because you can't make any plans at home, and

as a female you are expected to travel with a bag the same size as Edward's! He wears the same suit a lot and he can go to New York or to wherever else and change his clothes, whereas I couldn't! So I was always travelling with a larger suitcase than he, and he found this really mindblowingly annoying. Then of course I shopped all the way because what do you do when you are hanging around hotels all the time? It is very difficult not to shop.

He has a particular seat on the plane and he always seats me on the inside, and if there is a pretty lady he knows getting on the plane then I have to sit in another seat! And he says he is travelling with his grandmother. On the plane he likes to be on his own and be quiet; he does a lot of thinking on the plane. He had his Psion from the early days, and lost a couple on the way, leaving them in taxis or wherever. He used to have a lot of small bags with him and put knots in his hanky because he was always losing them. Very bag-conscious because he has lost so many. I think he has amalgamated them all into one now.

'The travel is extremely gruelling,' agrees Caspar, who accompanied Edward and Tom Farrell on an EC creativity project for the Europe-wide Year of Lifelong Learning in 1996.

It is a very punishing schedule, but when you travel with him he is very much adapted to it. British Airways at one time used to ask him for his advice about what they should be doing for their frequent flyers. He did have conversations with them about Fast Track, although he is always very specific that he does not claim credit for that initiative. He told them that they should focus on what goes on outside the cabin for the First Class business passengers, because it is a fat lot of good having all this luxury on board if there's so much hassle beforehand, but he doesn't claim credit for the idea. So, yes, the travel . . . he has his special gadgets and things that he takes with him and he is very punctual, as you probably know.

'It is a serious edginess,' agrees Linda. 'He has this need to be at an airport hours before the flight, he absolutely *hates* to be late.

He would say to me a time and I would arrive there *on time* and he would have been waiting five minutes for me and all of a dooh-dah. I remember in South Africa seeing him pacing up and down through the walls of a glass lift I was in. I was one minute late and as the lift came down I was two minutes late, and I was like – in the lift – going, 'I am coming! I am coming!' and I could see him pacing up and down the floor, getting more and more frustrated. I said, 'Edward, I could see you from the lift! . . .'

I notice it now when we are on the island off Cork. Say, for argument's sake, it is ten o'clock in the morning and he has a four o'clock flight. He is peppering a bit all that day because he knows he has to get to that airport about two, and he knows it takes an hour and a half to leave. So he says, 'Right, we need to leave the island for twelve to get there at two . . .' but when it gets to eleven he'd really rather he had said eleven and leave then, even though twelve was leaving us a safeguard of two hours.

It is almost like a nervous problem he has, a definite fear. I remember once in an airport in the States we had sat patiently at the gate for the best part of two and a half hours before the flight took off. I remember thinking, What are we *doing* here? I could tell he was getting agitated the more I got up to wander around, but as it was still half an hour before the flight was due to leave I got up to have a cigarette, and, you know, sometimes an air stewardess appears out of nowhere, and I was just walking back when I saw him get up. Now, I had told him to look after my bags, and I watched him get up, as this stewardess announced boarding, and push everybody at the top of the queue out of his way! He was standing there, breaking out in a sweat, as if he wasn't going to get on the plane! And my bags were still where we had been sitting, with no one paying attention.

I said, 'Edward, you are being absolutely ridiculous. Now you weren't even minding my bags and I saw you were trying to be first on the plane and the plane is not even taking off without you, you are sitting beside it!' And he didn't speak to me for the whole trip! He was booked on the first seat in the first aisle. He was the first person to get on and the first person to get off. And yet he is almost annoyed with everybody for taking so long to get on the plane.

That beautiful, still day on Tessera, far removed from angry airports and the ebb and flow of the multitude, I had a sense, as we walked through his rose garden, not only of his treasured freedom from control, but of a little loneliness, too. 'Do you ever get lonely?' I asked. He paused and said, 'Sometimes,' and it sounded true. Then he said, 'Come round here,' and we turned behind Bruno's house to a sun-soaked courtyard, where, on a step, sat a stunning Australian girl. Edward left us. I could have been Nicholas Urfe on the island of Phraxos in John Fowles's novel *The Magus*, she the mysterious Lily. I stood as he, rooted to the spot.

Just another travelling PA? What Aristotle said was, from the past let us create categories, definitions, boxes. Then when you come across something, analyse it first, then judge, 'Is it in this box, is it not in this box?' Recognise situations as standard, apply standard answers. What Edward says is, 'We are going to have to move to another kind of thinking, to what can be.' On such a day, I was not about to argue with that.

Months later, I asked Tom Farrell the same question, 'Does Edward ever get lonely?'

'Does he need company?' he translated. 'I think he probably does. I think that is why he has these secretaries running around him.' As it happened, the next day Linda Laird was due to take me over Edward's Irish retreat of West Skeam, and I asked her on the way down what these travelling PAs have to do. 'I travelled for Edward on and off for three and a half years,' she told me. 'I only did North America, Canada and London. Julia Pomirska does Australia. Celia Bartoli did Malta and the European countries. Nicola Tyler did South Africa for a while.'

I knew that Julia Pomirska had met Edward through mutual friends, and wondered how Linda had found her way to the job.

Basically it was an advertisement in a paper. 'Famous author needs assistant to travel extensively. Must have computer knowledge and good organisational skills.' Words to that effect. Tom Farrell and Ann Lynch [Tom's assistant] actually did the interview. Anyway, I went back to a second interview to meet Edward, and it was bizarre. It took place in the Leeson Park Hotel in Dublin. Twenty girls all brought in to talk with Edward around a table. All together! Anyway, he told us just to talk among ourselves. Yeah, it was so odd! Well, I started it off and I thought we'd talk about something topical, so I spoke about Princess Diana because she was in the papers at the time. I was really conducting this interview and saying, 'And what do you think, and what do you think, and have you anything to say on the subject?' And a lot of the girls had nothing to say. I suppose there were about three or four of us who did a lot of the talking while Edward sat up the top smiling and approving and not approving, and of course I kept saying, 'And what do you think, Edward?'

I guess this interview went on for the best part of two hours and it weeded out the good from the bad. He participated only minimally. If it went quiet he would lead something into it, but generally he kept quiet to see how we would get on with it.

Then there was a third interview, when he asked three of us to come back and interviewed us separately. Then he asked me to come back at half past seven. There was a dinner on that night, probably ten political figures and journalists were going to discuss the unemployment problem in Ireland. He was hosting it. So, anyway, I turned up and was terribly nervous. All the guests were bigwigs in Ireland and I would never have moved in such circles. I just spoke about things that I knew about. Then everybody stood up in turn to speak about unemployment, and I thought *I* was going to have to! It started at the top end of the table. I was at the bottom end. Edward had only announced that this would happen when we were already at the table. You know what Edward's like, he doesn't tell you what is going on. You are thrown into the pile and you just have to get on with it. By the time it came round to me, I had worked the sweat off myself, and had actually tried to put together a reasonable speech, and then he skipped me, and I thought, how could you skip me after all you had put me through?! To get me that far!

So, anyway, after the dinner Edward said, 'Why don't you come on a trip with me?' . . . So we went to the States, which was fantastic, New York and then up to Diane in Canada.

Now, his apartment in New York is only a one-bed apartment. I did stay on the couch at one stage, but it proved to be just too difficult, so I ended up staying with friends. His apartment's in Central Park South, a lovely location overlooking the park, beautiful, really beautiful, with a balcony, really terribly nice. It was a two-week trip, work and social. I think he did two seminars in that time. I remember thinking, 'Oh gosh, is this really what I want to do? . . .' But I thought I might as well run with this and see how it goes, it is certainly different and new and exciting.

I stopped travelling with Edward really after I met Roger, my husband. I suppose Edward had not so much tired of me, but he wanted to move on to new, different things. He likes to change the people who travel with him on a reasonably regular basis because obviously he gets bored and they get bored, you know?

In the 1980s, after Venezuela, the schools and business elements of Edward's enterprise continued to expand across the world. On the education side, CoRT had been introduced into Australia, New Zealand, Canada, Spain, Malta and Nigeria, besides Britain and Venezuela. Despite Odyssey, CoRT would find its way into schools in North America, eventually achieving award recognition in some. Indeed, such was the reputation of CoRT in the US, in spite of his exclusion in 1980, that Edward was invited to Minneapolis in April 1989 to address the Education Commission of the United States. This brings together all the governors and senior education officers in the entire US. Afterwards, he was whisked away for two days to give special CoRT seminars to senior educators in Minnesota. The governor subsequently made funds available for teacher training in CoRT.

Further north, in Canada, Norah Maier took Edward's schools programme deeper into the country. 'I travelled all over Canada to get it on the curriculum. It became very, very much integrated into a new movement in Saskatchewan, where they rewrote the whole curriculum, calling it the Common Essential Learnings, in which thinking was one of the five curricular areas – right up there with numeracy and literacy. Also in Eastern Canada. It really was quite across the board.'

In Bulgaria, Edward's CoRT experiment ran over twenty-five weeks in four schools: two in Sofia and two in Plovdiv. Later, Levcho Zdravchev at the Ministry of Public Education in Sofia confirmed that every child was tested at the start and on completion of the programme (also control groups of course) using Progressive Matrices of Raven, a well-known group intelligence test, and the Torrance Test of Creativity (see page 158). The results were so impressive that the ministry decided to spread CoRT to ten more schools. In a letter, Zdravchev invites Edward for a seven-day trip to meet the new teachers, and closes with 'best regards to your charming wife and hope she made an alcoholic revolution in England by introducing "drinking vodka straight"!'

Another favoured watering hole opened up by Edward at this time was Malaysia, where his work led to a personal friendship with Prime Minister Mahathir. The story began when the Islamic scholar Ungku Abdul Aziz attended his first seminar in Kuala Lumpur. 'I had read a number of his books and was very familiar with his work,' Professor Aziz told me. 'I was rather pushy perhaps. I sat next to him at the table during the lunch break and peppered him with questions. From there on we met again and again and again.' Before long, Edward had got CoRT into the senior science schools, MARA – 'a Malay acronym, they have schools all over the country,' says Aziz, 'and they teach in English right from the beginning. Their students – 10 to 20,000 at a time – go off to the US and go to Britain and so on.'

Malaysia is a federation of fourteen states, a number of which have sultans or kings – Aziz is himself of royal blood. 'They all get together once every five years and elect a Supreme King, the Agung, of Malaysia,' Aziz told me. 'The King of Malaysia has by law the right to appoint seven royal professors. I was appointed as one of them, and he hasn't appointed any more since, so I am known widely as *the* Royal Professor, and I appear a lot on television and in newspapers, etc.'

For twenty years, Aziz was rector of the University of Malaysia. The university had been established in 1960 in Kuala Lumpur, when he had been professor of economics.

Although I am a rural economist, thinking is an area in which I have tremendous personal interest. I even invented a Malay word for mind – *minda* – which is in the dictionary now, as of course is 'lateral thinking'. I was teaching in the Science School, the special foundation course that begins with logic and ends up with lateral thinking, the body/mind relationship and the philosophical and psychological implications of that. There was really no satisfactory word in Malay for the concept of mind. Now it is common for people, politicians and so on, in public, to use *minda*, and I am sure many people have forgotten who invented it.

The university's foundation curriculum at the Science School, into which Aziz inculcated Edward's lateral thinking, had a certain political significance:

Particularly in those days, it was very important to get the peasant children who were deprived of good schools, libraries, etc, into the university, and this course originally enabled this. I was Vice Chancellor by then and knew Mahathir very well, had a lot of things to do with him on and off. When we had this idea to set up this Foundation Studies Centre, he was Minister of Education. Many said, 'This is another of Ungku Abdul Aziz's great ideas, which are very difficult to put into practice; it won't work.' So we had a big meeting, and at the end of the meeting, as Minister of Education, Mahathir said, 'Let Ungku Aziz try.'

So, here they studied the subjects that were needed. We didn't

217

want to give them A level courses, which couldn't really prepare them for a university course, say, in medicine or engineering. So we asked the medics, 'What exactly does a student need to know in order to be a first year or a second year student?' We designed courses for this. They were taught how to think, how to study and put under enormous pressure to do this. Many subsequently have gone on to get FRCPs and FRCS – recently a dental student from the course became Chief Minister of the State.

To give you an eye into the problems we had, and still have, the Faculty of Medicine at the time I took over, had an intake of about 128 a year and of these only five or six would be Malays, yet they are half the population! So I thought this really was not on – there was a lot of political trouble – and what I decided was not to lower standards but to get these people in and just pump them up and tell them they are just going to have to study very hard.

As a result, Aziz is known 'among the peasants and the students and the trades unions and co-operators as well as university people, as Pak Ungku, which means (not quite in the English sense) Old Father William'. It is a word of respect.

Interest in Edward's programmes from as far afield as Russia and China had been sparked by the Venezuelan project, following an international conference, hosted by Machado in Caracas, which once again attracted Marjorie Wallace onto the scene.

I joined Edward on the plane at Paris. He travelled first class with his feet up, while I went economy, suffering like mad. I then try and creep up to get a glass of champagne and he doesn't quite want to know! We stayed at the Hilton. He had the suite. I had the standard single room. My worst memory was the Saturday night. I thought he would take me to wherever he was going, but no, he never materialised. And I sat there in the Hilton with nothing to eat all evening. That didn't endear me to the programme.

The interest of the Chinese, who made their own way over, was more positive. Straight away the Venezuelans jumped into the driving seat once more, taking their Venezuelan translation of CoRT, *Learning How To Think*, with them. 'For me one of the most important experiences was taking the de Bono programme to China,' Beatricz Capdeville told me.

I was part of the team that went to China to teach the professors at Shanghai University. That is where the training took place in May 1983. *Learning How To Think* was translated into Chinese. The Ministry of Education undertook to teach all the primary school children. Later on, by embassy, we heard for more than ten years all primary school children went through de Bono's method. I don't know whether it continued after that, my impression is that it did, but I have no information that it did.

Machado had preceded the training party, which actually set up training sessions at the University of Beijing as well as at Shanghai. Some 100,000 students are reckoned to have graduated from the subsequent teacher training programme. Capdeville told me,

I have the original paper, done by hand [Chinese translation], of the de Bono tools, and they have been using that *Learning How To Think* programme since then. I don't know how many millions of children were taught, but it was an official decision, not something in one school and not another.

We stayed in Beijing almost a month and trained about thirty-five or forty professors of that university. We did that with interpreters from Spanish direct to Chinese, three or four interpreters who spoke good Spanish. It was a little bit slow due to the language. We stayed in a hotel. At that time there was only one in Shanghai. We were a group of some ten trainers. Once there, we were distributed to work with the professors. One group stayed at Beijing, others went to Shanghai.

Five years later, Edward saw for himself how his reputation had spread. 'In 1988, when I was in Shanghai,' Edward recalls, 'they had a big meeting round my visit, where they brought 450 people from all over China, and in fact I was elected President of the Euro-China Association.'

Russia was also impressed, and this time Machado was not involved. 'I spent ten days in Moscow as the guest of Znanie, the national science society. They organise seminars,' Edward recalls. 'The Maltese Ambassador over there had been talking to them. So they invited me over. Then I talked to the Academy of Science – the philosophy, education, psychology departments. Then I gave lectures in Leningrad and so on. There was a very good response. In 1989 I was in Moscow twice and they asked me to train their teachers. They have a very special school project where they try new things and the rest of the education system watches, and if they like it they take it.' This was School Project One – ten leading schools test new approaches. 'I was also involved in teaching at School 57,' Edward went on, 'one of the most prominent schools in Moscow, a sort of Eton. Just as the Chinese High School in Singapore, which is the Eton of the whole Far East, they now teach my programmes too.'

School 57 is the oldest school in Moscow, and takes the most gifted students in mathematics. Mention of the Chinese High School in Singapore takes us into one of Edward's most successful territories, and not only for CoRT.

Singapore was starting afresh in the 1980s, and thinking skills for use in the real world were and are an important element in education. Linda Low explains why:

Singapore wants to be the human resource capital. This is a place where you don't even own your own water. I think that's very serious, we buy our water from our neighbours. We have no resources other than people. The human brain is the only thing we have to sell. So, training is of the utmost importance.

My earliest introduction to Edward was through Edna Copley in 1986. The Singapore government was interested in adding thinking skills to the education programme and Edna was taken in to introduce CoRT to Singapore schools [see page 150]. I happened to be one of the teachers who were selected to attend her training programme. Afterwards, of course, Edna went into the schools to see how we actually presented CoRT to the children. When she came to watch my presentation she was very impressed. She said it was an excellent programme, and wanted it to be videotaped as a sample programme to train other teachers. And I did that.

Now, at the end of the session with Edna, I went up to her on the last day and asked her for a testimonial. She wrote one on a plain piece of paper – no letterhead, nothing, and I still have that today. The letter said that if the government moved forward with this, I would be the right person to introduce it. Subsequently they set up a thinking unit in the Ministry of Education to introduce thinking. It was supposed to be the CoRT thinking unit and I was seconded as a resource person to develop that, but for personal reasons I decided not to take up the appointment. However, I was so interested in the programme that I did it anyway at no extra pay!

So, I was a teacher (at that time training ten-year-olds) and I was developing this and I was training teachers in my school! It was just marvellous. The children were looking forward to the thinking lessons. I was using the lessons as a bait! If you do this correctly, that properly, then we will have a thinking lesson. They were looking forward every week to the lesson.

I think what they liked was that in the thinking lessons they were not judged by how clever they were. All right, they may be very weak in mathematics or science, but this is an area where we could work on a clean slate. The children who were very inhibited because they were at the bottom of the class were now opening up. They went home and told their parents about it, and the parents came in and told me, 'Well, they look forward to your thinking lessons.' And I knew that I had hit it correctly. Every week we were just enjoying ourselves with our thinking lesson.

We then did a pilot study, because before introducing it to the educational system we had to do this – there was a fantastic difference between the pre-course and the post-course results. I presented the study to the school council and to the Minister for Education. Following that they decided to introduce it to more schools. So, I was in a way quite a pivotal influence in the introduction of this programme to Singapore schools.

Linda will have been referring to the Singapore government testing CoRT in twenty-five schools in May 1988, after which it was decided to spread CoRT's use through many other schools in the republic.

Then, in 1992, Linda and her husband Peter started their own school specialising in Edward's CoRT and Six Hats programmes.

When we introduced the business programme, the executives, realising how important thinking skills are, thought of their children and asked us, 'Do you have a schools programme too?' I told them about CoRT. That kindled the fire in us and made us think, why don't we set up a school of our own? So, from Mondays to Fridays we train only executives. On Saturdays, only students. One day a week, and a child comes for only one and a half hours per lesson for a duration of eight weeks, eight lessons. At the start, we asked only for children aged nine, ten, eleven, but soon they introduced their siblings, and now we have the school running from as young as six and a half to eighteen.

The Lows combine sensitivity with commercial nous in a way that is perfectly in tune with their culture. It works fantastically well.

In the years between the Albany dinners and 1992, when a seminal training session in San Francisco sent twelve of de Bono's disciples out into the world, Edward's appeal to business remained unique. On 12 December 1982, Kevin MacManus wrote in *Forbes Magazine*:

> For years, consultants have been making comfortable lives for themselves telling corporate managers everything they are doing wrong, from hiring and firing employees to buying and selling businesses. Now one has gone the ultimate. He is telling executives that they don't even know how to think properly. And judging by the reaction he is getting, a lot of corporate America must think he's right.

Increasingly, however, as his contact with top executives became closer, he began to be more sensitive to their needs. Where once he talked about 'a sense of immortality in a new idea', he now spoke of market strategies and opportunity seeking, and showed a knowledge of how the world of business had developed.

In an interview in *Success Magazine* in 1983, Edward showed that he had a clear sense of where his contribution would be made:

> In the 1950s and 1960s, when the business schools and the idiom of business training developed, the economy was growing and problem solving was sufficient ... Business has three stages. First there is the entrepreneurial stage – individuals, each with **an idea** and some measure of energy and drive. The next stage is **management** ... the efficient use of resources and problem solving. **The third** phase is the thinking phase. This is where we design our concepts, **our** market strategies and so on ... opportunity-seeking.

Another bridge with the business community was a growing treasure trove of instances in which lateral thinking had resulted in commercial value. An early example of this was the fishing industry in England, where a traditional method wasn't a problem, but a new idea turned out to work better. 'The old way of filleting fish was to pull the meat from the bone, until a worker who performed the task each day suggested that the process could be reversed. His suggestion was tested and it worked, and removing the bones from the meat became the standard method.

The old way wasn't a problem,' said Edward. 'If an idea goes on working we consider it a valid idea until it works rather less well. Only when it is in very bad shape do we question it.'

This kind of anecdote remains a feature of his seminars today. You might, for example, hear how at one of their senior labs, IBM claimed that Six Hats had reduced meeting times by 75 per cent. Or how at electronics and electrics giant ABB in Finland a project normally taking thirty days was reduced to two days through parallel thinking. Or how Statoil in Norway had a problem with one of their rigs for three weeks, costing them $100,000 a day, whereupon one of Edward's trainers, Jens Aarup, introduced parallel thinking through Six Hats – and within twelve minutes they had solved the problem, saving the company $10 million.

In 1980 Edward was still doing the odd public seminar in the States for $95 a head, but soon a far more lucrative strategy emerged – the International Creative Forum, involving a deeper dig in corporate pockets to the tune of $25,000 a time. In 1985 Edward's worldwide enterprise was seriously gaining ground, and he realised he needed more detailed day-to-day management. He turned to Don McQuaig, the man who had brought him to Canada nearly a decade earlier. Says McQuaig:

> When I said I was too busy, he said, 'Well, I was hoping you would offer your wife ...' Then, I remember him having this briefing meeting with Diane, it was about fifteen minutes long. He said it was simple, I'll send you these things and you just send these people an invoice. It turned out to be hugely more complex than that. Lawyers, accountants, book agents, business partners immediately started phoning her saying, 'What's this, what's that?' I guess it was trial by fire, she learned as she went. He has a way of setting his stuff up that only makes sense from his perspective, but it does work for him extremely well.

Diane remembers:

> I began managing Edward in 1985. In 1983 or 1984 Edward talked to Don. Don was very flattered but he was building his business. At the time I was an ex-nurse and had three children under the age of three and a half. I didn't really have any business knowledge, nor had I read any of his books, nor did I really know who he was. I first met

him in the basement of our home. Don and he had been out for dinner and discussed this and Don had said, 'Come on home and meet Diane,' so we met and shook hands on it in the basement. We spent about ten minutes together in true Edward style. He handed me a little piece of paper, which I have to this day, a list of some of his books, and at that time he took the list out and we decided to start two companies, and he just put a little letter beside each book in terms of where it had been written (whether inside or outside the UK) and which company it would fall under. And that was all I ever got from the man!

We started to work together by my fostering certain relationships that he had built up in different countries to enable us to develop a schedule that was more regular, so that when he was stepping off a podium, I was getting on the phone and booking him on there for the next year. So, I was getting organised around what he had been doing. Edward is a relationship builder. I don't want to take too much credit here.

I said, 'It has made him a very rich man.'

Said McQuaig, 'He has done very well.'

'On a scale of 1 to 10,' I asked, 'how motivated do you think he is by money?'

'That is a more complex question,' McQuaig replied. 'Edward is more interested in fairness than in money. He wants to be treated fairly. As I say, he has to be the most generous person I ever met [we had been talking about his unpaid work in education]. So he wants to be paid well. He doesn't want to be taken advantage of. There is a low bullshit threshold. When people are pulling the wool over, he is not happy.'

In the UK, Edward is constantly challenged about making money. Never in America, where success is allowed. 'If I were purely in the business world such comments would never arise,' he says. 'It is because people do not distinguish between my business activities and other activities that the resentment arises. Almost all the work I do in education is unpaid and often I even have to pay my own expenses. My policy is very simple: if someone is making money out of my work – as when seminars are set up and people pay to go – I want a fair share: $30,000 for a full day's seminar is at the lower end for American gurus. I am a philanthropist in education but see no reason to be so in business.'

The International Creative Forum, with which such giants as IBM, Prudential, DuPont, Merck, Nestlé, British Airways and BAA (the airport authority) were involved, was seeded 'in about 1987 or 1988' recalls Diane, 'in a meeting Edward and I had.

> We thought it would be a great idea to host in a forum arena some of his best clients. He had created relationships with the likes of Helmut Maucher, chairman of Nestlé in Switzerland, and Ron Barbaro of Prudential, so we thought, Why not bring them together and have them discuss business issues?
> At that time we were charging $25,000 for annual membership and we were having four meetings a year, each of three days, in different parts of the world. They would bring their business issues and Edward would teach the tools and they would send up to twelve participants from each company. It worked beautifully for the first year or two.

The first to sign up was DuPont. 'Edward and I were quite friendly because I had had him in quite often,' recalls David Tanner. 'I wrote out a cheque for $25,000 and that helped to set the ball rolling. We had about twelve companies. When I retired from DuPont in 1991, Edward asked me to become the executive director. Part of my responsibility was to bring in other companies.'

When Edward first went out into the boardrooms of big business, he used to say, 'I am the catalyst, the brain power is with you.' He was the facilitator, the midwife in the birth process of new ideas, and not personally concerned with sorting out problems or generating ideas of particular use to the companies. If they came up in seminar, fine. Seeding ideas for a company would, however, have had to be on a different basis, business-wise. More than this, it was always his opinion that getting involved with familiar content in seminar shifted attention from the tools themselves. If audiences get too close to the content, take up too much time discussing ideas of importance to them, little attention is paid to the process, and they find it difficult to transfer the skills to another context.

However, from the time of the Albany dinners, through his friendship in particular with Robert Holmes à Court and other high-level business people, and possibly sometimes through the International Creative Forum, the pressure to address issues of interest to these parties may have increased. Certainly David Tanner recalls him applying his techniques to particular issues, and certainly it was from this period that Edward's wealth soared.

> When Edward first came in, he talked about the techniques and said, 'It is up to you to apply them,' though later on, for example in the International Creative Forum, where my whole focus was on application, he began getting more involved in how to apply them. When we shifted into these companies they would bring at least one important problem with them to be tackled by the groups using the de Bono techniques. Edward was excellent, a very fast learner! He immediately did extremely well at that, though in the beginning it had just been lecture. We quickly changed that and he moved very nicely into that. When there were problems to be tackled he would teach the technique and then participate up front and apply that technique to a specific problem.

I asked Tanner why he thought Edward had agreed to change his way of working.

'He was well paid,' he replied.

As the decade drew to a close, Edward continued to be beset by post-Venezuela problems. Beatricz Capdeville, Luis Machado's assistant, first travelled to South Africa in 1988. The following year, Machado helped set up a non-profit-making company called the Upttrail Trust (Upgrading of Teaching, Training and Learning) at Kwazulu. The company aimed to supplement the 'three Rs' with the so-called 'three Cs' – classroom skills, communication skills and cognitive skills. And Edward's CoRT tools were made a part of it.

Upttrail was thus in the perfect position to enhance the education of the oppressed after Nelson Mandela was released from prison on 11 February 1990. As Edward himself pointed out: 'In South Africa, there is an urgent need for rapid education. Therefore, many subjects could be bypassed and a shorter, more powerful curriculum, which includes thinking skills, would fast-track the education system.' He himself was in South Africa maybe three times a year in those days: 'Before the first elections in South Africa they asked me to teach Six Hats to the heads of all the Peace Accord committees, solving the local problems in the towns and townships.'

Capdeville points out that funds were made available 'from a big NGO, an umbrella NGO used by the new government, which collected all the international funds. A lot of money was coming into South Africa at that time to support the different things that were happening. There were different education systems – for the whites, for the coloureds, for the blacks, and the worst one was for the blacks and that is where most of the efforts were directed.' After Mandela was released, Capdeville told me, 'we were working in the Cape region and also in Johannesburg. We had schools in Zululand, also Botswana and elsewhere, funded by some of the industries.'

However, Upttrail culminated in debacle, as Susan Mackie describes. Mackie was originally a remedial therapist by profession. 'I worked with very, very difficult children. I trained with Reuven Feuerstein [see page 188]. I started reading de Bono before I started teaching, when I was a young student, but before learning about CoRT I came across the Upttrail Trust. Edward had donated his tools to this Trust and it had been designed with work by David Perkins at Harvard University.'

One area in which Mackie was working for Upttrail was Sekhukhuneland, the far Northern Province, within the 1,000 schools programme [a government initiative], one of the big endeavours of the new government:

The area suffered under deprivation and lack of development as early as 1879 due to political oppression ... There is an estimated population of 50,000 people, with an average of ten members per household, 40 per cent of the population is under the age of thirty. There are only twelve primary schools and five secondary schools. Each school has around nine classrooms. There is no running water – water is drawn from a stream, which often dries up, and four boreholes. Malnutrition is rife among children under seven. The unemployment rate is estimated at 90 per cent.

Mackie became project director at Upttrail:

The old professor who ran it – Dr David van de Vyver – was wonderful, and they started to teach in very poor communities. Huge, huge money had been invested, but they hadn't produced much by way of results. And when I went in there I was told they were in a good state and they had a potential 2 million Rand's worth of work, but I discovered they didn't. There was a huge office, three secretaries and one old professor and no work. Money had come in from big companies to deliver work in communities, but the money had gone into the debt pool, so we couldn't do anything because they wanted to foreclose, and we were three-quarters of a million in debt. Now a non-profit company is not allowed to go into debt, and so I started to hunt around and I picked up the Lonplats project, which was Lonrho in those days and is now Lonplats – the Lonplat Platinum Mines. It was at that stage Eastern Platinum, Western Platinum, Karee, Western Platinum North and the Base Nickel Refinery – all part of one company. The entire unit is 16,000 people.

Mackie had landed a major commercial project, but she was worried. She could see that Upttrail was in difficulties, and believed that problems would increase because the fundamental reason for the difficulties was, she felt, that the teaching materials 'had been bastardised ...'

It is a complex and, in personnel terms, a sensitive set-up in the mines. Mackie says that probably 15,000 of the employees at Lonplats are –

illiterate, black, never been to school, no idea what school's like. They come from very rural communities, including Mozambique, where they have seen real poverty. They may be supporting between twelve and seventeen people at home. We have many official languages [Zulu, Xhosa, Sotho, Tswana and Shangani among them] and there are different dialects of Zulu and so on. So we are probably looking at twenty-two, twenty-three dialects. The translation of our questionnaire drove us mad. The dialect can change within 20 kilometres. Few can speak English or Afrikaans. We had translators and used sign language. There is a language called Kfanagalore, a mining language, which all the mining men speak, but it is an instruction language, not one for discussion.

What the company had been looking for was a way to improve human relations. In the Karee mine there would be up to 210 fights and disputes a month between the seven tribes working there. This sort of behaviour was hardly good for productivity. But there were other areas of concern within the company. Says Mackie:

On the whole, the middle levels in the organisation were white Afrikaans males. Now their whole lives they have been 'preferred employees' because they are white. Suddenly you have got all these organisations coming, called Equity and Affirmative Action, and these guys feel threatened. Also, in the old apartheid system their children's education was paid for. Suddenly their standard of living has dropped and they can no longer afford what their fathers could afford. Mining generally goes back generations and they come from these small communities where the watchword had been 'Be scared of the black-man'. So, suddenly you have got a company changing, and people saying, 'That behaviour is no longer acceptable'. That's the level on which we were batting in this project.

So, I started managing this. I was in my late twenties and this man I worked for was in his sixties, with quite an ego. It was not a good match and he wanted to control it. And the first bit of thinking we did, we had a major strike. He got the unions so up in arms they had this major strike! I had the human resources manager on to me at three o'clock in the morning, screaming blue murder and telling me to get the hell off his mine. I managed to calm it down.

What happened next was that Mackie got hold of Paddy Hills in London and said that she wanted to talk to Edward.

He agreed to dinner on the Friday night and David, the man I worked for, acted perfectly oddly that night. It was the weirdest dinner . . . he was acting really strange and I could never quite touch with Edward what the problem was. In the end, Edward suggested that I and Nicola Tyler, his South Africa assistant at the time, go with him to the Seychelles to spend some time. So we travelled there and one night he said very quietly, 'I have a licence agreement with the States. If Upttrail want to do commercial work then they need to get accredited.' He said he would help them. But this man upped and disappeared. The whole organisation vanished into thin air. In the meantime, the girl who sat on the Upttrail Trust board translated the book [based on de Bono's tools and being used by Upttrail] into Spanish and took it into Venezuela, and Edward did nothing. Edward is very forgiving. There is some very ouch politics in all this.

Capdeville tells me that permission for translation has been granted, and is anxious to give Edward the credit that is his due. 'De Bono was a very important component at that time in South Africa. He has done great things for the world and I am very eager to contribute something.'

Edward remains aloof from such in-crowd squabbling. His only interest is in the Lonplats work, which he took over after Upttrail collapsed. The project succeeded beyond their wildest dreams. 'Productivity is up at the mine,' Edward reports. 'An extra 65 million Rand last year. Absenteeism is down, safety is up, and so on.' The mine is itself publishing research undertaken into the success of the programme because it has had such an impact. Says Mackie: 'It is the first time we have ever researched using a good academic base. I trained practitioners in Action Research in how to research their own environment and we had a 100 per cent return of questionnaires, which is unheard of. The report will be massive – four mines and a base metal refinery. It will be published next year.'

It is possible to put together an impressive picture from information I have gleaned. At the Karee mine, worker grievances dropped from an average seven per day to four per month. Productivity increased by an average of 14 per cent per worker, and teams trained in de Bono techniques are 20 per cent more productive than untrained teams. 'On the worst case scenario,' says human resources divisional manager Greg Colin, 'there is only a 5 per cent improvement on centares per man ... [But] one of the greatest benefits of the programme is the increase in confidence and self-esteem of the employees. They see how they fit into the bigger picture ... Our absenteeism has also dropped substantially.' An Eastern Platinum miner, Antonio Salvador Bila, says: 'We never received bonuses ... With thinking tools we have a vision as a team to reach monthly targets. We used to think only about ourselves, we were narrow and unclear. Now we have applied the solutions to the traps – think clearly, don't rush, give thinking time, be clear and precise. We use the tools – APC, OPV, FIP, and PMI – in solving problems in daily production.'

Most impressively, social benefits have moved beyond the workplace. Said Bila, who is Mozambique-born and works at the Number 2 shaft at Eastern Platinum:

> I have a child and wife. The situation at home was not good, especially with my wife. In Shangani culture a man does not show his wife his pay slip. The man is responsible for the future – he makes all the decisions. When I started learning about thinking skills I realised I have to get my wife involved in setting a vision. There have been big achievements in my family since then: bank account grown, relationships have improved.

Herbert Mayeza, Secretary of the National Union of Mineworkers, speaks of workers becoming more involved in decision-making, and himself deploys the CoRT tools in resolving conflicts and crises: 'I have also taken the skills back to my community and even used them with the soccer club.' The tools' influence on life outside the mine is hilariously captured in a home-movie video that Mackie made. Mineworkers are talking and kidding about the differences the tools have made. In translation, one man says, 'At home I have got this big wife who is beating me up and since I taught her thinking she has stopped beating me up.' Another fellow, a Zulu, goes up to the teacher and says, 'Does this de Bono fellow have three wives?' The teacher says, 'Not as far as I know.' The man says, 'He must have, otherwise he couldn't think of these things. At home I've got three wives and my life was hell and then I taught them thinking and I have had peace for the last six months.'

Mackie herself spent several months in the mine shafts gaining workers' trust in the course of her work, and Edward went down in June 1998: 'History hasn't changed,' he said, on emerging, 'Human nature hasn't changed. *Behaviour* has changed very much just through teaching thinking – perceptions.'

Mackie is now on to another potentially huge project in South Africa.

Ingwe Coal – I got Edward to speak to them as a start and now I am doing work for senior management at Ingwe Coal. Upton Colliery is the pilot, it's about 4000 people. They have used the thinking tools to design and put the process together, and we have also used them to design the entire visual process to explain to people how to hook into it. So the tools have been thoroughly integrated into the whole project, and I go home now to finish that off.

Chapter Ten

Existential Ease

'Perceptions are real even when they do not reflect reality, just as fears may be unreasonable but not unreal.'

Edward's childhood had ended one day at Oxford, when, like so many before him, he 'suddenly thought grown-ups didn't know better'. For him personally, his independence, his autonomy, his freedom from control is all. These are qualities or states which seem to be attached to some sort of existential validity in his mind. They define the ultimate breakout, not just from the colonial cringe of Malta, but from the whole deep-truth, fundamentalist culture that engenders conflict in the world.

In *The Happiness Purpose*, he observes that man is 'an anonymous creature in a large urban society', no longer the man within himself and within a community, the small society with its own community beliefs ... The community as meta-system is no more, its religion, its clearly defined expectations are gone ... Communities have been destroyed by ease of movement and communication and mass cultural influences (advertising, records, television). 'Technology denudes our sense of community,' agreed Australian producer Steve Vizard in a conversation with Edward during an Australian TV pilot called *Food For Thought*.

The genesis of modern/postmodern man is tied up with the movement of people from country to town in the Industrial Revolution, which caused great social change. Inevitably, the great shift from rural to urban Britain led to artistic narratives of nostalgia and loss, most famously by Thomas Hardy, who watched as the rural community culture into which he was born was laid waste. Hardy was born in 1840 and died in 1925, and thus saw inordinate change, as industrialisation and the new technology overtook the old rural traditions – even, near the end, having to duck behind a hedge in his Dorset home to avoid being snapped by Japanese tourists!

It is important to understand what *was* lost. It wasn't just the old rural crafts and skills. The novelist John Fowles understood and expressed what it was perfectly in *Thomas Hardy Country* (1984): 'It is ... a complete tradition of surviving in rural conditions, not only a whole manner of life, but an unconscious philosophy of it, also disappeared.'

Edward, far from bemoaning this loss, welcomes it. Postmodern man no longer feels the need for community to protect him against his worst nature, which he sees as the community's original purpose. Postmodern, urban man, alienated from the land and his rural community's simple values, has come to terms with his fate. 'To be modern is to know that one's fate is to become outdated, that one's doings will pass on into obscurity; yet it is also, in a sense, to embrace this, to eschew the illusory charms of otherworldly hopes,' as John Jervis put it in his excellent book, *Exploring The Modern* (1998).

Now that we know our natures so much better, now that we are so much more civilised, enjoyment can be a legitimate aim. This is the theme of Edward's *The Happiness Purpose*, written nearly a quarter of a century ago.

As pertinent to the development of modernity as the 19th-century alienation from rural values was the connected, more intellectual move away from the notion of 'true nature', 'true self' and what Edward discards in his methodology as 'deep-truth thinking'. John Jervis traces this back to the 18th century, to the increasing theatricality of dress, of speech, etc, a movement which reached its height of expression a century later in Oscar Wilde, for whom to be human is actually to be *un*natural, to play endless roles – 'The first duty in life is to be as artificial as possible.' Human nature is constantly changing and 'cannot be anchored' to truth: 'It is only shallow people who do not judge by appearances. The true mystery of the world is the visible, not the invisible,' he writes in *The Picture of Dorian Gray* (1891), and elsewhere: 'Truth is entirely and absolutely a matter of style.'

Today, to be human *is* to be unnatural. In his film, *2040* – ninety minutes of Edward looking into the future through his concept doodles (he stars, but his face is never seen) – he introduces conceptual 'you-masks' instead of deep soul-searching. To become a thinker, he writes in *Tactics*, you must role-play being a thinker (this would become his Six Hats methodology, see page 248). Edward sees the 'natural' not as an absence of artifice, but as a state in which artifice is so completely absorbed that it has become natural. Natural – artificial – new-natural: stable – unstable – stable. It is the development of ideas, man turning the world to his purpose.

There is no God, there is no true self, so what is there?

Recently I misquoted what a wise cleric from Palmers Green said to me about modernity. 'In pre-modern times, God knew best; in modern times, I knew best; in postmodern times, no one knows best.' Edward capped it with, 'So, I suppose that in post-postmodern times there is no best.'

The latter was in fact the priest's postmodern category. The times in which we live, while not countenancing that there is an absolute best way forward, have one last obsession – project, which Jervis describes as 'purposeful future-orientated activity, geared to the achievement of practical, secular goals, and capable of elaboration into life-governing values and priorities that can make sense of – and in – individual life narratives.'

This, the project of postmodernity, is precisely Edward's mission. Amidst the violent dislocations of modern life, Edward's 'purposeful, future-orientated project' is to reconstruct our thinking and discover what can be.

Why he appears alternately shy, arrogant, restless, impatient, stand-offish, why he dislikes sharing a platform with others, why he shrugs and fails to chase people who rip him off, why he is furious when they adapt his methods, are all the result of his determination to preserve the purity of project and not to be sidetracked from that. Because, in the absence of deep-truth culture, for Edward, as for Jervis's postmodern man, project ensures and defines identity. Project (mission laced with a strong dose of ego-drive) and identity are now indistinguishable.

In *Conflicts* (1985), he attaches a sense of urgency to his mission:

Consider a heavy SKF ball-bearing suspended by a cord directly above a delicate Baccarat crystal goblet. The cord is on fire. There is a certain logical inevitability that the glass is to be shattered ... Something untoward might happen: a breeze may extinguish the fire. If you owned that glass would you wait for something unexpected to rescue the glass or would you want to be rather more constructive? The most hopeful thing about the human race is its relative stupidity. If I had to believe that humanity was operating at the full throttle of its intellectual potential and still producing the crises, mess and dangers of today's world, then there could be little hope.

This is the first book to take his thinking model into the political arena. His constructive, relativist approach (that there is no right nor wrong, only different perceptions – 'I find no villains but intelligent people locked by the logic and continuity of their positions into the argument/clash mode') gained him admission to all camps, as for example in Northern Ireland (page 24), although his concept of triangular thinking, as detailed in *Conflicts*, was no more than the interpolation of a neutral third party whose job it is to design a way out, using his constructive and lateral thinking techniques. It was *Six Thinking Hats* (1986), which organised the techniques into a highly usable structure, while *Parallel Thinking* sets out the new paradigm – his relativist, non-judgemental, practical alternative to right/wrong conflict thinking.

To begin with, however, he planned a more dramatic move beyond the literary world – to set up the neutral, third party himself. He had tried for a while to get the UN interested in a 'new ideas' group, 'but it was like dancing in treacle. Koffe Annan attended one meeting and was most disappointing,' Edward recalls. In a letter to *The Times* in October 1985, he wrote: 'The UN is not a satisfactory body for this purpose [as a neutral third party] because it is a representative body and must ultimately reflect the wishes, sometimes partisan, of its members.' He went on to say that the collapse of talks with the PLO and the collapse of the Berne talks with Argentina suggested the need for 'a sort of intellectual Red Cross'. Then, when nobody did anything about it, he promptly went ahead and tried to set up just such a body on his own. Registering it in the Hague he called it SITO – Supranational Independent Thinking Organisation. From the start the idea smacked of his mother's political idealism, and five years later, in the *Guardian*, Edward had to admit that he had discussed SITO 'with various heads of state and at the most senior level in the USSR and US. There was support for the idea, but a feeling that local diplomats would always feel capable of carrying out all required negotiation.'

SITO started with good intentions. 'We had a meeting at Palazzo Marnisi,' Edward told me last summer.

> Then it just seemed awfully difficult to get people. Then I was involved through the University of Malta and we got people from Cyprus, people from Northern Cyprus, the Turkish side, but then when the Greeks from Southern Cyprus heard they were coming they said they couldn't come. So in the end we got one or two people from the south, some trades unionists, but it was a pity because it could have been an opportunity.

It is easy to scoff at this enterprise, which didn't work, but then how many people would have gone to the expense (and stuck their necks out) personally to promote world peace in any way at all? 'It was his wonderful idea of changing the way leaders think,' recalls John Edwards.

> He funded this organisation out of his own pocket. I meet a lot of people who say what a money grubber he is, and you just roll your eyes. They know nothing about what he does and he will never tell you. I remember him taking me into the big dining room at Marnisi, where he had this huge table, and he said, 'This is where SITO is going to meet.' You know, if they would let Edward help them he would help them enormously. The point about Edward's things is that they are simple, powerful and elegant, and I love things that are simple, powerful and elegant. They are so deceptive. They appear so simple but once you work with them you begin to appreciate the power in them. It is quite incredible the way his simple tools work.

Professor Aziz was among those who attended one of the SITO meetings.

> I went to Marnisi, spent four or five days there. There was a guy from the Red Cross, I remember. SITO was interesting and I was familiar with the background of what Edward was trying to do. The problem, I think, was some of the participants. The German guy – huge ego – he had his own system. Edward couldn't get the people to form a team. They were not completely sold on the idea. I thought it was a very good idea and would have been very happy to have collaborated with it, but it just didn't take off. The wrong people were selected. In their countries or in their institutions they may have been very outstanding, but collectively they didn't gel. That was part of the problem. The other thing is that these sort of things are very difficult to set up. I am immersed in lateral thinking. I find I am doing things all the time and wonder why other people don't think like that. But it takes time to get to that stage. You really have to understand the thing, really practise it a lot.

Politics is obviously an area which would benefit from Edward's thinking, and there have been occasions, as in Northern Ireland, where he has been called upon, but the mechanism of politics is such, and the sensitivity, that people are bound to be wary of independent operators (not that I can think of any, other than Edward, in this field).

Nevertheless, both in Ireland and in Israel around the same time, Edward discovered that the fundamentalist cultures were interested in his ideas.

> I half suspected before I went to Israel a couple of years ago that they would be fairly chauvinistic about thinking – you know, 'We're the bright guys' – and I thought that my work would not do well. On the contrary they were very enthusiastic. I had a session with Begin, who was the Minister of Science at that time, and with the Minister of Education, who called in all his advisers and said, 'We must do this.' Then, this May I was in Jordan and met with the Palestinian education authorities responsible for teaching all the children in the refugee camps, about 400,000 of them, so that is beginning now too. But I haven't tried to get involved politically. I think that it is a situation that might benefit tremendously from parallel thinking, but I don't go knocking on doors.

Before the recent appalling events between Israel and Palestine, I was speaking to Dan Sharon of the Branco Weiss Institute in Jerusalem, who told me he is 'close to the Prime Minister, the Minister for Education, first names. The Minister for Education is a big fan of Edward.' I heard how the institute was disseminating Edward's books, had CoRT with a few hundred schools and used some of his lateral thinking tools, such as the Concept Fan. So, why didn't he get Edward involved politically? 'Politically the situation is not right at this moment for Edward to come,' Sharon said politely. 'It is too deeply entrenched in religious extremism. Right now people expect Arafat to make concessions. He cannot. It is very complicated. I am afraid to waste the good will at this moment.' Days later the situation exploded.

I pressed Edward for information about other approaches. 'I am cagey about sharing some things,' he said. 'I must not seem to be using connections for publicity. There is a perceived danger that groups that have consulted me will be attacked for not being able to think for themselves – "Why do you need de Bono to show you how, etc?"' I then asked him about a meeting at Newport, Rhode Island, last year, which I had heard about by chance when he hadn't been able to make a meeting with me. His manager was unable to help me beyond saying: 'The Newport thing was the think tank for the navy. I really don't have those things. If he does those things – Ireland, etc – he does them on his own.' In the event, Edward was happy to oblige: 'I can talk about that, it wasn't a classified meeting. It was with the US Navy. The Under-Secretary of the Navy was there, about twenty admirals, ten marine generals. I was the only non-American, non-navy person – to look at possible effects of Y2K outside the navy. In the end, we decided it wouldn't be very important.'

On another occasion, outside the mainstream political context, he was asked by Prince Philip to intervene in an ongoing quarrel between the World Wildlife Fund and the World Conservation Union (IUCN). 'I went out to Switzerland and they all came from the four corners of the earth. I think it was due to go on for three days, but after the first morning we had got it all sorted out.' There has, I gather, been perfect peace between the two organisations ever since.

In 1989, Edward undertook his most public foray into matters of world policy at the Seoul Symposium of Nobel Laureates, which took place in both Seoul and Pohang, Korea, from 29 October to 3 November. Topics ranged through Third World debt, AIDS, world trade and economic development, education, unemployment, ecology and pollution, human values, world peace and arms spending and conflict. The Nobel laureates invited were: Physics: Murray Gell-Mann (the quark and the Eightfold Way), Ivar Giaever (electron tunnelling and super-conductivity), Brian David Josephson (tunnelling supercurrents), Burton Richter (from the PSI to charm) and Sheldon Lee Glashow (towards unification of the forces of nature). Chemistry: George Porter (flash photolysis), Herbert C. Brown (hydrogenation), Walter Gilbert (DNA sequencing and gene structure), Dudley R. Herschbach (measuring chemical reactions). Physiology/Medicine: Daniel Carleton Gajdusek (virus infection), Rita Levi-Montalcini (cellular growth). Literature: Wole Soyinka (Africa). The sponsors were the *Korea Economic Daily* and the Korean Broadcasting System in cooperation with Pohang Iron and Steel Co.

This was a very big project and it did take quite some fixing. What emerges is a picture of what is required behind the scenes to keep Edward's show on the road – a process Edward prefers not to know about. Fortunately, in this instance, Tom Farrell was close at hand.

At the time I was re-opening up Japan. Edward hadn't been to Japan for about twelve years. I was trying to open up Korea as well – much more difficult because Korea hadn't heard of de Bono. He had been to Japan after lateral thinking became popular around 1969, 1970, but nothing major since then. I made it major, OK? So, there I was, working between Japan and Korea, going round various companies in Korea, and one particular company, the *Korea Economic Daily*, a financial paper. I always believed it belonged to the government and I am sure it did. By then, I had got them to publish some of his books. I met the president of that, Lee Kyu-Haeng, and he said, 'We are having a 25th anniversary and I want something very special.' I said, 'Such as?' I didn't at once know what could be really special. I said, 'Let me talk to de Bono and come back to you.'

So, I met Edward in London and told him they were looking for something unusual. Well, he already had in his mind he'd like to bring some Nobel laureates together – he had a great friend, Murray Gell-Mann.

The Koreans responded warmly to the idea, and Farrell was pleased, if curious to know why.

I said to Lee Kyu-Haeng, 'Why are you doing all of this?' 'Well,' he said, 'We want to inspire our young physicists and our young medical people.' They planed in 1,000 students to Pohang, each group of 100 students had a morning with a Nobel laureate. They then put those interviews away to be shown in the year 2000. They also ran interviews with each laureate and their opposite number in Korea – each one hour on camera, again to go in the can for the year 2000. They made a Laureate Park in Pohang, a big one, trees were involved – eleven Nobel laureates and de Bono shovelling a tree. That's the first time in history that eleven Nobel laureates have come together to look at world problems.

I asked Edward what he recalls of the conference. 'What sticks,' he said, 'I think there were eleven Nobel prizewinners – there was only one who said he had got his ideas by systematic analysis, every other one came by their ideas by mistake and omni-speculation.' I asked how they were as thinkers outside their fields of expertise. 'When they were talking on subjects that were not their own they were good, but not as outstanding as when they were talking about their own subjects,' he replied. 'I don't want to give the impression they were bad thinkers. They were not.'

'It was a helluva business,' recalls Farrell.

It took us, myself and Ann Lynch, about eighteen months to put together. Why did it take so long? I was going backwards and forwards negotiating the deal. I actually made eighteen round trips in six months to Seoul. I'd go out, we'd make the deal. I'd go back, they'd change the deal. You can't deal with Korea over the phone or by fax. On the plane, backwards and forwards, backwards and forwards. One day I said to Edward, 'This is getting ridiculous.' He said, 'OK, what are you going to do about it?'

So I called a lawyer in New York – he spoke Korean, was married to a Korean, and I said, 'This is my problem, what do I do?' He said, 'Listen, leave it with me.' Called me back the next day and said, 'There is a guy in Seoul. Take $1,000 in your pocket with you. Go and see him. He will meet with you and you will both walk into that office and the deal will be done.'

I put $1,000 in my pocket, went to Seoul, saw this guy at ten in the morning, we were in the office by half ten, by eleven o'clock the contract was fully qualified and signed. That was done, the contract called for twelve laureates. I had booked all the tickets via American Express, etc, against the contract . . . I showed Amex the contract and they said everything was fine. Then I had a fax in from Korea telling me that Gell-Mann wasn't turning up. He had sent his ticket back . . . The contract called for twelve Nobel laureates and now I am left with eleven. After eighteen months' work, I am left with eleven people.

In the event, all was fine with the Koreans about Gell-Mann's absence and the day of the laureates' arrival approached. Meanwhile, Edward, knowing that he would need publicity for the event if any of what was discussed was to bite, approached Marjorie Wallace to cover it.

She recalls:

It was about the most stupid thing I did in my life because my mother had just had a stroke. Edward assured me she would be all right and at the last moment I tumble onto the flight. This time I am first class with him because I said I wouldn't come otherwise. I sit beside him for the whole flight! He falls to sleep of course . . . We arrive at the airport and they mistake me for the twelfth Nobel prizewinner that didn't turn up. I was Dr Wallace! That is how they got me in there. As I arrived, they gave me a bouquet. Sadly, they then realised I wasn't a Nobel prizewinner and that a wife of one of them didn't have a bouquet, so they snatched it out of my hands!

Continues Farrell,

So there's a car to meet them in the first class with their wives, and there is a reception in the hotel when they arrive, and from then on it is nothing but outriders, cars, receptions, talks. We had a set time for everything and I thought the Koreans would be much like the Japanese – but no ... We were in serious trouble one night. The minister for science was hosting a dinner and Josephson from the UK wouldn't come down. I had the heavies on me. I am not joking, the heavies! They said – 'You get him down here.' I said, 'Excuse me?' They said, 'The Minister will be embarrassed!' I said, 'Excuse me, gentlemen, but f ... the Minister!' Very rarely do I swear, it is not in my nature to swear, but that is exactly what I said to them.

I was so uptight. I had lost twelve pounds that week in weight. And Edward was doing his thing and didn't know any of the background. I am the bunny, you see. I had two other staff, but that didn't matter. I mean, one guy, Gajdusek, called me at two o'clock in the morning and said, 'The ribbon of my typewriter has run out, can you get me one?' I had to find him a ribbon that hour of the morning, would you believe? He is the same guy who is coming in the car with me and the owner of the *Korea Economic Daily*, saying that he doesn't like newspaper people! He brought with him a black guy from New Guinea and said, 'This is my son,' and the Koreans couldn't figure out that one at all. They had a real problem. Now every laureate has a suite. So he arrives with his son and the Koreans say, 'Will we get a room for your son, Professor?' And he says, 'No, he will stay with me.' For days they had this problem. They couldn't come to terms with it at all. Maybe now they would.

So, that was an extraordinary event, but not only that, it was historic. At the end of it all they gave Edward a standing ovation, and three of them wrote a foreword to his book *I Am Right, You Are Wrong*.

Five years later, in *Parallel Thinking*, Edward set out in an historical context the paradigmatic shift which is inherent in all his thinking programmes – the shift from the system rules of logic (which hurry us towards making judgement of a situation) to the system rules of perception (which give us pause to consider that there are other points of view and may be alternative ways of going about things).

He proceeds by making his target the truth merchants, the Gang of

Three – Socrates, Plato and Aristotle – the fathers of logic and absolutist, good/bad, right/wrong fundamentalism, a way of thinking that he considers to be not only at the root of conflict in the world, but also the reason why we lurch endlessly through successive states of stability and chaos. 'Medicine lets babies live and keeps people alive longer. There is then chaos until improved food supplies and birth control catch up.' In the 19th century, better transport brought in cheaper food from abroad, hastening mechanisation and heralding the exodus of millions from the English countryside to cities and towns, which in turn led to serious urban problems until services caught up.

Edward pictures a self-organising system served poorly by thinking which hasn't changed in thousands of years. For example, the benefits of nuclear power are threatened by the terrors of nuclear war grounded in an adversarial concept as current in the Stone Age as in the 20th century. 'There is a gap between the system we have and the one we need . . . Our technology has changed, but our basic thinking tools have not.' That is his message. 'People say, if you learn the mistakes of history you'll learn how to handle your own life. I say, if you learn the successes of history you'll be trapped into repeating them.' This is like French Academician André Maurois' 'Endless Recurrence, which marks out the history of the world', with Edward as provocateur, whipping us out of our repetitive orbits. And it works, as Nobel physicist Sheldon Lee Glashow agreed after spending a week with Edward in Korea: 'The old habits [of thinking] seem confining, inadequate and perhaps even dangerous, since our social conflicts are as primitive as ever while our technical ability to pursue them is unconstrained.'

As we have seen in discussion of lateral thinking and CoRT, fundamental to Edward's thinking is the concept of 'movement' as an alternative idiom to 'judgement'. Now, in parallel thinking, 'Argument – the basis of our parliaments, our courts and our discussions – is an extremely limited and inefficient method of thinking. It is an extension of judgement-based thinking.' The judgement idiom recognises, identifies, locates and keeps us within the old patterns of thinking. The movement idiom allows us to skip across patterns to discover alternatives, other people's views, new possibilities, hitherto undreamt-of ideas, and so on.

Argument is the tool of judgement. Says Edward:

Instead of argument, let's move to parallel thinking. The protagonists, instead of arguing, look in the same direction at any one of a series of moments. Imagine we have a building and four people, each standing looking at each of the four faces of it, each arguing that he or she has the right view. Parallel thinking means everyone comes round to one face, then to the next and the next – every side, every aspect comes into view one by one – at the same moment. All are looking in the same direction at any one time. Thinking in parallel, not arguing.

At this point I am reminded of the difficulty I have with the goats and Porsche game show business, and conclude that some discussion may be needed to ensure that everyone is in fact seeing the same thing when they are looking in the same direction at the same time. It is this very point that the methodology of his Six Hats thinking programme addresses, as we will see.

'Every serious intellectual advance has had to begin with an attack on some Aristotelian doctrine,' said Bertrand Russell, and Edward's problem with the Gang of Three is fundamental: that they set in stone the judgemental attitude in Western culture. Socrates was heavily into argument (or dialectic). In Plato's dialogues, someone puts something up and he knocks it down. He is a skilful wordsmith. Edward describes his approach as, 'That's wrong, that's wrong, that's wrong.' So what's right? 'Not my business!'

Plato, influenced by the mathematician Pythagoras and believing that as there are ultimate truths in mathematics, so there are ultimate truths in life, gave us his Doctrine of Ideas or Forms, essences out of reach of our senses, whose imprint is inscribed on our minds at birth. All things participate in these forms. All that we can know we know of these forms, which transcend being (and are thus not susceptible to proof or denial). They are the source of the existence of all that is knowable and the means of its apprehension, a bit like the sun is to visible things. With his Doctrine of Forms, Plato denied human knowledge the evidence of the senses and at the same time promoted the judgement mode. There was bound to be conflict.

Edward challenges the notion of these basic, unmovable truths, which are deeply embedded in our culture, in religion, in aesthetics, in ethics, in law, and in our day-to-day thinking. Society, one might say, has for thousands of years been rooted in them.

Aristotle, Plato's pupil, didn't toe the line on Plato's Forms, but invented the syllogism, which was an attempt to bring the certainty of mathematics to argument and ensure that ethics, law, religion, aesthetics, and so on worked with the certainty of $2 + 2 = 4$. Given clear categorisation of premises and a few axioms or rules, like the Law of Contradiction ('A cannot be both B and not–B,') and the Law of the Excluded Middle ('A must be either B or not–B'), civilisation would be sorted. The syllogism has dominated the science of logic for more than 2,000 years:

> All men are mortal
> Socrates is a man
> Therefore, Socrates is mortal.

The validity of the entailment (last line) is dependent on the validity of the premises from which it is deduced. Aristotle was very keen on classifying things according to their attributes because that way, the validity of the premises was clear and he could put his logic to work.

'Aristotle invented a kind of inclusion, exclusion, logic,' as Edward describes it.

> What he said was, from the past let us create categories, definitions, boxes. Then when you come across something, you may have to analyse it first, then judge, 'Is it in this box, is it not in this box?' Something was either in the box or outside it, it couldn't belong partly to one box and partly to another. A good model of it is medicine. A child is brought in with a rash and the doctor has to decide what is his condition. The doctor has possibilities. He then judges, what box does this fit? When the judgement is made, you know what to do. The prescription is on the side of the box.

But as soon as we try and define and categorise everything in this way (which we tend to do even in our relationships), we deny possibilities. Analysing, defining, categorising has formed the brain's tendency to fit what we perceive into familiar boxes, which closes the door on possibility and keeps us firmly in judgement mode. Consider how many of our thoughts and conversations each day are judgemental. 'That is the standard model for most of our thinking – 100 per cent of our education, 90 per cent of our behaviour is about recognising situations as standard, and applying standard answers,' says Edward. 'We are going to have to move to another kind of thinking, to what can be.'

There is nothing wrong with Aristotle's analytical judgemental mode, says Edward, in the sense that there is nothing wrong with the left wheel of a car. Excellent, but inadequate. Where the axioms impinge on perception they do not hold good because perception and logic operate in different systems. Perceptions cannot be judged true or false like mathematical propositions. Being relative to conditions and circumstances, they may be true and false at the same time. The Law of Contradiction ('A cannot be both B and not–B,') and the Law of the Excluded Middle ('A must be either B or not–B') do not necessarily apply in the universe of perception. A new highway into a city holds different values for landowners who have sold their land for development, for locals whose lives are blighted by its noise and pollution, for commuters who can now travel more quickly into the city, for inner-city dwellers who now have more traffic congestion . . . And so on. The new highway is both good and bad at the same time. It is unclassifiable as falling into one box or the other. Logic works well in maths because maths is a closed system, with everything neatly defined. We have defined 1 and 2 before deducing that 1 + 2 = 3. In real life, definitions/ perceptions differ and are relative to circumstance, to where the protagonists are coming from. A can be, and very often is, both B and not–B.

Relativity is the reality of perception. Absolutism is the reality of the system of logic. Perception is no less real for that. In fact, it is more real because logic is a closed system divorced from reality, a system in which everything has to be defined in order to work, and life isn't like that. So Edward can enjoy the paradox: 'Perceptions are real even when they do not reflect reality.' Whether they do or do not reflect reality is not the point. Another similar proposition is: 'Fears may be unreasonable, but they are not unreal.'

It is the axiomatic unreality of the analytical judgemental mode – the very fact that 'A' can be both 'B' and 'not–B' in reality – which invites conflict between two agents boxed up in the logic of their own positions, each blind to the logic of the perception of the other.

Edward's beef with the Gang of Three is their fundamentally authoritarian approach to determining what is. With parallel thinking, Edward sets a different purpose. Within the idiom of movement – creative, constructive, design thinking – let's discover what can be. That is the nature of the paradigm shift that he proposes.

With the move away from deep-truth thinking, which has to be defended at all costs, 'arrogance and righteousness disappear and with them persecution'. With the move to 'proto-truth', a contingent truth, a notion introduced in *The Happiness Purpose* in 1977, there is a constant readiness to change, but also a willingness to use the contingent truth as absolute, provided the perception of a situation is the priority, and is tackled in a constructive, creative fashion.

The Sophist Protagoras's 'What seems to me is so to me: what seems to you is so to you,' historically suppressed by the Gang of Three, is thus Edward's starting point. But he harnesses it to the design idiom – thinking in parallel with Six Hats, all thinking in the same direction at one time (see below); thinking constructively with the CoRT tools, broadening perception and seeing others' points of view; thinking creatively with lateral thinking, and finding not compromise – this is not consensus politics – but a new way forward.

Parallel Thinking is his clearest statement of the paradigm shift that is his mission to effect. The *Financial Times* described the book as 'his boldest attempt yet to change the way our minds work'. But the book isn't in itself a radical shift. He is really just easing our minds further along the path on which they were set in *Conflicts*, the same path he took as a teenager, sitting in the family dining room, with his chair back perilously on its heels, silently getting his mind around the polarised arguments of the assembled throng.

As he pointed out in *Conflicts*, our thinking is already changing in the direction in which the new idiom will take us. He wrote, 'In Europe today it would be unthinkable for England to declare war on France or for Germany to attack Austria. Yet, less than a lifetime ago, wars on this scale were very thinkable. The superpower bloc is the next logical progression. After that the technology of communication, the interlocking of economies and the cost of war should make the idiom obsolete on any major scale.'

Some of this was prescient in 1984, when he wrote it. The Berlin Wall didn't come down until 9 November 1989. In fact, Edward visited the Kremlin shortly after publication of *Conflicts* and discovered that his work was part of the shift in attitude. 'I had a meeting with the Foreign Affairs Committee of the Politburo in the Kremlin in Moscow,' he told me, 'and the top chap was sitting reading a copy of *Conflicts*. I noticed it was heavily annotated in the margin and when he saw me looking at this, he said, "This is not the only copy, Gorbachev has got his own!"'

Dr Eric Dosmukhamedov, now ensconced at the Socio-Legal Centre at Oxford University, confirmed to me that Edward's books were part of the reading in the Kremlin at the time of perestroika. I went back to *Conflicts* with renewed zeal and came to the quote above. So prescient did it seem that it struck me with unease that the notion of 'interlocking economies' made Britain's adoption of the Euro inevitable too.

Diving back into the mid-1980s for the tools to implement parallel thinking, SITO having failed to take off, Edward emerged with Six Hats as the constructive, role-playing, non-adversarial way forward. It is not different from CoRT or to lateral thinking. It is simply a different arrangement of what he has given us before. Designed to be applied to conflict situations and to the creation of new ideas, Six Hats lays down six sorts of thinking to be engaged, one at a time.

In Six Hat Thinking, the hat is not a thing to put on, but a signal that a person or group is about to direct attention towards the matter in hand from one of six points of view. Black-hat thinking gives *carte blanche* to tear an idea to shreds, but the essence of Six Hats is objectivity, and there is no place for emotion under the black hat. Personal feelings can only be expressed under the red hat. Whatever may be said under the negative auspices of the black hat can have nothing to do with feelings and may end up not bearing much on the decision at all. Everyone must contribute under each hat, and under the blue hat (managing the thinking process) there is skill in drawing up an appropriate order of hats for a particular purpose.

Usually, when we are thinking, we are trying to do a whole variety of things at the same time. We may be trying to be creative, cautious, intuitive all at the same time. If, as Edward claims, there is a change in brain chemicals in the neuro-transmitter balance when you are being cautious or positive or creative, there may even be a physiological reason why Six Hats works. So, for very practical reasons, it is important to do these things separately. 'You cannot maximise in different directions at the same time,' as Edward puts it.

In particular, the Six Hats programme is designed to remove what he refers to as 'the main restriction on thinking . . . ego defence . . .'

> With the hats the ego doesn't come into it. The ego is the big problem in thinking. If you are against an idea you are not going to look at it closely; if you are enthusiastic you may be insufficiently cautious. With the hats, supposing you don't like the idea, you are invited to be as critical or cautious as you like, but then when the yellow hat comes round you are expected to look for value and if you sit there and refuse to find any value when all around you are finding value suddenly you are shown to be inadequate as a thinker. The whole dynamic has changed. If you want to show off now you don't show off by winning or losing an argument but by performing

better under every hat. The dynamics of showing off change completely.

White Hat

Wearing this hat, players can only present facts and figures, absolutely objectively, absolutely neutrally (hence white). There is no place for proposals, arguments or judgement, for extrapolation of figures into trends, for statistical analysis of any kind, for opinion, bias or emotion, for anything other than the facts, plain and simple. Indeed, the white hat is very useful to focus on the very process of separating facts from extrapolation and interpretation. As Edward points out, 'It might be imagined that politicians would have considerable difficulty with white-hat thinking.'

Under the white hat, you ask, What information have we got? What is missing? How do we get what we need? Which are checked facts? Which are merely believed facts (what he calls second-class facts)?

In amassing facts Edward recommends asking two types of question, fishing questions (exploratory) and hunting questions (assessment-type, yes/no-answer questions). Should you find difficulty in checking whether a useful piece of information is a fact, frame its likelihood as distinctly as possible.

The idea of Six Hats is to build up a thinking map of the matter in hand, to come to a meeting not with proposals, but like the Japanese do, with facts that enrich the mapping of a situation to suggest a route through.

Red Hat

Under the auspices of the red hat you may do two things. You may let rip your true feelings about an issue – this response is invited under the red hat and is characterised by its fiery colour – or you may offer an intuition or gut feeling. An intuition may be a sudden insight or a judgement grounded in experience, the logic of which is too complex to disentangle for checking. Intuitions can be taken onto the map but only under the auspices of fallible, red-hat thinking.

Negotiation is the trading of the value of a situation from two points of view. These values must be expressed under red-hat thinking. The important thing is to give vent to feelings early so that their influence on the map can be tracked and to consult them again in relation to outcome.

Edward recalls that when he was in South Africa teaching the peace accord committees Six Hat thinking, 'they always started the meetings with the red hat, allowing everyone to express their emotions. Then they could get on with the meeting.'

Black Hat

The black hat concerns negative assessment, and the objective values of the matter in hand. Only the red hat allows a subjective, personal response. So there is to be no mordant negativity here, only logical negativity, although it seems that certain people fall into black-hat thinking more readily than others and the black hat performs a useful function in 'segregating the negativity of naturally pessimistic thinking'.

Edward's caveat is that the black hat gets overuse. 'Criticism is very natural because the brain has a powerful mismatch mechanism – it's a very useful survival technique, but prone to overuse. Criticism is all right if we proffer something else.'

Yellow Hat

The yellow hat encourages the listing of benefits in a situation – very often hidden benefits. Value sensitising is an important part of it. It is a constructive attitude of mind. It takes the ego out of negotiation. It takes the ego out of thinking. If you attach your ego to a point of view you're going to attack many other ideas. Under the yellow hat, ego is shown up by the emergence of value (if everyone else is finding value).

In the mid-1980s, *Tactics* revealed that the one defining characteristic of success was a willingness to make things happen, which is fundamental yellow-hat thinking.

Green Hat

Green is the colour of spring and growing plants. This is the hat for possibilities, creative and lateral thinking. Alternatives, new ideas, change. 'Just as logical thinking is based on the behaviour of symbolic thinking (a particular universe), so lateral thinking is based on the behaviour of patterning systems (also a particular universe).' Out of one box, into another? The green box has no lid. Fundamental to it is the search for alternatives, but the green hat takes us into a territory devoid of safe logic and far away from the cosy feeling so many choose to chase, of always being right.

Blue Hat

Under this hat, you focus on the strategy or structure for discussing the job in hand. Edward favours appointing a concept manager who looks after the blue hat, like a finance manager looks after the money. The blue hat is a job for the orchestral conductor, the choreographer, the orchestrator. Under the blue hat we customise the software for the mind. If intelligence is the engineering of a car, the blue-hat thinker is not in the car, he is watching from outside and directing the process.

Sequence varies as to purpose. For example – seeking an idea:

White – gather information
Green – creating alternatives or new ideas
Yellow – benefits and feasibility
Black – weaknesses and dangers
Red – feelings
Green – further developing alternatives and ideas and making a choice
Blue – look back and assess what thinking has been done
Black – final judgement/choice
Red – feelings on the outcome

Whereas reacting to a presented idea might be: Red, Yellow, Black, Green, White, Green, Black, Red.

Six Hats is used in a variety of contexts, but it is especially flexible in a judgement context. The law is an area in which Edward has done much work, but it remains relatively untouched by his thinking. The relationship between perception and reality is clearly an issue. At a seminar in 1999, Edward began:

Last year I was asked to give one of the opening talks at an Australian constitutional convention about the future of the federation after 100 years, and I told this story: This [he drew the picture on his OHP] is an overhead view of a motorcar, which the owner had painted half black and half white. When his friend said to him, 'Why do you paint your car half white and half black?' he replied, 'It's such fun, whenever I have an accident, to hear the witnesses in court contradicting one another.' One witness said that it was a black car that came round the corner and knocked a cyclist over and another said it was a white car. At the end of the convention Sir Anthony Mason, one of their top judges, came up to me and said, 'I am going to use that story again and again, so often do I come across people arguing about a situation only because they are looking at different parts of it.'

There is, on the one hand, the question of a witness's perception of a situation, and on the other, the key question of lawyers forming or altering or seducing jurors' perception of a situation, which takes us back to Owen Fogarty, Father Peter and the University of Malta Literary and Debating Society in the 1950s, when Edward would love deliberately to argue the weaker case. I asked him whether he might have liked to be a lawyer. 'I can never ever imagine wanting to be a lawyer because though I can see it is intellectually stimulating, it is so unconstructive. Well, you may say that's not true, because each separate case successfully prosecuted is an achievement, but you are not really adding anything to the world at all.'

Nevertheless, he enjoys speaking at legal conventions. 'Last year, I was asked to San Diego to speak to the American Bar Association about how lawyers could be more creative,' he told me. 'I think there were ninety deans of law schools and law professors and top lawyers, so I do get involved. I am on the Council of Dispute Resolution and in Australia, the head of it, Sir Lawrence Street, is a great friend.' In 1990, a friend of mine heard Edward speak at the Commonwealth Law Conference and recalls his taking the lion's share of the audience – 1,500 compared to 300-odd for Geoffrey Robertson and others. I asked Edward what he had addressed. 'I was talking about the limitations of the adversarial system. There was huge interest. A lot of these lawyers and judges came up afterwards and said, "We agree with you. It's an awful system. We're just trapped in it." I am not against the system, just the way we revere it. I think perhaps it has 10 per cent usefulness, but we esteem it far too highly and use it far too widely.' On another occasion, he said to me: 'In a court of law everyone is case making – if the defence notices something that will help the prosecution he'll keep quiet about it, and vice versa – they are not exploring the subject.'

On the face of it, the case-making system, as opposed to the inquisitional system, which they have in France and which is increasingly used in other countries in administrative law and tribunals, does seem less fair. When I was twelve, I was on holiday in the Lake District with a party which included David Calcutt, later Sir David Calcutt QC and one of the government's designated members of the Panel of Arbitrators of the International Centre for the Settlement of International Disputes. One evening at dinner, after climbing Sca Fell, I asked him whether he had ever 'got anyone off' that may have been guilty. My memory is that he said that he had, though very probably he couched it in stainless, lawyer-type terms. I then asked him whether, in his role as prosecutor, he had ever convicted anyone that he thought may have been innocent. Most boys of twelve were still in the grip of the awesome black-hat scene in David Lean's film of *Great Expectations*; and when Calcutt confirmed that miscarriages of justice did inevitably occur – I believe I lost whatever vestige of childhood innocence I had left at that time.

The point is that with Six Hats a verdict does not depend on argumentation skills, the situation has to be explored from every point of view by all parties at one and the same time. Every constituent of the jury's perception of the situation, emotion included, must be given due weight and not be allowed to have an inappropriate or dominant influence on matters. Biases and prejudices must be scrutinised as keenly as the facts, and all of it by lawyers looking in the same direction at the same time, such that eventually the law no longer depends on argument skills. 'Not adversarial, not confrontational – full exploration,' as Edward would put it.

Since Caspar de Bono used Six Hats on British jury service, one of Edward's trainers, Grant Todd, has been working with the US judiciary, piloting its use with juries there.

'People in juries in poll after poll have said they wish they had more help and guidance with discussion,' Grant told me.

Six Hats takes out all the distractions, all the differences – you have reticent people and people who are forward. It takes out all those sort of imbalances. I simply say that it is the most balanced and comprehensive way to look at any issue, whatever it is. The great thing about parallel thinking is that it allows jurors to pull themselves together, too. We allow them temporarily to change their behaviour, in a group setting, in a positive, quality way. Taking a course in Six Hats might cost an ordinary person $400. I say that we can train jurors for less than the price of lunch. There isn't much money to spare in the judicial system and we are not looking to make money, though we are not looking to lose money either. I am now in discussion with three states, Wisconsin, Arizona, Washington, and we are going to do pilot programmes to show the efficacy of the programme and are aiming to have the results available in time for the Jury Summit in New York City at the beginning of next year.

The story that had sparked Todd's interest was not in fact a thorough-going use of Six Hats in a jury's deliberation of a case, but it is worth telling nonetheless. Said Caspar,

> The defendant was accused of beating up a taxi driver. The taxi driver was on the phone to his wife in a public phone booth on Oxford Street, and this guy was putting up prostitute cards while he was on the phone. There was an altercation and this guy proceeded to beat up the taxi driver. There was a retrial because, after two days, the first jury hadn't been able to come to a decision.
>
> The judge was quite specific in his summing up at the retrial: we should make our decision as to whether the defendant used reasonable force, because the defence claimed that the taxi driver started the fight. When we went into the jury room everyone round the table gave their view and it was increasingly clear that what everyone was saying was that whoever it was who had started the fight was basically guilty, but it wasn't clear who had started the fight. In fact it was this that was disputed.
>
> When it came to my turn to speak, I didn't actually use the Six Hats out loud, but it was clear to me that what was missing was some blue-hat thinking – focus. I simply said that I think we are debating the wrong issue, that we will never come to agreement if we discuss who started the fight, and that is probably why the previous jury took two days not to arrive at a verdict. I said, what the judge actually said to us was, answer the simple question, 'Did the defendant use reasonable force or was it unreasonable?' And it was fairly clear from the amount of damage done to the taxi driver that he hadn't used reasonable force, and we all went round the table agreeing and in five minutes it was done. I used it as an example to Grant because in my head I said, 'I can see why this isn't working. What's missing is the blue-hat thinking.'

Like Demajo's use of CoRT at the match between Galatasaray and Leeds, the method, thoroughly internalised, enabled Caspar to get to the heart of the problem immediately. The blue hat, in this instance, was all that was needed.

Six Hats attracted media criticism when it was first published, partly because it is so simple an idea. But on its success in a variety of arenas – schools, overseas development, business and industry – Edward has built an international distribution business, APTT, which employs more than 900 trainers worldwide.

In 1989, before APTT was up and running, the programme had already started to gain ground in the area of business. I have a published list of Edward's seminar invitations for that year, which included Hoechst-Celanese (largest chemical company in the world), Citicorp (leading US bank) L.M. Ericsson (leading Swedish electronic company), Total (major French oil company), Mondadori (largest publisher in Italy), Zegna (leading Italian fashion house), Kuwait Oil Company, Barclays Bank, Midland Bank, Weston Group (leading Canadian food company), Smurfitt (largest company in Ireland) and Prudential Insurance (leading insurance company in Canada/US). In Milan he taught business school professors from all over the world at Bocconi University. In Japan, where Farrell's ground work clearly paid off, Hisashi Shinto, chief executive of Nippon Telephone and Telegraph (NTT) with 350,000 employees – at the time the total value of the top five US corporations was less than that of NTT – liked Six Hats so much that he ordered several thousand copies for his executives to read. 'Before that it was not done to attack the boss in Japan,' says Edward, 'but now executives can ring up and say, "I want to do black-hat thinking."' With the success of the book in that market came an invitation in 1989 from the *Nihon Kezai Shinbun* (equivalent of the *Wall Street Journal* in the US) to address a seminar with 400 executives. In Lahore, Pakistan, Edward spoke at ADASIA, the leading marketing and advertising conference in Asia, as well as meeting with senior education officials. In May he gave the keynote address at ADARABIA conference in Cairo, and as October turned into November, of course, he ran the Seoul Symposium of Nobel Laureates in Korea.

Recently, I spoke to Andreas Novak, who is currently de Bono master trainer for Six Hats in Germany. Novak has the programme with two European giants, Siemens and Bosch. 'Bosch is innovative and extremely successful,' he told me.

It is a highly technical engineering company. We have a car-makers' boom, which makes it a Bosch boom, because most of the parts in cars are made by Bosch. The Swabian people (where Bosch head-quarters is situated) are technical, driven people, very very bright, but they do not make much fuss about themselves, and even in Germany few realise that the company has 190,000 workers world-wide and a turnover of some 50 billion Deutschmarks annually. More than 2,000 people in Germany were trained in Six Hats within

Bosch. The company is committed to the people they employ, in that they keep them on, but not so, until recently, in training them. What happened was that this CEO attended a seminar given by Edward in 1995, and subsequently tried to get Edward to HQ. For two years he tried. Finally Edward agreed to go in December 1997, and returned in March and April 1998. After that, Bosch started on a larger scale to teach the programme to management. This was done by a colleague of mine and myself. Altogether we had 600 people at courses. There is no doubt that company performance is better, otherwise we would not get so many people in seminars here.

For Siemens, which is by far the biggest corporation in Europe worldwide – it has something like 325,000 on the payroll and the product is everything to do with electricity – the facts are that Edward was at their HQ Research and Development two or three times in the mid-1990s. At that time the company was in urgent need of an infusion of creativity and innovation (it was far behind, for example, ABB or General Electric – not in terms of turnover, but in terms of what money they earned). I will not go into the reasons, but fact was that they started a programme to be TOP again (this was the name of the programme as well). Part of this initiative was to invite Edward into the R&D department. Soon afterwards they drummed up thirty-seven in-house trainers to get certified, which was happening in 1996.

Although it is not possible to measure the specific impact of Six Hats in TOP, Edward can justifiably claim that since the programme was introduced, 'Siemens' share price has doubled, which for the biggest company in Europe is quite something. Their profits are up 98 per cent.' There is, however, much more to Six Hats than big business. Noted Edward:

A couple of years ago, I had two letters on the same day. One was from the Head of Research at Siemens, saying how well Six Hats was working, and the other was from a young fellow, Simon Batchelor, on an aid mission to Khmer villages in Cambodia to drill for water. He had his daughter with him and one of my books, *Teach Your Child How to Think*, from which he began to teach the villagers about Six Hats. They became so enthusiastic that the whole mission changed. Thereafter, he was invited to Vietnam and Afghanistan to do the same.

Simon Batchelor's story is so compelling that it confines hard research data to a back seat in the evaluation of the Six Hats programme, though it contains plenty of that too:

There is a history to development. In the 1950s and early 1960s you get these huge dam projects by the government and the World Bank, intended to generate massive electricity but now said to be white elephants. My favourite example is a little place in northern Kenya, in the middle of the desert, where they built a factory for freezing fish because there's a saltwater lake there teeming with fish. The local people are walking around in animal skins – literally – and they are expected to manage this fish freezing factory and run the frozen fish down to Nairobi. I don't know what people were thinking of. A lot of it is politics, bribery, whatever.

Then, in the late 1960s, you get Schumacher [Ernst Schumacher, British economist, best known for his book *Small is Beautiful* (1973)] saying what is needed is intermediate technology, as they can't cope with massive technological stuff. What they need are small things like hand pumps. My business partner, Professor Dunn who was my PhD tutor, was a colleague of Schumacher's, so I am on the edge of that shift – wind pumps, hand pumps, etc. Then, by the mid-1980s we were starting to read that intermediate technology is not the answer, it's about *people* and people participation. It takes about ten years after the thinkers and academics write stuff for developers to catch up, so this Cambodia project, which began in 1992 and was and is completely people oriented, is actually very new.

So I had this opportunity to go to Cambodia with an organisation that is predominantly involved with relief. Christian Outreach goes into an emergency situation, feeds people, sets up shelter, water supplies, etc. They had been working with Khmer refugees on the Thai border for, I think it was, thirteen years in total. The Khmer finished, well supposedly finished, ruling the country in 1979. But of course there had been a civil war going on through the intervening years and people had not returned. There were around half a million people sitting on the Thai/Cambodia border in refugee camps. Christian Outreach had been there all those years running health services, food distribution, etc.

The perception of the political situation in Cambodia depended on who you spoke to. Originally, people spoke of an invasion from

Vietnam and a puppet Communist government in Cambodia. In hindsight, most people would say that that view was based on the paranoia of American government. Vietnam had just beaten America, and America was pretty pissed off about that, therefore they labelled the strife in Cambodia as an invasion from Vietnam.

With hindsight, we know that what actually happened was that a faction of the Khmer Rouge ran off to Vietnam, raising themselves a small army. Then, the Khmer Rouge from inside Cambodia attacked Vietnam and tried to expand their borders. Vietnam retaliated, pushing them back, and also backed this other Khmer Rouge faction that came back into Cambodia, captured about half the country and set up a government.

So this invasion was not quite what the world press painted it. Unfortunately, what it meant was that for the next ten, thirteen years Cambodia was suffering an embargo and there were only a few agencies, like the Mennonites (a religious group in America that originally came from Prussia and the Netherlands, sort of Baptists) and Oxfam, who were prepared to break the embargo and try and help rebuild the country. There was huge poverty. Then, in 1992, there was UN-brokered peace in the civil war.

The important thing, from a de Bono point of view, was that because of their background, Christian Outreach knew very little about development process, rebuilding a country. They were mainly refugee orientated. But they wanted to do something and so offered me a position as programme manager, saying, 'Simon, you know more about development than we do, why don't you just go for a year with a blank sheet of paper and a budget line and after a year you tell us what you want to do?' Very nice brief and incredibly unusual. That is a key point. I had had two other offers for UNDP posts, one in Vietnam as head of renewable energy and one in Solomon Islands as head of energy. I had to make the choice: 'Can you make more of a difference sitting in a government office somewhere making policy or in the bush somewhere, working intensively with a few people?' I decided I would go for the bush option.

So, I and my family – ten-year-old daughter – set off for Cambodia, lived in Prey Veng, which at that time had no electricity, no other expatriates. I had read a lot of books about development work being more people orientated than technology orientated. Now, here was an ideal opportunity to ask the question, 'OK, what does that mean in practice?'

You must first appreciate what I had walked into. All the intellectuals had been systematically wiped out. They always talk about how 'their minds were trained to be numb'. During the Khmer Rouge years, if you were standing next to somebody that the Khmer Rouge shot, if you flinched you were likely to get shot as well. So they trained themselves not to think about it, not to think of the human cost, the human suffering. Although we are talking thirteen years later, those thirteen years have been in limbo. Most people would talk about the KM as though it were yesterday. Take language learning: our teacher could not teach us about rice. In the Cambodian language there are about twenty-five different words for rice and it is important to get the right one for the right stage. But she couldn't actually tell us anything about that because as soon as she mentioned rice she broke down in tears because it reminded her of the KM years and all the hardship that she went through. She was a doctor, one of the few surviving intellectuals, but she just couldn't get past the word 'rice'. We had to keep turning over the pages of the book to avoid it.

So we started this project, started working with the villagers, trying to stimulate them to think creatively about what they could do with the resources they had. Our programme was not going to give them very much, rather accelerate from and multiply what they already had. There were basic problems. Population increases had wiped out the trees in the vicinity, so now rather than travelling half a day for firewood they were travelling three days for firewood. How are you going to prevent it becoming a desert?

The problem was to motivate, to get the village to trigger itself into action, to get its own momentum going. It was not going to be enough simply to tell them or even show them how. Batchelor could reason with them logically till he was blue in the face, but it wouldn't change their behaviour. They'd say, 'It's your pump, your well, not our business.' Somehow he had to change perceptions, trigger patterns that would rearrange all the complex interrelationships within village culture so that they would begin to operate (in Edward's terms) in design mode. These people were psychologically devastated and they also had their own cultural patterns which seemed to vie with progress. 'Khmers are useless at decision making,' Batchelor continued.

If they made a decision during the KR years they were shot for their trouble, so they learned to put their hand up, not to volunteer any of their ideas. They also have the whole 'face' thing of Asia very, very strongly, so that if you make a wrong suggestion you lose face. That means, again, you don't volunteer ideas. You also have an extremely hierarchical society so you would never contradict your boss if he makes a suggestion. So there is very little mechanism within Khmer society for getting a sensible decision out of things where people have volunteered their true opinions.

In de Bono terms, Batchelor was to become the 'provocation' to the self-organising system of the Khmer village with all its special biases. He went on:

> To start with, I just handled questions from instinct and experience. We worked with six villages to start with. It is a very slow process. After I had worked with those six villages for a year we wrote up the promised plan to work with fifty-two villages over the next five years. Because it then took a while to get that funded, it has effectively taken seven years. So we are talking about 22,000 people over a seven-year period with a planned exit strategy, to get out in such a way that people are not dependent on us. A lot of the objectives and the goals in the plan were about changing people's thinking or helping people's thinking to change. That is very unusual. Normally it will be, 'We'll put in fifty wells, etc.' So we were very surprised when the British government paid for 50 per cent of it. There was no hardware guaranteed – there is hardware involved but it wasn't the priority.
>
> I had some staff – some given me by the government (and I had no choice over these) and some I had hired from among ex-workers on the border, whom Christian Outreach knew were trustworthy. I had spent a year working with the six villages and doing it from instinct. Then I began trying to communicate to my new staff what we were doing and how to do it.
>
> You start with dialogue. Most of the books on the shelf talk about 'open questions' and 'closed questions'. You must have open questions not closed questions [if you want to get an active dialogue going]. You don't go into a village and say, 'Do you want a new water supply?' Because if you do, they will just say, 'Yes.' Rather, you go in with open questions, like 'What is the biggest problem in your village?' That's the first open question and that is obvious, but where

do you go after that? If they say, 'Water is the main problem,' you say, 'What sort of water supply do you want?' But the problem with that is that they may have experience of only one sort of water supply [straight into a cul de sac]. They may have dug open wells for the last 2,000 years and they are not going to think of hand pumps or water pumps or whatever.

So, there was no framework for guiding that discussion, and I was simply telling my staff, 'You must ask open questions.' Depending on the staff member, either they started with an open question and very quickly funnelled down to their own experience, bringing things to a close, or, as was the case with a couple of staff members, they were very good at keeping the questions open ... and it never closed. Discussions would then go on and on. If people had been talking about water, they would ask other open questions which would make sure water remained the absolute priority and of course that would lead on to discussions about buffaloes or whatever.

I went through a phase when I was letting the staff run discussions and then I would try to postmortem them afterwards, saying things like, 'At that point, you shouldn't have asked that question,' and they would say, 'Why?' And I would struggle. I had no framework to discuss these things. I just had a gut feeling, if you like, that at that point the discussion went off down a blind alley. I had no guidelines to communicate to them what I knew instinctively.

Then I read Edward's book.

As I said, I had taken my family, and I read *Teach Your Child How To Think* in the process of home schooling for my ten-year-old daughter, Diana. This was a back-to-the-bush job. We didn't sign on for correspondence school. Everyone moans about the National Curriculum in Britain. For us it was great. It had just come in. We bought a copy, which said what you had got to learn. It also forced a lot of publishers to publish new books. So we went to Foyle's or Dillons and went along and grabbed books off the shelves. We went out with 40 kilos of books or something, and while we were doing that we saw the *Teach Your Child How To Think* book and thought, 'Oh, well, that'll be an interesting sideline. It's not on the NC but it'll give us a break from the facts and figures of geography and history.'

Eventually, I had begun to say to Diana, 'Let's read this book together for an hour a week,' and we hit the Hat thinking at precisely the time I was struggling with how to describe to my staff how to run discussions and so on. It was, of course, exactly what I needed. Tailor made. So I began by teaching the staff Six Hats thinking ... Culturally, in fact, the colours of Edward's model don't work in Cambodia. Yellow doesn't work here because of course they are not looking for the sunshine, they are desperate for the rain. And the black hat doesn't really work because black and white have a funny relationship, it is not the good/evil meaning it has in our culture. And they don't have a black hat of judgement either. But they were happy to remember the colours based on my amusing anecdotes about how they worked in British culture.

Initially I used it only amongst the staff. But of course the staff are going to the villages and running discussions, using it in their brain to guide their questioning. So during my mentoring of them I would listen to them and say, 'Right, at this stage you'll be needing a green question,' and so they would begin to phrase a green question, like, 'We have been talking about spending $500 on a water supply, what else could we do with $500?' Yet the villagers at this point don't know anything about the hats. Indeed, the first thing they ever knew about the hats was fairly near my leaving time when we printed up T-shirts as a leaving present to all the village committee members (six or seven people in each village, without whom we always said we would never take a decision). The T-shirt has the hats on it, they are sitting on teapots because we are always going into the village drinking cups of tea. People used to say, 'OK, we can see the villages improving, but all you seem to do is drink cups of tea!' I have a terrible reputation in Cambodia regarding tea.

The committee members all accepted the T-shirts and thought they were beautiful with nice colours, etc. They hadn't a clue what it was about, but that was what I wanted because I knew that over the following weeks, the committees would turn round to the Khmer staff and say, 'These are great T-shirts, what do they mean? What is it all about?' And then the Khmer staff would say, 'Well, actually this is what we have been using in all our discussions and let me explain it to you.'

That is exactly what happened. The original nineteen villages all know the Six Hats thinking model. Some use it more than others.

Results? Let's make a cost comparison. Another NGO was doing a water programme, hand pumps, they had hand pumps at the centre of the agency agenda. Now, the hand pump programme cost the same as our entire people programme. Yet, in our programme we did everything from contraception through to schools to water supplies to small businesses, the whole culture thing. On water alone, that other programme generated 648 hand pumps, 70 per cent of which were working one year down the line, which is actually very good. But in the same time period, with our money doing all these other things as well, we have 2,200 pumps! Basically, people started to put their hands in their pockets and finance their own pumps. They had talked through the benefits and *they could see.*

You know the phrase, 'Give a man a fish and you feed him for a day; teach a man to fish and you feed him for life.' We say, 'Give a man a fish, you feed him for a day; teach a man to fish, you feed him until someone comes along with a better fishing technique or until war overtakes him and he becomes a refugee or until somebody builds a factory and pollutes out all his fish. But, if you teach a man to think, then you feed him for life, because if he becomes a refugee then he will think through his new situation and work out a new situation for livelihood.' He is equipped for life, which is de Bono's thing.

An example of how the whole system was galvanised, and both personal and community benefits accrued, is in the area of contraception – '80 per cent of the eligible women now undertake contraception,' says Batchelor.

When we started, there was one lady who was trying contraception. In project proposals you have to indicate what your achievements are going to be. The funding bodies, like the British government, want to know. I guaranteed a 50 per cent increase in the number of women undertaking contraception, so that wasn't promising much! It was a complete con, we only needed one more person. In reality, we have thousands more and the clinics are all run by volunteer women from the villages, who saw their own need and set it up. They turned it into a little business. They found they could buy the contraception – they used Depot, a three-month injection – from a nearby town for 1,700 riel and sell it to the villagers for 2,500 riel – about $1 or 60p. We are not talking vast profit, but what that meant was that they got something out of the day and they also have money for buying rice and so on. While other contraception agencies round the country were not having any impact, ours was taking off like wild fire.

Why? Because the problem with Depot is that the first time you have it you get more intensive bleeding than you do normally and the women often don't return for the second jab. So it fades out after an initial burst of enthusiasm. But our three ladies were systematically going to their neighbours. They lived in their villages where the customers were and they'd go round and say, 'No, I know you've got more bleeding now but if you have that second injection you'll be all right.' So they captured all those drop-outs and brought them back into the programme. And once they'd done that, it became a self-perpetuating thing.

We turned the villages from a situation where there was a shortage of water and food and dirty water, where there were no mechanisms for small businesses, intense child deaths under five, to a situation where they have all got water, they have all got food, there are opportunities for business and the child mortality rate has dropped dramatically.

Now the Khmer staff have formed their own Khmer organisation. They are seeking funding to expand beyond the fifty-two villages. There is an acceleration effect beyond the control villages anyway. When a good idea comes up it spreads over the borders. The treadle pump has gone berserk! It just sells in its thousands, particularly suited for Cambodia, originally made in Bangladesh. We brought it not to the village but to the nearby town so that the villagers still had to make an effort to go to the town and purchase it. All the time we are trying not to do it for them.

One begins to understand why all those years ago, Edward would teach but refused to do the nannying!

As I left Batchelor, I asked him whether, back in 1993, his ten-year-old daughter had benefited from reading *Teach Your Child How To Think*.

'A statistical sample of one is not a valid sample,' he said. 'But she is a straight A student who has just got an offer to Oxford to read psychology. She can articulate.'

Chapter Eleven

Value X

'What is going to change human behaviour is changes in human thinking. Not changes in human values.'

De Bono PLC is not a concept that this master of de-centralisation likes to entertain. 'It has always been a sort of loose network,' he admits. His manager, Diane McQuaig, has a vision for him of 'a solid team, who would just put all its energy into getting him the recognition he deserves,' but that is not his style. 'He captures the moment, he is in the Gold Coast, he and somebody say, "Let's do this," and I hear about it a year later, when the paperwork hits my offices. He really is his own man ... Stephen Covey, all these people, have organisations, they have machines. Now Edward has never wanted something like that ...'

'On that subject,' said Paddy Hills, 'it goes back to Edward not really wishing to be controlled.' On the other hand, he is scrupulous in his time-keeping and, once he has agreed on something, in never letting anyone down. He likes a team around him, but he likes to think of it as a global family, from which he can escape at any time onto one of his islands. He does not want the team to organise him, he does not want a machine driving him.

In business, as in life, there is minimum emotional trade. Personally, he rates respect over love. Love is 'fine in theory but rarely reached in practice ... Respect is my ability to see [a person] as an entity,' he writes in *The Happiness Purpose*, 'it has nothing to do with how they react to me. Respect is a much more usable currency. Unfortunately, poets don't make much of a fuss about it.' In the business context he does not acquiesce in something because someone, who has done something for him, wants him to, but because that something is in itself worth doing.

Jealous of his independence, he demands of anyone that works for him the same self-reliance and disinterested dedication to project that is his obsession. He doesn't always get it.

His management style and expectations do frustrate some people who work for him, and it might be expected that people not used to working independently will find it difficult to succeed. However, the Lows are among those successful in the organisation who promote integration. Peter Low, who has become a millionaire working solely on the de Bono thinking programmes, advises 'that it is not enough for a person to be a trainer full stop and have no idea what the network is doing, or the place of a trainer or a master trainer in the whole network. In something like this you can't be self-sufficient ... Linda and I are pretty unique in the sense that we are master trainers and distributors and we run a school and so we have a much more comprehensive picture of who is in the organisation, how it is run and what some of the difficulties are. That I think is the point of advantage that we have, and Edward I think is aware of that.'

The Lows believe that creating a culture around what you are doing is important. When their students pass out of their school, they keep in touch. 'The Edward de Bono graduate alumni have like a credit card, and they can buy his things at a discount. There is also a newsletter. Then two or three times a year we meet with them and we mentor them. Why? Because these are going to be the future of Singapore, yes?'

Singapore is of course a particular environment, but what is relevant globally is the way this extraordinary couple relate to Edward. They appeal to what drives friendship in Edward – trust, and to what drives respect in him – autonomy and self-reliance.

Edward trusts us a lot because we have always opened all our books, displayed our honesty with him. Also, we respect that he has been a one-man show all along, with Paddy's help. When he comes out to places like Singapore you can't hold the man back by giving him all the problems you face with the business. I mean, once in a while you might ask him for his counsel, you know? But he has given you the package. Go, do it well! We don't give him problems. We only give him good news.

Edward's own itinerary, complex as it is, is kept free of problems by regular communication between Diane McQuaig in Toronto, Julia Pomirska in Sydney and Paddy Hills in London. 'I only remember one ghastly moment,' says Paddy.

He was coming into London and had agreed to do a talk whilst having to leave almost immediately to do another talk further afield in England, and then to fly out that night. That was a bit like an Anneke Rice scene? Getting him from A to B, telling the people where he was giving his talk, about the car that would be sitting at a particular time, on a particular corner with the engine running as he came out, and so on. There are some fairly hairy moments, but he never panics. He knew it had become a problem. He then required me to unravel it for him and make sure it was as smooth a passage as possible both for the people he was with and him.

Six Hats brought the first signs of organisation in the shape of a worldwide distribution and training network. 'I was a teacher in the 1970s and was assigned to develop a Creative Writing curriculum for high school kids,' Kathy Myers, who put the deal together, told me. The teaching was loosely based on de Bono's ideas and proved popular and successful. Years later, she left the teaching profession and took a job in Des Moines, Iowa, with a company publishing teaching materials, eventually becoming Editor-in-Chief. 'It was about a $12 million company, specialising in teaching English, language arts, literature, reading. So, I wanted to try to give teachers something they didn't have, and the one thing I knew that was new was Edward. This was 1984. I knew about CoRT, and I started to write to the Institute of Creative Thinking [Edward's base in New York], to Paddi Demattio, but I could never get through to Edward.

Then, Edward appeared at a National Catholic Teachers' Association conference in California. Christine Maxwell was in charge of CoRT at that time. I watched Edward perform and I was thrilled. That was the first time that I had seen him head-on talking about schools. But I still hadn't had any direct communication with him, and I have to admit I was afraid to talk to him. So, I went over to the booth and Christine Maxwell was there and one other woman. They had two people looking after a mob of some fifty people wanting to buy, so I couldn't talk to them either. Then someone gave Edward my letters and I began to be in touch with him directly. He invited me to hear him speak in Kansas City, to another group of educators, and that was the first time I met him face to face . . . I have never seen him as anything other than encouraging. His underlying philosophy, which he has stated to me several times, is that people won't do you any harm and they *might* do you some good, and you never know who is going to emerge as one who will contribute.

Myers was handed over to Diane McQuaig, who kept her hopes up that something would eventually materialise from her meeting with Edward.

Diane, early on, was the reason I stuck it out. She taught me to persist. She showed me that when Edward didn't follow through, it wasn't that he was rejecting but because he was just not focused on whatever it was you wanted him to do. So I met him in Toronto, and we pinned down the project ... a set of books called *Think, Note, Write*, and then we were field testing and using a team of editors and teachers and writing additional material, and I had a call from Pergamon saying that we couldn't publish it and I just about died. But then it turned out that we could publish, but had to change the names of the tools slightly.

We got pilots in forty-eight of the land states, before he asked whether we wanted to do Six Thinking Hats. Six Hats was big, but long before we knew it would be a success, the owner of my company and Edward and I met in San Francisco and agreed to do his corporate training. So, that was when APTT (Advanced Practical Thinking Training) was born. That meeting was on 1 July 1991. We incorporated it in September, he wrote the first of the instructor and participant manuals over Christmas 1991, and we got them on New Year's Day, 1992. Our first seminar with published materials was held on 17 February. It had been a huge scramble to get that manuscript edited, designed and published. We called the birth of the course Forty Days and Forty Nights. A dozen people attended that seminar. We certified people from three countries – Singapore, Canada and the United States – and some of them are still among the most active trainers in the whole network.

Two of the original twelve disciples were Peter and Linda Low. Linda recalled:

I was by this time a corporate trainer in a multinational, the American International Group. Edward invited me to a seminar of his in Singapore. He knew that I was very interested in his work and he introduced me more and more to them. I started looking after his business in Singapore, making arrangements as a friend. Then at the end of 1991, on one of his visits, Edward popped the question. He said, 'I have decided to train trainers worldwide and the first training will be done in February 1992.' I said I was very interested, I had already said I would just like to carry your bag all over the world to learn. So I was on the first team. There were twelve of us. We went to San Francisco.

We twelve didn't know what we were getting into. Edward is famous. His methods are world renowned. But how do we know whether this is going to take off? Who is going to believe our marketing? We had a certification programme and at the end, I remember, we sat together with Kathy Myers – Kathy will remember this very well – and said, 'Where do we go from here?'

By the end of that month I had tendered my resignation and told Edward we would set up a company solely to represent him. Very brave. Throwing ourselves in the deep blue sea. It was tough. Edward gave us lots of moral support, but in the first six months we were bringing in no money at all and we had a family.

At that time Edward said, 'Why don't you just operate from home?' But I said, 'That will not do in Singapore. If you are working out of the garage, no one is going to take you seriously.' So we invested a fair bit of money then. We picked a prime area of business at retail level, and actually built a resource centre on Edward. So, when you enter the office the first thing you see is a portrait of Edward smiling at all visitors. We believe that you want a focus, the whole set-up is only on Edward, all his books, paraphernalia, tapes, his games – and we build it big. When executives walk by the office for lunch they say, 'Edward de Bono, now let's find out a little bit about this,' and they walk in. And they purchase the books or they sign up for the seminars, and we run student programmes and they sign up their children for that. It is so well known that when anyone wants to look for something creative – creative thinking – they come to my shop. The adult programme fits into the children's programme and it spreads to other children by word of mouth and the children recommend it to their parents. It is a whole thing, a circle. Every day when I go on a seminar, I have no break at all. When there is a tea break I am there marketing our tools.

How do you start? You pick up the Yellow Pages and you ring the company and you say, 'Have you heard of Edward de Bono? We are now representing Dr de Bono in Singapore,' and out of twenty calls you make you can only get one that will agree to allow you to make a presentation. It was just knocking on doors that would either not open or would open and shut.

I was just using my Visa card and making payment with payment, but once we started you can't believe it. We had our first contract in September that year, 1992. In the first year we made our first million profit! Profit. Not turnover, profit! We were not working twelve hours a day, it was something like sixteen or eighteen hours. In the day you do the work and in the night you prepare, do the marketing and all. And you have got bills to pay. But I owned my first Mercedes in the first year.

Every time we get a new car we make sure that it is delivered when Edward is in town and he will be the first non-family member to sit in it. Peter's birthday is in September. Last year I bought him the Jaguar S Type, but they didn't deliver until November. I told the dealer, 'If you can't deliver by the 12th, forget it because Edward is leaving on the 12th.' Peter now drives the S type and I drive the Mercedes E200, which has those lovely eyes.

Now, nobody is going to pay money into a programme that does not work. We would like to put on record that what we have today, the house in London, the house in Singapore, God made possible through Edward. That's the thing. And now we have trained more than 290 corporations, and the pride today is that we don't do presentations anymore.

I have trained more than 25,000. Today, as we speak, Peter is training sixty at Citibank in Singapore, and in the last six months both of us have hit more than 1,600 people. We conduct seminars at the Singapore Institute of Management and they are always successful, even during the economic crisis. Once a year they organise a seminar for Edward, but we have one there every month.

In the beginning we were taking country by country, beginning with the nearest, Malaysia. Then we went on to Indonesia. We train in all kinds of industries. In Singapore Airlines, around forty-eight of the captains of aircraft attend our programme. Peter even had a one-to-one personal session with the Auditor General in Singapore. Very often the CEOs of companies won't attend with their subordinates 'because of time constraints', you understand? We go in and do a four-hour session, working through the tools with them and working out some problems with them.

Later, I asked Peter and Linda how they survived the steep economic downturn in Asia.

During the crisis, when they talk about budget cuts they tend to get us in. Either you can get in a consultant, which is expensive, or you can bring us in and give the people, who may not be so busy, thinking skills so that the ideas are in place when the turnround comes. We pulled out of Indonesia because of the current turmoil. Hong Kong was not as badly affected. Our Hong Kong strategy increased sales by 56 per cent. When Indonesia went down and the downturn came, Hong Kong came through at that time. The Hong Kong Jockey Club, a very prestigious club, have taken the Six Hats and lateral thinking. Even today I went into the board of management there and did the tools with them and I am having Edward address them in November this year. Now, China Light & Power, who control the electricity generators in Hong Kong and China, have also taken it for their senior management. Let me say again, nobody, no company, is going to put money into programmes that don't work.

Back in 1992, McQuaig and Myers worked together to set up distributorships all over the world. 'The three top networks at the beginning were the US, Canadian and Singapore (Asian) networks,' said Myers.

And then we just started adding country by country. Edward would go out speaking and people would want to know how they could get more and he would then hand them over to me. I would sort them out and find a distributor. The distributor is responsible for being APTT on the ground in another location. They order books, find trainers, certify them, market the courses, manage the trainers, they make the business happen. It is a huge job.

Now there are 925 trainers and we are going to conduct certifications in June and July. As we add we decertify or we cause them to go dormant. If they are on the books and haven't ordered manuals for two years we take them off the list. So probably there are 1,200 certified, but more than 900 active. The training is all for corporate business. APTT do not certify for schools.

Says McQuaig:

> Even so, I would say we are capturing only a tiny bit of the market, and people have pirated his work. All the time corporations using Six Hats independently are brought to my notice – actually creating materials on it. Lateral thinking is different. Unfortunately, in the early 1970s nobody copyrighted or trademarked lateral thinking, so it is out there and nobody can do anything about that. But we have trademarked Six Hats. What I prefer to do is to bring copyright transgressors on side. Recently we found this big company – huge – a well-known worldwide consulting company, teaching it formally, and rather than go after them we paired up with them. And now they are doing it properly.
>
> There is a great market out there. No one else is touting thinking tools. Edward's work is unique, and this is really his time. I have seen a tremendous increase in interest in innovation and creativity over the last three or four years. Any business magazine you pick up today is about creativity and everyone is developing strategies which are bound to rely on Edward's tools. I would say first of all Australia, second Singapore, third Canada (Edward over the years has had a lot of exposure here). After Canada, South America, then Europe.

In Australia things are organised in such a way that, if they get it right, the De Bono Institute in Melbourne could be the blueprint for the future. The idea is to combine an aggressive sell to the corporate side with a considered strategy on the educational and sociological side – in effect, to put commercial revenue right back into the non-profit mission. The De Bono Institute enjoys almost legendary status – rumours fly that an endowment from the Andrews Foundation, variously touted as $6.5 million and $8 million, came as a result of a dinner with author Bryce Courtenay, President Bill Clinton and Edward. They are not true. Julia Pomirska tells me that it kicked off after a preliminary discussion with Bryce Courtenay, who then floated the concept at a keynote address. 'It was Bryce who got up and publicly spoke about it.' The original institute director Max Dumais, when he was director of the Australian Association of Philanthropy, approached the Andrews Foundation and clinched the deal in 1996, when the family foundation put a similar amount into helping preserve the history of Australia. There is plenty of money, but it is not all available at once; they have to live off the interest. The institute has much to do. There is enthusiasm, but as yet not much to show for it. 'They are never in our top group,' says Myers of the royalty revenue, which may be out of step with Edward's popularity in Australia. However, this is only on the commercial side. The institute does a lot of work in education and this year top-flight master trainer Susan Mackie, from South Africa, is set to take over.

In February 1998, Australian magazine *The Bulletin* declared that 'when de Bono gave his imprimatur to the institute, he did so having declined similar proposals from Malta, Portugal, Ireland and the United States'. There is in fact a foundation in Dublin, which Edward has subsidised to the tone of about $400,000 over the years, two in South Africa (one dormant but in existence with a board of trustees), another in plan in Belfast for the UK, not to mention the International Centre for Thinking in New York. There is also a foundation in Malta, on behalf of which Edward and Daniela Bartoli are currently looking to raise £25 million to turn the ancient Fort Ricarsoli there into a World Centre for New Thinking. Tom Farrell also tells me of a foundation about to open in New Zealand and the possibility of another in Germany. 'The foundations are not designed to make money,' Farrell explained, 'only to make money to do other things.'

Some projects currently deserving of this kind of investment, besides education, include one of Farrell's, in South Africa.

This involves 'outfitting a huge truck, making it into a classroom and wheeling it around the country,' projects with the unemployed in the UK, and an interesting one in Cork, Ireland, with disadvantaged youngsters.

The National Youth Commission gave Tom Farrell the go-ahead to introduce CoRT into three South African prisons. He said,

I visited one in Durban, met a lot of prisoners, young and old, and then we had a two-hour satellite link between the three prisons. I was on a panel of six, and a prisoner asked me, 'Is it possible for me to be trained in the CoRT programme and then for me to train other prisoners in the system?' Subsequently the National Commission agreed to train 176 prisoners. We sent the programme from the United States to the Commission, paid for by the Edward de Bono Foundation in Dublin, to train those prisoners, and that is an ongoing situation right now. This is a current event.

Then, what followed from their understanding of what the CoRT programme is about was an idea to train teachers and people in the townships and in the villages, to put it into programmes for drug abuse, alcohol abuse, the HIV programme, with funding from the government. That's going to take a little time.

How is it relevant? The CoRT programme enables people to work things out for themselves. CoRT makes no value judgement on whatever their situation is. If we say, 'Is it a good or a bad idea to use a condom?' you will find that they always come out on the interesting side of the PMI that it is a good idea. So they have made the decision, they have themselves altered their perception. The PMI is the tool or the catalyst to bring out that decision which they make themselves. All the tools bring about a change of attitude or a mindset.

So, we will, over the next five years, put in that programme across South Africa. Then I had this idea, and it *is* my idea! I don't have too many of them – Education on Wheels, that's a 16-metre trailer that will be converted into a proper classroom. It will open out on the sides. It will have thirty-five chairs and five round tables. It will be fully equipped, lighting, cooling, overhead projector, the lot. It will travel anywhere. We estimate we can teach 900 children on a monthly cycle, using the first ten tools of the CoRT programme at any spot we want to go to.

South Africa don't have the money for education. They just downsized about eighteen months ago to some 30,000 teachers, and 95 per cent of the budget goes on administration. Only about two years ago did the supermarkets give the 'sell-by date food', which is collected by another organisation, to the kids in school who just don't have enough food. We want to start school at seven o'clock in the morning up until late in the evening with young children first, then youth in the afternoon, and then adults and teachers in the evening. Then, at the weekend, only teachers.

I have got ninety radio stations ready to report on this on a daily basis. Not only is the idea good for CoRT, but for what I call 'primary help' – you know, wash your hands after going to the toilet and before eating. Eventually, I would like to transfer ownership of the project to Lions, to Rotary, to volunteer organisations. Let them take ownership of it, so that it becomes a whole community effort. The De Bono Foundation will still go on, training the people, but I want these organisations to own the thing and raise funds to train the teachers. If the model works well in South Africa I can take it to

India, to Pakistan, to other African countries. So, education is now mobile!

I want the next five years with this wagon to become the chequebook for industry, government, commerce. Each wagon will be sponsored by a corporation or an organisation. For the first time they will see Education on Wheels with their ads on the side of that truck. They will pay on an annual basis for the teacher, for the upkeep of the wagon, for the new wagon, and this will be controlled by the Foundation.

In Ireland, work with disadvantaged kids in Cork is already spreading countrywide. When I heard about it, I was reminded of something that Edward noted down in the early 1980s, at the time of the Venezuela experiment: 'Poverty is often psychological. People think they can't do anything, they can't change their destiny. But if you can break through that and give them the confidence that they can do things, then they can make the best of what they have.'

Barry Lynch is a trainer in Six Hats, DATT and lateral thinking. He trained while working for ALPS Electric, part of the Japanese-owned ALPS Corporation, which employs 20,000 people worldwide and has sales of around $4 billion.

I was working in process engineering, maximising output and quality. Then the managing director of the plant, a man called John O'Sullivan, attended one of Edward's seminars in London and came back very enthusiastic. John sent me and the personnel manager to be trained. I have to be honest, I was not very enthusiastic at all. I had never heard of de Bono or lateral thinking. I wasn't even involved in training people. So I went in a very negative frame of mind, not least because I had had to drop my holidays to go on it. When I arrived in Brussels for the training programme, there were about twenty-five others, some of whom were willing converts and knew a lot about it. Having done the course I was more enthusiastic, but when I came home, I put the book and the folder in the drawer and other, more pressing, things took over.

This was 1992/3, just before de Bono's network really got going in Europe, though it was well established in the States. I was on a five-day 'train the trainer' course: Six Hats and lateral thinking. At this stage licences were only available in Europe for corporate trainers which meant that I was not licensed to train anyone outside the company. I could do nothing outside the company. Then, pretty soon after that, around 1995, people like the Holst Group started running programmes for independent consultants, and programmes were very much separated into Six Hats, lateral thinking and the DATT programme.

A year passed and John came back to me and said, 'Look, you've done the training and nothing has happened for a year, do it – or else!' At the time I was working with a team of production people, trying to design a new production layout and not getting very far, and I thought, well, I might as well try this Hats thing, give it a go if for nothing else than get my boss off my back, you know?

So, I introduced this team of people to Six Hats and the immediate result was that it stopped them talking round in circles and fighting and roaring. They played the game really from the start, at least once the initial embarrassment was over. It probably took one meeting to get it really going. I had the advantage of knowing the group fairly well and they were open to my guidance. They had no option, but in a way they felt the need themselves because they were getting pretty browned off not making progress. Anyway, the whole thing worked very well, the arguments ended and we got very focused and produced results very quickly, and it became the standard way of doing things.

So, that really rekindled my interest in de Bono and I went back and started reading a few of the books, voluntarily going on some of the courses between 1995 and 1998, both on Hats, lateral thinking and the DATT programme, and ALPS were very supportive of me. They sent me to Venice on a five-day advanced course on lateral thinking for management – on the island. It was a bit of a reward from the company for me persuading the rest of the factory to use the techniques. It was great – five days on the island with Edward and only ten other people. We got a chance to pick his brains and really go through the techniques.

Lynch is now a full-time independent trainer and introduces the techniques to people involved in various projects designed to get disadvantaged youngsters into work. One pilot took place in Cork. Funding came from the Irish government through an organisation called Fás, the National Training Authority. 'They place a training levy on manufacturers and the levy goes to fund Fás,' Lynch explained. I asked him how the pilot had shaped up.

Initially I trained teachers from various centres, who then taught the techniques to their students. But the results were not as good as we had hoped, so I began to go round to each centre one half day a month and meet with the instructors. There might be five or six per centre. They would report as to what they had been doing and I would retrain them on a particular tool or technique, as required. They would then try that out the next month and report back, and so it would go on. Doing it this way really made the thing start to work. Now the instructors had regular back-up.

A lot of these youngsters suffered from very low levels of literacy, came from very deprived backgrounds, and overall would have achieved little at school. The first month or two when I was going around, I thought this is not going to work because teachers would go in and talk, say, about the PMI technique and they would be met with huge waves of apathy, or even resistance.

These kids get paid a weekly wage by the government to actually attend the workshops and in many cases they had little or no interest in learning. And where there was interest it was generally in manual skills, also taught in the centres. So, you can imagine the environment these teachers were going into and I had nothing but admiration for them.

Because of the literacy levels they had to make it more accessible. Some of the kids would not be familiar with words like 'consequences' so a C&S was a tough option. Together, with great care, we worked on the way the tools were presented. For example, in the PMI we would use + and − signs on the board − a visual use of PMI. C&S short-, medium- and long-term consequences became definite time spans − tomorrow, next week, and so on.

After a couple of weeks, one of the teachers got the kids over the resentment and we saw that a lot of it was fear of being exposed. I had a few of the students − tough-looking youngsters − sit in with a session when I was training their teachers. Initially they were very suspicious as to who I was and why I was there. They had assumed I was from the police − I actually look a bit like a policeman. Once they saw that I wasn't trying to catch them out, that I didn't want to highlight a lack of academic ability, things changed. You see, although they come across as violent and aggressive and arrogant, a lot of them have serious problems of self-esteem. Some, maybe, have failed every exam they have ever attempted. Maybe others have been kicked out of every school they have ever been to. Lots of negative feedback. So their immediate reaction to everything new is, Why bother? What is the point? I'll only make a mess of it. Now, here was something they could do straight away, once they saw that they could do it, once they saw that they didn't have to have a leaving certificate, like an A level, in it. Interestingly, the time limits for coming up with ideas in CoRT were not really a problem to them, a lot of them are fairly streetwise, used to thinking on their feet and for themselves. The problem was to get them to open up and do it in a formal environment.

I asked Lynch what kind of hard results were achieved.

Cork City is pretty small 150,000 or something, and geographically it is quite small, but at the same time as far as these youngsters were concerned, if you live in one particular neighbourhood that was where you stayed. Now, there was one group which had finished some sort of computer course, and there was a job advertised in one of the papers on the other side of the city, which is like only two miles away, but none of the kids wanted to go near it. It was like a foreign country. They would never leave their own neighbourhood. So, the teacher got the class to do a PMI on whether they should or should not apply for the job. At the end of it they did apply for it and one of them actually got it, and a month later he said, 'If I hadn't done that PMI thing I'd never have got it.' That was a major change in perception. Before that, travelling across the city for a job wasn't worth thinking about.

One centre that caters only for female students also did some great work. They were using the techniques for staff and pupil meetings, trying to design a new disciplinary code. The staff made a draft proposal and then the students did a PMI on it, and a C&S, etc, and they used three or four of the techniques on it and came up with a final version which was quite different from the original and much improved. The code was based on a points system, with various points for various misdemeanors up to a threshold, after which privileges would be withheld or whatever. I remember when they came to the 'I' in the PMI, one of them suggested that it would be interesting to run the scheme for a trial week, run up points, but at the end of the week not to do anything – just use it to see how bad is bad behaviour, etc. This was an incredibly sophisticated suggestion, something that neither the instructors nor myself would ever have come up with. And of course, the good thing was that they got the rest of the kids to buy into it because they had designed it themselves.

Another instructor used the techniques in a metalworking class, I remember, using them to evaluate what they were making, because again the pupils would say, That's stupid, no point in making it, no one will use it ... So this instructor would get the kids to think through it using the tools.

Today, in England, Edna Copley is dismayed that CoRT is not required study in schools up and down the country, and she blames Edward for not concentrating his efforts on implementing it. You could look at it like that, or you could begin to appreciate the broader, deeper picture. Today, for the first time in British history, the Department of Education has a committee on thinking skills, and the Education Secretary has promised teachers training in thinking skills. And, following a report called *All Our Futures*, made for the Department for Education and Employment (DfEE) by the National Advisory Committee on Creative and Cultural Education, chaired by Warwick University Professor Ken Robinson and published in 1999, thinking skills will become part of the schools curriculum. How has this happened?

Edward's testing of CoRT in British schools in the 1970s was the spark that inspired this development. No work of this sort was done prior to that and no testing as thorough has been undertaken since (pages 129–155). Only one evaluation showed negative results. Unfortunately for CoRT, it was carried out by the Schools Council (Hunter-Grundin, 1985), and one has to wonder how far it contributed to any decision to let de Bono's influence slide. The report did show a statistically significant increase in the number of *relevant* ideas following the use of CoRT training, but, since the difference in *total* ideas was not statistically significant, the report was perceived as negative. 'This is manifestly absurd,' says Edward, 'since *irrelevant* ideas have no value.'

The study was year-long, involving ten primary schools, each with one treatment class and one control class. Twenty-two CoRT lessons were taught. The whole thing was then repeated in the second year, with slight changes in the control group structure. Assessment was via a reading comprehension test, a mental arithmetic test and a logical reasoning test, a creativity test, listing possible uses for a brick or a matchstick, two essay topics (a pre- and post-test) and recorded group discussions.

In addition to this point that the assessment had been about totals of ideas and not their utility, Edward objected that a reading comprehension test, a mental arithmetic test and a logical reasoning test were irrelevant to CoRT teaching, and Hunter-Grundin accepted that. There also appears to have been a problem with the training of the teachers in the test. The study concludes by noting that while the great majority of students enjoyed the CoRT lessons throughout, the teachers 'became somewhat disenchanted' as the lessons progressed. No attempt was made to transfer the skill-teaching to other sectors of the curriculum.

Today, however, there is a very different climate. Now, for the first time in all British schools, there will be a concerted drive to teaching creativity – not just art or music, but creativity across the board. The principles of the section of *All Our Futures* on creative education owe much to CoRT. Among the key points of agreement are: emphasis on outcome involving action (Edward's 'movement' or 'operacy'), emphasis on value outcome, on deferment of judgement and on transferability of thinking skills across different fields. This should not surprise, because Edward has done more than anyone during the last thirty years to create the environment for this initiative to go forward. Perhaps in recognition of this, the DfEE asked him to train their own staff at the end of 1998.

Nearly a decade earlier, in July 1989, at an OECD conference in Paris focusing on international education, Edward had acidly observed that CoRT had been taken up more readily in the developing world, unblemished by 'educational complacency, inadequate leadership, jealousies, political in-fighting and confusion'. That conference of the academic establishment was the first time the Europeans had got together to look at the whole thinking movement, but Edward found himself facing, not John McPeck this time, but an Australian called Professor Malcolm Skilbeck, Vice-Chancellor of Deakin University in Victoria. No international conference since Bill Maxwell's 1982 conference in Fiji was to be deemed complete without an argument between the boffins and Edward, the entrepreneur whose product is thinking. *Learning to Think, Thinking to Learn* (1991), edited by Stuart Maclure and Peter Davies, is the record of that conference.

Maclure was editor of *The Times Educational Supplement* from 1969 to 1989. In his introduction he differentiates between the skills approach to teaching thinking, into which he lumps both Edward and Reuven Feuerstein, and those who favour an 'infusion' model – introducing materials and method focused on improving reasoning, problem-solving and analysis *within the curriculum.*

In the course of the conference, one Dr Philip Adey, very much part of Maclure's second category, though apparently rooting for Feuerstein too, looked at an attempt to improve thinking among twelve-year-olds in eight secondary schools over a period of two years. 'The aim was to test hypotheses relating to the acceleration of cognitive development through the teaching of science.' The experiment led to 'some real gains' in levels of cognitive development, 'but no measurable improvements in their science achievement. One year later, the gains in cognitive development have disappeared, but all the experimental groups show a significantly higher proportion of pupils achieving high results in science.'

The work that Adey described at this conference now has a name – CASE: Cognitive Acceleration through Science Education. Today, Philip Adey is director of the Advancement of Thinking at King's College, London, where the CASE project is based. Adey and colleague Michael Shayer began training in 1991 and, as I write, more than 400 British secondary schools are working with them. In May this year, *The Times* reported that the results 'are irrefutable, showing gains of up to 20 per cent in the proportion of teenagers reaching at least grade C in English, maths and science at GCSE.'

Edward dismisses 20 per cent as a very slight improvement, compared with the performance of CoRT. Back in 1989, after Adey had set out his stall at the OECD Conference, Maclure concluded that 'the work which Adey described is unlikely to have widespread influence'. However, Skilbeck argued against CoRT because it was 'a method to promote rather than a subject to examine'. Why, when the curriculum has been for so long subject-content based and has effectively taught thinking as a by-product, are we suddenly to accept thinking, which is method rather than subject, as necessary? Surely 'thought must address content'?

Edward agrees that thought must address content, but queries the CASE notion that thinking can be taught effectively in a school curriculum subject context. The content with which the skills are taught and rehearsed needs to be bland enough not to inhibit focus on the skills *per se*. Maclure brought Skilbeck up to date on the idea that the curriculum already teaches thinking as a by-product: 'In many education systems, the classics – Latin and Greek – used to be presented as disciplines of peculiar significance because of their transfer potential as a training of the mind in the accurate use of language and precision of thought. Psychologists discounted these claims.' Any special aptitude is now reckoned probably to have predated these claims.

Edward's view on this absolutely fundamental point is:

> It is perfectly true that some thinking skills are being taught implicitly while any curriculum subject is being taught. But these skills are very limited – they are confined to information sorting and analysis, as well as some debating skills – and fall short of the range of thinking skills required both as life skills and for development (decisions, priorities, alternatives, other people's views, etc).

The shift of education from ivory tower to vocational since 1972, when Edward was calling British universities 'irrelevant centres of mental masturbation', is clear in Britain, where polytechnics were elevated to university status ten years ago. Not only did this elevation increase the number of vocational subjects and courses for study at undergraduate level, but throughout the sector it threw a new emphasis on extra-curricular activities for undergraduates that involve skills that would transfer to the workplace, as well as more widespread consultation between the industry and education sectors about the curriculum and the kind of skills industry is looking for. A recent survey of 250 British firms by *Signposts to Employability 2001* shows that university degree classification is now only the third most important graduate recruitment criterion, almost equal with problem-solving skills. 'Most importantly, applicants have to show they can deliver,' said Robert Bowler, recruitment manager of a leading telecommunications company. 'Perhaps they have organised events at university, or even set up a small business. That is more valuable to us than someone who sat in their bedroom and got a First.' Says Edward, 'In the UK youngsters leave school knowing the names of Henry VIII's wives and even the date of the Treaty of Utrecht, but have no idea how the corner shop works and how value is created in society. Education is a locked-in system and not really concerned with the outside world at all. The CASE work is an example. Teaching children to do better at exams. What about the real world?'

In the early 1990s, yet another acronym was commonly heard in the corridors of university sector colleges anxious to achieve university status – PTS, or Personal Transferable Skills.

This is precisely the move that Edward anticipated with CoRT. There has never been a closer involvement between higher education and the workplace. Preparation for the real world has become a prerequisite of university status, yet few universities are doing it well. The National Union of Students and the UK distributor of Edward's thinking programmes may some time recognise the opportunities implicit in that.

As Edward said twelve years ago, 'In an increasingly complex world, students need thinking skills to use as life skills.'

While academics remain stuck in the conceptual rut of vocational courses as subject based – business or event management, media studies or even pop music – it may be that student demand will favour a course with an element, such as CoRT, which teaches vocational *method* applicable to whatever subject or career a student has in mind.

In the mid-1990s, Diane McQuaig suggested to Russell Chalmers that he might take on the UK distributorship of de Bono. 'Russ had been in Toronto – he was a client of ours,' explained Diane. 'He returned to London and took over the business that represented the McQuaig Institute for us in the UK. Subsequently, once he had got settled in, we recommended Edward's work to him and he became the UK distributor. That guy is like a dog with a bone. He grabs the tools, he sees the applications. The UK was dead for us before. Russell is a sales machine.'

I visited Russell Chalmers at the offices of his company, the Holst group, and asked him why, when we have a government that is accepting the idea of teaching thinking in schools, an educational culture increasingly in favour of real-world/vocational education, and one of its own departments inviting Edward to train its staff, is CoRT not part of the National Curriculum.

'Alongside the commercial business, we have in fact been doing a lot of work in the education area,' he replied. 'We have got an enormous number of contacts.' He has been working with Gideon Meyer who is on the DfEE committee concerned with introducing thinking skills to the curriculum and

a bunch of academics, including Professor Philip Adey, who has developed CASE and who disappointed me so much in a meeting we had in the Design Council. I was talking about research undertaken by John Edwards on Edward's stuff and he said, 'Has this been done with children with a minimum IQ of 114?' I said, 'a. I don't know and

b. I thought we were doing this for all children and particularly those who need help.' All I got was raised eyebrows. We are outside the academic establishment. You see, Edward has made a lot of money and there are people who resent that. He has been very critical of the education system, the educationalists. He is always at pains to say education is full of great people but if you look at what it is actually doing, sustaining divisions among people ... So they don't like that. Finally, Edward's stuff is simple and I don't think they like that! I wouldn't mind if they said, 'We have looked at the de Bono stuff and it doesn't stack up because of these things...' I might disagree but I could understand the logic.

But we are starting to make some inroads. We are working with some independent people, like Sally Ann Eisenberg at Broadfields Junior School in Edgware, Patsy Kane at Parrs Wood School in Manchester. I went to a school in Leeds on Friday, Benton Park School, to do a taster session. King Solomon's School in Ilford work with us. Someone else came to us from a school in Derby. We trained the Thomas Hardy School in Dorset in July. And so on. We have trained around 100 trainers in the last six months, and have now developed a high-quality, comprehensive programme for schools which is generating tremendous interest.

On another level we have a relationship with people on the QCA (Qualification and Curriculum Authority) and Demos, the think tank. Also, through a friend of mine, Linbert Spencer, who is one of the country's leading authorities on equal opportunities and is actually working at the moment at the Foreign Office, we found our way to Michael Bichard [Permanent Secretary for the DfEE]. Bichard said he would see us, said he was interested, that he'd like me to talk to his head of training and development to see how this might be moved forward inside the department. Out of that we managed to get Edward in for a lunchtime session. They had a series of people like Colin Marshall, David Puttnam ... 'Would Edward like to do something like that?'

So, basically Edward was in the DfEE in October because we arranged it, and the interest level was such that they had about twice the take-up they normally have. In fact, they were so full in London someone jokingly said, 'I could have sold my ticket for this!' Bichard did the introduction. Edward did his usual excellent job on thinking skills in about an hour, then a bit on education, touched some hot buttons without alienating people, which can happen – he talked about literacy, numeracy and operacy. He did a super job. We then followed it up and so far we have trained about 300 people in the DfEE. The trouble is that they are individuals and we really need to train teams. It is difficult for individuals to make change on their own. So they haven't, in my view, seen the kind of impact they should have done. With the Foreign Office, on the other hand, we have started with a different position. We have much more of an implementation plan with them, they focus on doing it with teams, etc. We have been training the department to come up with more breakthrough ideas on intractable problems.

The DfEE talk was a huge success and widely publicised in the press, with Edward far and away the most popular speaker they had had – 200 officials squeezing into a room for 120. Chalmers' view is that there seems to be no reason why Edward's CoRT and Six Hats cannot be put into the curriculum, even with the CASE experiment up and running. I asked for detail about the Manchester Comprehensive where Holst had just been training.

Ian Hall, the headmaster, went to Australia, managed to get himself on to a couple of visits that Estelle Morris [Education Minister] was making to schools that were using Hats. He was just blown away by how well it worked for them, what it was doing for them. Took him five months to find us after he came back. One of the teachers has a tutorial group with major behavioural difficulties and he decided to use Six Hats and there was a huge shift of behaviour immediately.

I spoke to Patsy Kane at the school, who is responsible for the programme. She told me they were using Six Hats both with staff and kids.

We are now working on a scheme of work for tutor time, which will involve every tutor in the school – that's a huge number of teachers being trained in the Six Thinking Hats – and the heads of every year. There are 1,800 pupils in the school. I did it for two lessons – I have a year 9 group (fourteen-year-olds) for just one lesson a week – and their full-time teacher did the evaluation for me in the following lesson, asking the kids to say where they thought it could be useful. 'We needed each other's opinions, we worked more quickly, we thought more clearly.' They were clear what it was helping them with and they remembered what each of the hats was for, they remembered what the purpose was. The teacher was so impressed that she came to me immediately and asked to be trained! Which is why I invited the English adviser to the second day of training because it is a really good technique for group work and discussion work.

Now, we are thinking of having the hats painted as a mural in the school as a reminder. We used it in our senior team management meeting and that went down really well. The meeting was quicker and more positive, and the social science faculty have used it in their faculty meeting with good results. What I liked about it was the comments the children made – 'We needed each others' opinions, it was a structured way forward, more people contributed.' The kids liked the discipline of it. It kept them really focused. It really sharpens things up. That was on very little trialing and the kids were recognising the results, which really impressed me.

I asked whether she had looked at CoRT.

The government is starting Learning Support Centres for kids that would otherwise be excluded. I would like to try CoRT in there. I have talked with the coordinator. Often their social relationships are very poor and if they can begin to think of themselves as thinkers and contributing, then it could be very helpful.

I have put in for a Best Practice Research Scholarship with the DfEE, looking at de Bono skills and incorporating it into the curriculum. This is what the government wants, some thinking skills ... When they have been taught Six Hats you can use it with the kids as a kind of shorthand. People just use the language so easily – 'Come on let's use some green-hat thinking!'

There's not many things that you do as a teacher where the kids comment on the difference so explicitly! I was really impressed with the feedback.

Chalmers' own enthusiasm is to spread interest from a conspicuous success in the government area – his New Deal initiative for the unemployed.

It has taken forever to get to the point where we are going to roll it out across six, seven employment districts. Our statistics show that those among the New Deal unemployed who have had Edward's training are between four and five times more likely to find work, that six to nine months after the initial pilots, 90 per cent are still in a job and 85 per cent are off the register and off benefits. So, the results are dramatic, and that is for just three two-hour sessions. Now there's a shift from local to rolling it out nationally, and someone has been assigned to us. We are going to run our first pilot for New Deal 25+ in Reading in July.

We are also at the Schools Exclusion Unit on Monday, because I think Edward's programmes can help significantly reducing exclusion in schools and truancy too. So my vision for New Deal and exclusions at school and young offenders in prison is that we get Edward's training to them and people see the dramatic change. I think there is also huge leverage with the charities. If we can capture the imagination of Oxfam, Save the Children, NSPCC, etc, people will learn how to help themselves.

Beyond Britain, the spread of de Bono programmes continues apace. This summer I learned that master trainer Sunil Gupta had placed CoRT in Dubai schools and had trained inside HSBC, British Petroleum, Intercontinental Hotels, Unilever and Bahrain Telecommunications in Bahrain and Lebanon. It may seem incredible that a rich, fundamentalist culture should welcome a framework which specifically opens minds to other points of view, inhibits bias and suspends judgement. Not only is this happening but it is being paid for by business, by this link between the corporate world, commerce, and value measurable in other than hard cash.

I raised this Middle East development with Edward and he confirmed the importance of this territory.

I was talking in Saudi Arabia, and this fundamentalist got up and he was quite polite. He said, 'I am not sure about teaching thinking. People should read the Koran and do what they are told. Let's see what the great prophet Mohammed has to say.' Now, there is a saying in the *hadith* [the life and sayings of Mohammed] – I keep getting different versions of this – I was told it says, 'One hour of thinking is better than one year of prayer,' [which is what Edward said at the talk] but now I hear that it says, 'One hour of thinking is better than seventy years of meaningless prayer.' Immediate silence. Everyone sits down. But another time I said this in Bahrain. The head of the Islamic Centre came to see me and said, 'You are absolutely right, people don't know this.' So one of the things I want to do is to have a major Islamic conference saying, 'We are the thinking religion.'

With visions of a *fatwah* looming, I asked Professor Aziz to dig out the correct quote. 'The actual quote from the *hadith*,' he said,' depends of course on the translation. In effect, the prophet said: "One hour of thinking is better than one year of meditation," because meditation takes your mind into a state where you are not using logic . . .'

Edward is sixty-eight. With the post-Hats organisation in shape, the retirement question arises. What will survive? 'On the business side there's Kathy Myers and APTT, we have about 925 trainers,' Edward said to me this summer.

> On the educational side clearly there are a lot of able people carrying on. Caspar is very good at it. So there are people in place to carry on. One of the things I am trying to do in Malta is, I have an option from the government on Fort Ricarsoli, this huge fort on the other side of the harbour. The idea is to create a World Thinking Centre, where different companies, different countries, NGOs and corporations would have their intellectual ambassadors, and these people would meet together formally, informally, task forces, round tables, they might fly in their ecology experts for a week on ecology . . . And so it would be a permanent thinking interaction, but mixing in business. I will probably have to raise about $25 million to make it happen. It's a nice site, needs a lot doing to it. It's a big concept and it is needed. I tried for some time through people in New York to encourage the United Nations to set up a think tank, but dealing with the UN is like dancing in treacle. So I dropped that idea.

Shades of SITO? Or perhaps a hint that he may soon be going to ground in Malta? There is certainly enough going on on the island to keep him occupied. Daniela Bartoli and Sandra Dingli have recently secured his programmes a place on the schools curriculum, there is Charmaine Ferrante's school for Down's syndrome and autistic children, and foundation course possibilities opening up at the university. And there is the success of his training at Brandstätter Group's Playmobil – Susan Mackie, Sandra Azzopardi and John Camilleri trained a company of more than 700 employees from top to bottom.

I visited them in July while I was on the island, and saw for myself how

DATT and Six Hats are used by workers on the production line right through to senior management. There has been 'reduction in conflicts, reduction in disciplinary action, increase in the number and quality of suggestions – all these have happened and more,' I was told. 'The best piece of feedback we got from the workforce was that they were using the mnemonics at home.' Azzopardi is now so taken with the whole thing that she is introducing the tools to the General Workers Union Shop Stewards in Malta.

I asked what becomes of a GWU member who no longer wants to argue with anyone. I wasn't the first to ask, and it is, of course, a measure of how deep the change in our culture might be.

So, with his father involved with all this, and the international dimension at Fort Ricarsoli, would Caspar be tempted away from the *Financial Times* to take over? 'We have talked about what would happen when he steps down,' Caspar said. 'I am very enthusiastic and interested about the work and have enjoyed teaching it and find it useful personally. But it is also important to develop my own skills and credibility and value if you like, rather than be a carbon copy or be in the shadows. I guess the real crux would be if I felt that the thinking was being misrepresented or compromised in some way and then we'd need to do something about that.'

My thoughts were on Edward's retirement – in particular the love and goats' cheese aspect – when earlier this year I was transported to his island, West Skeam, by local fisherman John Pyburn and we were greeted by a herd of goats on the cliff above the natural harbour. Edward had introduced a couple of the beasts to the island and now they and the following generation have gone quite wild.

However, I can't see him retiring to West Skeam, any more than to one of his other islands. There is the softer beauty of Tessera, of course, but it is very small. There is Little Green Island off Mackay, Queensland, Australia. This is larger – some 150 acres – but somewhat mangrovey, with just the one solar-powered building, made out of corrugated iron, steel and wood by Julia Pomirska's brother. (It won an ecology award.) There is a conference room, of course – 'We use the helicopter to take them across' – and Edward's bedroom, but little else. He told Australian TV that it is 'my own special island', but he is notoriously unfaithful when it comes to islands.

I haven't seen his island in the Bahamas, but Linda Laird, who has, tells me that it is –

about five acres, a small house, two up, two down, two bedrooms, if I remember. There is no way you could do conferences on it. The most you could fit in for dinner would be about ten, squashed around the table. Nothing much grows there, it is connected to the mainland by a spit at low water, where the sand has built up over time. When I was over there he had me looking at properties on the mainland. I don't know whether that was because he was thinking of selling. They were fairly expensive.

West Skeam has altogether more character, but would Edward be up to the challenge of the rugged Atlantic coast for more than a few days at a time? It lies a good way from the mainland, maybe fifteen minutes by boat. The strong, stone buildings – croft-like, single storey – housed two families at one time and make three houses now, but Linda counsels caution:

> I know that if I stopped working for Edward and I had to choose someone else to look after the island it would have to be a man and someone who knew about boats, because there are very few women who would do what I do. It is wild and wintery and difficult to deal with, hauling the groceries over the rocks up and down the pier. We used to have this old fishing boat when we were doing it up. I'd go off in the car, fill it up with stuff and come back down to the pier, load it into the boat by myself, take it across to the island, wolf-whistle up to the others to come and help me bring it up to the house.
>
> One time when we were coming off the island there was a storm brewing and you have to look smartish in a storm or you won't get off. Michael Coughlan was with us, a typical guy from West Cork – 'Ah, sure, whenever.' So he loaded up the boat and he loaded up the boat and he continued to load up the boat, and I said that I thought there was too much in the boat and that we wouldn't all fit in. 'Ah, not at all, Linda, not at all, you're fussing again.' Same man doesn't swim. None of the fishermen do, you know. They have this myth that if they can swim and they are way, way out to sea, then it prolongs their life in the cold, cold water, whereas if they can't swim they just drown. Gone in seconds instead of hanging around for six hours. I understand the logic unless you happen to be just 100 yards away from the shore. There was also a seventy-four-year-old man with us, a good worker but getting frail.

So we all – there were six of us – headed back and about a third of the way across I said to Michael, 'There's black stuff left behind in the water, what is it?' And the boat didn't sound too healthy. I said, 'Michael, I really prefer if you turned back.' Michael said, 'Not at all, it'll be fine, fine.' And what made me trust him, I don't know. He kept saying to me that the black stuff in the water was coal dust from when we brought a ton of coal over, and said we were nearly there. As we were going past East Skeam I said that I hoped the boat would break down there because we could swim to that island from where we were. But the boat kept going and we seemed to be getting there, though she was getting sicklier and sicklier as we went. I'd say we were about fifty yards from the pier when the engine just stopped. And as the storm was brewing, the wind was picking up and the waves lifted us up off the rocks and bounced us back off the rocks. We had maybe got a ton of scaffolding on the boat, planks of wood, all the guys' tools, all our clothes, cameras, computers, the works. I started pegging the camera and the computer bags up as far as I could throw them up onto the shore as we were bouncing down off the rocks. As the waves threw us up I would throw something off and then we'd go du, du, du, du, back down the rocks again. And the old man had terror in his eyes, and every time we got to the top rock I knew I had to push someone off, right?

Meanwhile I am trying to dial John Pyburn on Hare Island. His dad picked up the phone, a very quietly spoken man, and says, 'Oh, I'll get John for you now,' and I am screaming at him, 'Get him now! Get him now!' And then I am pushing people off the boat as a wave takes us up, shouting, 'Down! Jump off the boat when it's up the rocks!' I was terrified if they jumped at the wrong moment they'd be swept under the boat and the boat would come crashing down on them. Then, all of a sudden, I could see John Pyburn heading out from Hare Island in his little dingy to get us. I realised at this stage that the boat, with a fair few holes in the bottom of it, was not rescuable. Michael decided to stay on it with Brian, one of his workers. John Pyburn came across, slung over a rope and tried to pull it off the rocks, but as she came off she was so top heavy, she just turned over, upside down, and all the stuff just piled out. So they towed it across to this bay like that, upside down, and of course all the bags popped up from the cuddy, and then became so waterlogged they sank to the bottom like stones.

West Skeam is hewn in a wild workshop. You can be solitary here, certainly, but solitary as on the wild moor. This is not the fertile, rural English cultural heritage that was Hardy's. It is rather the harsh beauty of the Brontës and not to be tamed, the sort of place where even postmodern man, for all his autonomy and obsession with project, might yet find something of which he is not master, something that strangely wills and works for itself outside man's little system and inspires his values. Is that, after all, what draws Edward here?

Defining values is, he accepts, the necessary modern focus: 'Why do we need new processes in thinking?' Edward asks a seminar audience rhetorically.

> In the past, the emphasis has been on housekeeping, price advantage, increased efficiency, and so on, but what happens when everyone is equally competent? If your only hope for survival is for your competitors to continue to be more incompetent than yourself, that's a pretty weak basis for survival. So, at this point you need to be in value creation ... Technology is ahead of the value concepts we provide. Technology will amply and ably deliver value but we have to design the concepts to deliver. Devise the value concepts and technology will support and deliver those concepts.

That is the area which Edward's thinking – all our thinking (and some might say, not a little feeling) – must now address. But where does postmodern man find his values, in a world where no one knows best? In the pilot programme for the Australian TV series, *Food For Thought*, Edward is having dinner with six others at the luxurious home of Jean and Richard Pratt, an industrialist and one of Australia's richest men. Also in attendance are ex-Prime Minister Bob Hawke, TV producer Steve Vizard, bestselling author Bryce Courtenay, and Tan Le, introduced as 'Young Australian of the Year'. At one point, Bob Hawke said to Edward, 'In this last century we have seen the most explosive output of technical genius, but it seems to me we have had a collective lobotomy on the other side of the brain – the social engineering side has been relatively dead.'

Tan Le agreed: 'We are going to have to think about how we ascribe value to our lives. We value things like power, like money, influence. Even our GDP measures consumption, but is that really measuring *growth*?'

The conversation continued with a suggestion that technology might somehow be used to recreate values traditionally inspired by community. But Edward says, 'Technology is the opposite of community. Because we have the telephone we can have friends hundreds of miles away. If there was no telephone you would have to go down to the pub and talk to your neighbour.'

With no need to feel that he belongs, Edward seems unable to detect any advantages in community, even misinterpreting Tan Le's desire to immerse herself in the new community culture when she arrived in Australia as a cry of loneliness, rather than cultural interest, and suggesting that she should have simply got together with fellow immigrants. The perception of values describing the spirit of a culture seems already lost. Technology – clinical, random, designed for one person – has taken away any sense of it.

Weighing anchor altogether may not be satisfactory to the young, however. 'Postmodern culture,' wrote Professor Andrew Henley, an economist and editor of the Association of Christian Economists, 'is telling them they can think what they like and that's okay, but actually it's a very insecure answer to an emotionally and financially insecure student.'

By imagining his own roots not as the roots of a tree but as tributaries of a river, Edward challenges not only the old idea of identity rooted in a culture, but also the idea of values, beliefs and ideas infusing a community. This is John Fowles's 'unconscious philosophy of life', lost to modernism (page 234) – the spirit of place, the spirit of a people.

For postmodern man, community spells limitation – box culture. It is the essence of lateral thinking to encourage new perceptions, not once but as a constant refrain. Edward's rootlessness gives postmodern man his emotional detachment and calls into question the notion of values arising in *un*thinking fashion, inspired by culture, art, religion. There is, for example, no place for traditional metaphors of inspiration like this one, used by D. H. Lawrence in *Fantasia of the Unconscious*: 'I come so well to understand tree-worship. All the old Aryans worshipped the tree. My ancestors. The tree of life. The tree of knowledge ... Here am I between his toes like a pea-bug, and him noiselessly over-reaching me, and I feel his great blood-jet surging. And he has no eyes. But he turns two ways: he thrusts himself tremendously down to the middle earth, where dead men sink in darkness, in the damp, dense undersoil; and he turns himself about in high air ... A huge, plunging, tremendous soul. I would like to be a tree for a while. The great lust of roots. Root-lust. And no mind at all.'

Here is a deep-truth metaphor of the spirit, sensuous, bubbling with fertility, but deliberately *un*thinking ('no mind at all') – emotional, primitive, tapping into a collective subconscious spirit. A postmodernist might choose John Jervis's words to dismiss it as 'the meaningless residue of the Romantic myth of the artist.'

But in the novels of Susan Hill (*Strange Meeting, The Bird of Night*, etc) we can see the same unconscious inspiration achieving value definition of an impressive kind. In the creation of her story, *The Albatross*, 'I know only that the book wrote itself,' she records. 'All the best writing does that and speaks the truth and could be in no way other than it is . . . the story unwound itself from me like a thread and knitted itself together into paragraphs before my astonished eyes. I felt as if I were having no part of it, as if I were taking down dictation from some inner voice . . . It is an awesome experience.'

The Albatross was inspired by the spirit of Aldeburgh, first captured by Benjamin Britten's 'Sea Interludes' in his opera *Peter Grimes*, which she heard as a child. Hill recalled this much later on a visit to the Suffolk seaside town. What is *The Albatross* about? 'It is about the misfit, the odd, the simple, the strange one in the midst of the rest of ordinary humanity, and about the power of love and pure goodness, shining through all manner of human exteriors. It is about possessiveness and cruelty and oppression, about fear and pride . . .'

'I would not get into the literary argument mode,' says Edward. 'That dilutes the point that thinking is an operational skill . . . which is key.' Edward remains wary of the power of words. He once wrote that 'the literary writer creeps into the soul of man'. Words have associations deep down in our culture. Words 'freeze perceptions at one moment in history,' he complains, 'and then insist we continue to use these frozen perceptions when we should be doing better.' Others would argue that the best fiction provokes new perceptions as happily as lateral thinking and with the bonus of a value dimension. In *Wormholes* (1998), John Fowles defines the novel's purpose as 'to entertain, to satirize, to describe new sensibilities, to record life, to improve life . . .' and writes, 'A novel is a hypothesis more or less ingeniously and persuasively presented – that is first cousin to a lie.' In Edward's vocabulary, hypothesis is the very 'driver of thinking', the possibility system depends on developing provocative hypotheses. Investigating a hypothesis enables a creative framework for exploring information, as opposed to pre-empting exploration with judgement based on old, worn-out concepts. When, in defence of the provocative, hypothetical, deep-truth values of fiction, I suggested to Edward that in a sense all fiction is a deliberate, provocative lie, he looked through me and said, 'And biography?'

In non-literary, but similar terms, the working-class values of northern Britain arose as an expression of community caught in the jaws of the 1920s Depression. In Blackburn, they arose so forcibly that even in penury a worker's pride persuaded him to refuse money from a prosperous brother, as William Woodruff tells in the autobiographical *The Road to Nab End* (1993). The values of the British northern working-class culture, epitomised by the Woodruff family, rose up within the community and were its deeply felt, unthinking expression. We have come to laud such values, but William's sister Brenda saw the limitations of coming upon values in this way, and later called their father 'a gaumless creature. He had the head and brains of a brass knob. He didn't foresee anything because he never *thought* about anything. He was a grand worker, nobody better, but where brains were concerned he was lost.'

Edward's CoRT programme was tailor-made (alas, too late) for William and Brenda's father, whose deep-truth value system was so exploited by mill owners in 19th- and early 20th-century England.

So where will our values come from amidst the 'violent dislocations' of modern urban life?

Of all the traditional philosophers, Edward favours William James, brother of Henry. 'Henry James was the writer, they were brothers. I like his pragmatism, where he would say, "Look, what is the cash value of it? What difference does it make if it is true or not true?" That's water logic really, in that it is not "what this is", but "what does it flow on to?" I had a lot of sympathy with his approach.'

So are we looking at the pragmatic approach of a type espoused by Lord Chesterfield in the 18th century, when he scandalised his contemporaries by advising his son to be morally pure for no other reason than that no one would trust him if he was not?

James's 'cash value' sounds like that of the banker at one of Edward's seminars, who cared for his low-paying customers only because there weren't enough high-paying customers to go round. But in fact, James allowed that mystical states 'open out the possibility of other orders of truth, in which, so far as anything in us vitally responds to them, we may freely continue to have faith'.

Edward picks up on the 'cash value' image by prizing integrity, trust and respect, and describing the latter as a more 'usable currency' than love. He is at pains to point out that 'cash value' is not material value.

Though he is rarely drawn on the subject of faith, he has said, 'I have the view that believing and thinking are completely separate systems and can easily coexist.' Indeed, it is belief in his unproven model of the mechanism of mind that enabled him to develop his thinking tools and techniques in the first place.

We have the technology to do virtually anything we need. What we need to do now is to apply technology in ways that will add value to our lives. Edward's contribution is intended to be more fundamental and liberating than telling us *what* our values should or should not be. It shows us *how* to look for and broaden our perception of the alternatives. He shows us *how* to think rather than telling us *what* to think, because we are going to need to, now that the right/wrong paradigm is no more. He said:

> What is going to change human behaviour is changes in human thinking. Not changes in human values. For instance, in the CoRT programme we teach something very simple called an OPV – Other People's Views. OK, so two people are having this fight, then one of them says, 'Wait a bit, we've done these thinking lessons. Let's do an OPV.' In thirty seconds the fight is over. Operational! The story I tell about values, is that when I had done my training of teachers in Venezuela, at the press conference some of the journalists said, 'Well, I am not sure you are teaching thinking, maybe you are just teaching Western bourgeois values.' So I said, 'Suppose you have a table with a glass of milk on it and a glass of Coca Cola and a glass of pisco or tequila. Supposing you have poor eyesight. You don't have any choice. If we give you a pair of spectacles I am not telling you to choose the milk or the Coca Cola or the tequila, I am giving you the choice in the spectacles business.'

His thinking programmes put the individual in control, so that while he himself hails the passing of community culture, in line with his personal autonomy he personally sees no reason to adopt such incursive technological innovations as a personal e-mail or mobile phone. He has no car, even.

The real shift, then, is not from logical to lateral thinking. He never meant to replace the one with the other, rather to release the stranglehold of logic by defining the creative alternative and showing us how to do it. The real sea change was his challenge to absolute criteria that impel our judgement and inhibit possibility.

In place of the absolute values of art, religion and political theory he returns to us this unique 'Value X', *the freedom that thinking brings.* Recently he said to me: 'The last time I was in Istanbul I gave a seminar to some 250,000 people, after which I gave an interview on their main television chat show, and the interviewer said, "We are so tired of *isms* – Marxism, capitalism, fundamentalism – what you are doing to teach thinking is important because it shows us how to escape all these *isms*." That's not bad. I'd be happy to leave it there.'

Bibliography

Borges, Jorge Luis *Labyrinths* (New Directions, 1964; Penguin Books, 1970)

Barbour, Julian *The End of Time* (Weidenfeld and Nicolson, 1999)

Close, Frank *Lucifer's Legacy: The Meaning of Asymmetry* (Oxford University Press, 2000)

Dawkins, Richard *Unweaving The Rainbow* (Allen Lane, The Penguin Press, 1998)

de Bono, Edward *The Use of Lateral Thinking* (Jonathan Cape, 1967)

—*The Five-Day Course in Thinking* (Basic Books, 1967)

—*The Mechanism of Mind* (Jonathan Cape, 1969)

—*Lateral Thinking: A Textbook in Creativity* (Jonathan Cape, 1970)

—*The Dog Exercising Machine* (Penguin, 1970)

—*Practical Thinking and Different Ways of Being Right and Wrong* (Jonathan Cape, 1971)

—*Lateral Thinking For Management* (McGraw Hill, 1971; Penguin, 1976)

—*PO: Beyond Yes and No* (Simon and Schuster, 1972; Penguin, 1973)

—*Children Solve Problems* (Penguin, 1972)

—*Eureka! An Illustrated History of Invention* (Thames & Hudson, 1974)

—*Teaching Thinking* (Maurice Temple Smith, 1976)

—*The Greatest Thinkers* (Weidenfeld and Nicolson, 1976)

—*Wordpower: An Illustrated Dictionary of Vital Words* (Pierrot Publishing, 1977)

—*The Happiness Purpose* (Maurice Temple Smith, 1977)

—*The Case of the Disappearing Elephant* (Dent, 1977)

—*Opportunities: A Handbook of Business Opportunity Search* (Associated Business Programmes, 1978)

—*Future Positive* (Maurice Temple Smith, 1979)
—*Atlas of Management Thinking* (Maurice Temple Smith, 1981)
—*de Bono's Thinking Course* (BBC Publications, 1982)
—*Tactics: The Art and Science of Success* (William Collins, 1984)
—*Conflicts: A Better Way To Resolve Them* (Harrap, 1985)
—*Six Thinking Hats* (Key Porter Books, 1985; Viking, 1986)
—*Masterthinker's Handbook* (Penguin, 1985)
—*Letters to Thinkers* (Penguin, 1987)
—*I Am Right, You Are Wrong* (Viking, 1990)
—*Positive Revolution for Brazil* (Penguin, 1990)
—*Handbook for a Positive Revolution* (Viking, 1991)
—*Six Action Shoes* (HarperCollins, 1991)
—*Sur/Petition: Going Beyond Competition* (HarperCollins, 1992)
—*Serious Creativity* (HarperCollins, 1992)
—*Teach Your Child How To Think* (Viking, 1992)
—*Water Logic* (Viking, 1993)
—*Parallel Thinking* (Viking, 1994)
—*Teach Yourself To Think* (Viking, 1995)
—*Mind Power* (Dorling Kindersley, 1995)
—*Edward de Bono's Textbook of Wisdom* (Viking, 1996)
—*How To Be More Interesting* (Viking, 1997)
—*Simplicity* (Viking, 1998)
—*New Thinking for the New Millennium* (Viking, 1999)
—*The de Bono Code Book* (Viking, 2000)
Dingli, Sandra *Creative Thinking, A Multifaceted Approach* (Malta University Press, 1994)
—*Creative Thinking, New Perspectives* (Malta University Press, 1996)
Fowles, John *Wormholes* (Henry Holt, 1998)
—and Draper, Jo *Thomas Hardy's England* (Jonathan Cape, 1984)
Gardner, Howard *Frames of Mind* (Heinemann, 1983)
Greene, Brian *The Elegant Universe* (Jonathan Cape, 1999)
Hay, George (ed.) *The Edward De Bono Science Fiction Collection* (Elmfield Press, 1976)
Hill, Susan *The Albatross* (Longman, 1988)
Jervis, John *Exploring The Modern* (Blackwell, 1998)
Johnson, George *Strange Beauty* (Jonathan Cape, 2000)
Koestler, Arthur *The Act of Creation* (Hutchinson, 1964)
Kuhn, Thomas *Structure of Scientific Revolutions* (University of Chicago Press, 1962)
Lee, M H and Marudarajan, A R *International Journal of Man-Machine*

Studies (Vol. 17, pp189–210; Academic Press, 1982)

Machado, Luis Alberto *The Right to be Intelligent* (Pergamon, 1980)

Maclure, Stuart and Davies, Peter (eds.) *Learning to Think: Thinking to Learn* (Pergamon, 1991)

Maxwell, William (ed.) *Thinking: The Expanded Frontier* (Laurence E Erlbaum, 1983)

McNeill, Daniel and Freiberger, Paul *Fuzzy Logic* (Simon and Schuster, 1993)

National Advisory Committee on Creative & Cultural Education *All Our Futures* (DfEE, 1999)

Perkins, David *Outsmarting IQ: The Emerging Science of Learnable Intelligence* (Simon and Schuster, 1995)

Pinker, Steven *How The Mind Works* (Norton, 1997; Penguin, 1998)

Ridley, Matt *Genome: The Autobiography of a Species in 23 Chapters* (Fourth Estate, 1999)

Russell, Bertrand *Our Knowledge of The External World* (Open Court, 1914)

Ryle, Gilbert *Dilemmas* (Cambridge University Press, 1954)

Tanner, David *Total Creativity* (APTT, 1997)

Woodruff, William *The Road to Nab End* (Eland, 1993)

Index